# GRAVEYARDS
*of*
# TRINITY CHURCH
***and***
# ST. PAUL'S

# GRAVEYARDS *of* TRINITY CHURCH *and* ST. PAUL'S

## A HISTORY AND GUIDE

ADAM SELZER

Published by The History Press
Charleston, SC
www.historypress.com



*Maps used by permission of Trinity Archives.*
*Photographs were taken by the author unless otherwise noted.*

First published 2025

Manufactured in the United States

ISBN 9781467155946

Library of Congress Control Number: 2024945421

# CONTENTS

# PREFACE

One day in the mid-1800s, Reverend Robert Hallem said, "I wonder if we shall have to live in the next world with the sort of cherubim that we see carved on tombstones. I really hope not, for I fancy that it might be disagreeable."

To some, this was a scandalous thing to suggest. But one listener, journalist John Flavel Mines, later wrote, "The fancy might be readily forgiven by one who has made a study of the winged heads that adorn the funereal slabs in (New York's) Trinity churchyard. They are every degree of gruesomeness, only each a little more horrible than others."[1] In 1846, a reporter (likely Walt Whitman) called the skulls adorning Trinity gravestones "[decorations] which the rude and unhappy taste of former times made appropriate....It is a bad philosophy which identifies the passing away of our friends with such horrid tokens of fate."[2]

Even as far back as 1822, when in-ground burials at Trinity were stopped, the older headstones there were seen as hopelessly old-fashioned, with their skulls and morbid epitaphs. Visitors today often remark that the headstones there look like something from cartoons.

From 1800 to 1820, Manhattan's population had more than doubled from 61,000 to 123,000, and the pace was accelerating. Though much of the city was still concentrated in the southern tip of the island, where the roads are still a medieval jumble, in 1811, commissioners had plotted out how the city would grow in a neat grid of numbered streets above Houston Street, starting with 1st Street and going all the way up to 155th.

There were graveyards everywhere in lower Manhattan in those days. Besides the still-extant Trinity and St. Paul's, there were churchyards lining Nassau Street and scattered elsewhere throughout the island. By 1822, many of them were in poor condition. People complained that there were terrible odors emanating from the stone burial vaults beside the New Dutch Churchyard on Fulton, as well as from the graveyard attached to the Presbyterian church on Wall Street. St. Paul's churchyard on Broadway was said to be slightly better, but the yard there still "emitted unpleasant effluvia."[3] People began to worry that these reeking burial grounds were hazards to public health (see page 91) and called for them to be closed. After all, they were full. Despite its small size, some said that more people were buried at Trinity than lived in the city (see page 63), and every new burial seemed to turn up stray bones from old ones, which were tossed in the charnel house or "bone pit."

Burials in lower Manhattan were soon stopped, and the boundary quickly moved farther north.

Of course, there may have been other motivations for halting burials. The city was moving into the future, and churchyards were not just old-fashioned and smelly, they were also sitting on land that was growing ever more valuable. One appalled 1838 commenter wrote, "A full-blooded speculator never passes a church yard in this city that his bowels do not yearn and his mouth water to see the ground thus lying unproductive. His imagination runs riot with the vision of streets and six story stores, rising as it were from the dead."[4]

Already by then, a number of graveyards had been paved or built over (sometimes with the bodies removed and sometimes not). By the end of the century, nearly all of them were gone. Burials now took place in the park-like expanses of Woodlawn and Green-Wood in other boroughs, and graveyards themselves were a relic of an earlier time. "People were not as ambitious then," the *New York Tribune* noted in 1890, "and did not call every school a college…they spoke of graveyards and burying grounds where nothing less than 'cemetery' will answer now."[5]

But Trinity's and St. Paul's graveyards endured. Over time, they came to be spoken of as symbols of American history—below the bustling skyscrapers of Wall Street were a connection to the city's colonial and Revolutionary past.

Many of the epitaphs ask us to consider the dust beneath them. Who were these people? Articles and pamphlets written about them tend to reduce them to their military achievements, the offices they held, the people they married, the land (and people) they owned, and their connections to prominent families. But people are more than their bullet points; most of the people buried here who lived to a reasonable age sang songs, played games, and had favorite foods and best friends. They fell in and out of love. Though many soldiers and statesmen lie in these two graveyards, so do poets, scoundrels, and perfectly ordinary, everyday people. Or, anyway, perfectly ordinary by 1700s standards.

In this book, I'll look into some of the most interesting stories from these two graveyards. I will also examine their epitaphs (including many that are now illegible) and their often-surprising sources.

Like all burial grounds, Trinity and St. Paul's are filled with mysteries. There are lost headstones and many unidentified monuments (though I've been able to identify a few of them in the course of researching this book). There's even at least one marker for a fictional character.

It isn't exactly true that "everyone has a story." Everyone should have *lots* of stories.

Here are a few.

—Adam Selzer, 2024
Adamchicago.com

# ACKNOWLEDGEMENTS

I wish to thank Kathryn Hurwitz at the Trinity Archives, as well as former archivists Miriam Silverman and "Whitey Sterling." Thanks for the Richter's Box, Mr. Sterling. And Sam the Eagle, whose one line in *The Great Muppet Caper* ("You are all weirdos.") ran in my head throughout the writing of this book.

# COMMON MONUMENT STYLES AND SYMBOLS

Some of the styles of grave markers and symbols at Trinity and St. Paul's:

**Box Graves**: Though these can appear to be tombs encasing a coffin, they usually did not have stone floors; the bodies were buried beneath them. Covering the whole grave theoretically protected the grave from both the elements and grave robbers.

**Ledger Grave**: A slab laid on the ground. Some of these may have been box graves whose sides decayed or sank.

**Vault Marker**: These smaller markers cover a buried staircase leading to the door of one of the underground vaults that lie beneath the ground.

**Death's Head**: The skull, sometimes with wings to represent the fleeting nature of life, commonly seen on eighteenth-century graves. They were meant to be scary reminders of mortality, inspiring viewers to be more religious.

**Soul Effigy**: A face with wings, representing the soul's flight from the body, gradually replaced death's heads in popularity. One could say that it represents the Enlightenment era's view of religion replacing the fire-and-brimstone style of an earlier day.

**Headstone**: The most common gravestone style, often with ornamentation in the top portion (known as a tympanum). Most here are made of limestone, marble, or sandstone.

*Note: Records on birth and death years—especially birth years—can be very hard to determine. In most cases, I have based estimated birth years on what the epitaphs say, though records are often wildly contradictory.*

# PART I

# TRINITY CHURCHYARD

Trinity Church in 1922, before the Manning Wing was added. *Library of Congress.*

Introduction

# TRINITY CHURCH

When Trinity Church was given its charter from the king of England in 1697, the paperwork called for a nominal rent of one peppercorn per year to be paid to the Crown. It was never paid until 1976. That year, the church wrote to Queen Elizabeth II, offering to pay up at last, and she "thought it was a fitting idea."[6] On a trip to New York, the queen walked to the steps of the church, where Reverend Robert Parks gave her a glass vessel containing 279 peppercorns, covering the back rent.[7] It's technically in arrears again today.

The graveyard on the north side of the church is among the oldest public places in Manhattan, in operation as a town burial ground since the seventeenth century. The oldest headstone is dated 1681 (see page 117), a full sixteen years before Trinity Church was founded. New York was then a village of a few thousand people, almost all concentrated on the southern tip of the island. When the first Trinity Church was built, only a generation had passed since the English seized the city from the Dutch. The church added its own burial ground—now the south churchyard—when it was built and, a few years later, took over management of the old town burial ground, which is now the north churchyard.

The church was a part of the Church of England. Though other Protestant denominations thrived in the young city—and a small Jewish congregation even raised money to help build the church—in 1700, a law was passed making it illegal, on penalty of life imprisonment or death, for a Catholic priest to set foot in New York.

Early New Yorkers were raised to be terrified of Catholics and spoke of them the way the English a century before had spoken of Jews. Many were

Protestants who had fled from France or Spain, both of which recognized James Stuart, the Catholic son of King James II, as the true monarch of England (the exiled Stuart was derisively known among Protestants as the "Pretender") and were actively battling with England for control of North American territories. Partly from genuine fear for their safety and partly out of prejudice, New Yorkers taught their children to hate and fear "the Pope, Devil and Pretender."

The first Trinity Church was destroyed in the Great New York City Fire of 1776, along with its burial records. A second church—now facing Broadway, unlike the original—opened on the spot in 1790. That building lasted less than half a century before it was torn down due to structural problems. The third (and current) church opened in 1846, featuring a Gothic design by architect Richard Upjohn. The spire instantly became iconic; it made the church the tallest building not only in town but also in the entire United States, a distinction it would hold for more than two decades.

In-ground burials largely ended in 1822. During the construction of the third church, the burial ground was left in disarray. Journalist John Flavel Mines recalled, "Many tombstones were broken, others were moved out of place, and confusion reigned."[8] In 1866, a wire fence was replaced with an iron railing, partly "to prevent little boys from playing leap-frog in the churchyard in church time, and demolishing tombstones."[9] Little care seems to have been taken of them in those days, and no one can guess the number that were lost.

As of 1897, when Sexton Phillip G. Walter (1860–1916) attempted to transcribe the remaining monuments at Trinity and St. Paul's, there were around 1,200 stones and monuments at Trinity, of which about 1,000 were still legible. Many more would become illegible in the coming years, and many of the inscriptions he wrote down can't be matched to any stone today. In the 1980s, Jerusalem-born preservationist Miriam Silverman (1923–2012) found that acid rain and other factors were causing the remaining monuments to decay at an "appalling rate." Many previous attempts at preservation, such as adding resin coatings to marble urn-topped monuments, she described as "disastrous." She launched a massive project to document, map, and preserve the remaining stones with more modern technology, and changes have been relatively minimal since.

Still, with so many burial records lost in fires and even many documented burials not appearing in the surviving records, there are countless unanswered questions. The interment books never gave specific burial locations, so it's unusual to know even generally where a person with no headstone was buried. In many cases, no record survives to show whose grave a now-illegible stone marks. It's even difficult to know if the legible gravestones accurately mark the spot where a person is buried—in some cases, they certainly don't, and in many, they probably never did.

Records are also sparse and contradictory as to who was and wasn't interred in the dozens of brick subterranean vaults under the graveyard. Sometimes, metal coffin plates were all that remained of a coffin just a few years after they were interred, and those were sometimes illegible.

But the people interred here represent a unique view of New York—and the United States—from a critical period in history. From the scattered remaining stories of the people interred here, one gets a fascinating, up-close look at a lost society.

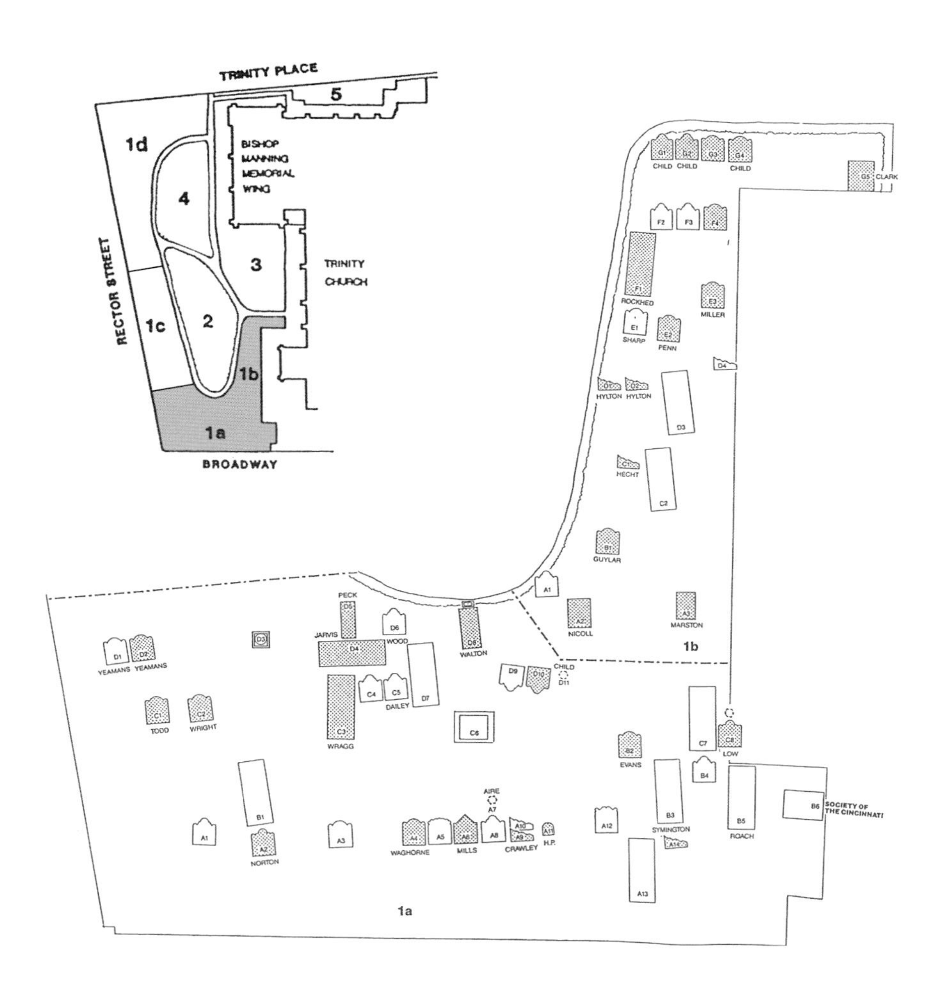
TRINITY PLACE
5
1d
BISHOP
MANNING
MEMORIAL
WING
4
3
TRINITY
CHURCH
RECTOR STREET
1c
2
1b
1a
BROADWAY
CHILD
CHILD
CHILD
CLARK
ROCKHED
MILLER
SHARP
PENN
HYLTON
HYLTON
HECHT
GUYLAR
NICOLL
MARSTON
PECK
JARVIS
WOOD
WALTON
CHILD
YEAMANS
YEAMANS
TODD
WRIGHT
DAILEY
WRAGG
LOW
EVANS
AIRE
SOCIETY OF THE CINCINNATI
NORTON
WAGHORNE
MILLS
CRAWLEY
H.P.
SYMINGTON
ROACH

# SECTIONS S1-A AND S1-B

## JAMES LAWRENCE

*In regard to the commanders of gun boats (whom you are pleased to term "swaggerers"), I assure you that their sabres are sufficiently sharp to cut off your ears, and will inevitably be employed in that service, if any future remarks, injurious to their reputation, should be inserted in your paper.*

—*James Lawrence to the* New York Advertiser[10]

Among the first things one sees when entering the grounds of Trinity Churchyard is the large monument to CAPTAIN JAMES LAWRENCE (1781–1813). He is best remembered for saying, "Don't give up the ship," in his final battle, but his career was far too tumultuous and controversial to be contained in one catchphrase.

In 1807, when Jacob Frank of the *New York Advertiser* published criticisms of navy gunners, Lawrence not only sent a letter threatening to cut off his ears but also stormed into Frank's office demanding a reply. Frank wasn't in at the time, but a clerk, Mr. Murphy, said, "Mr. Frank will stand in his own shoes." Another clerk said, "This is an independent paper, and the press is free; your threats won't intimidate him."

When one of the clerks added that Mr. Frank had *laughed* at then-lieutenant Lawrence's threats, Lawrence punched that clerk in the mouth, and shouted, "You damned rascal! Laughed at it? God damn you. I'll be damned if I won't serve Frank in the same way!"[11]

His use of the phrase "damned rascal" was a message that would have been unmistakable at the time: he was looking for a duel. But the staff simply ignored the brash young officer. Lawrence eventually apologized, but the hotheaded episode foreshadowed his demise.

Captain Lawrence, by Gilbert Stuart.

Lawrence had already had an adventurous naval career. In 1804, when the USS *Philadelphia* was captured by Barbary pirates, Stephen Decatur recaptured and burned the ship in Tripoli Harbor, following a raid that British vice admiral Lord Horatio Nelson was said to call "the most bold and daring act of the age." Lawrence was second-in-command. During the War of 1812, Lawrence was in command of the USS *Hornet* when it sank the British *Peacock*, making him a national hero.

Months later, he was given command of the *Chesapeake*. Though he was under orders not to engage in combat if he didn't have to, he and Captain Phillip Broke of the British *Shannon* agreed to a "ship's duel," in which they'd meet "ship to ship to try the fortune of our respective flags."[12]

As spectators gathered on the shore to watch the planned battle, Lawrence dressed in his best and told his crew they would "have blood for supper."[13]

He had reason to be optimistic: the U.S. Navy had been racking up victories, and the *Chesapeake* had more guns and more men than the *Shannon*. But his crew were unfamiliar with the ship, their new captain, and even each other. Broke's crew and ship were, in contrast, a well-oiled machine. Fifteen minutes after the first shot was fired, the British seamen had disabled, boarded, and captured the *Chesapeake*. Lawrence was shot twice, and his wounds proved to be fatal. Before his death, he was heard to say, "Don't give up the ship."

In some accounts, he later changed the order to "Blow her up!" But by then, it was too late. The ship had already been given up. Dozens were dead as a result of Lawrence's reckless agreement to fight.

LIEUTENANT AUGUSTUS LUDLOW (1792–1813) briefly took command when Lawrence fell. He had gone to sea at the age of twelve and saw service in the Tripoli War only a year later. Now, attempting to repel a boarding party, his head was cut nearly in two by a saber blade. He died days later in a Halifax hospital.[14] "Poor fellow!" his brother wrote. "It is the fortune of war and what we must expect!"[15]

Captain Broke, for his part, sustained a sword wound to the head that left his pulsating brain exposed to view. He somehow survived, but his career was over.

Lawrence and Ludlow were initially buried in Halifax, but two months later they were exhumed and buried in Salem, Massachusetts. A month after that they were moved to Trinity Churchyard.[16] The funeral and reinterment was a major public relations move by the navy, spinning Lawrence's foolhardy loss as martyrdom.

A monument resembling a broken marble column was built in 1816, but it was apparently not built to last; within a decade, its decaying condition was a common topic in the press.[17] Some found the complaints disingenuous; one paper wrote, "Whenever an editor has been hard run for a subject, the ghost of the naval hero has been 'trotted out,' his battles fought over, his dying words repeated—and all because the pile above has crumbled away."[18] It was replaced in 1847 by the current monument, designed by Richard Upjohn.[19]

JULIA MONTAUDEVERT LAWRENCE (1788–1865) outlived her husband by more than half a century. She was a New York girl, living near Bowling Green at the time of her wedding, which took place at Trinity Church in June 1809. She gave birth to a son a month after her husband's death and had only just recovered physically when she attended his funeral at Trinity. The child, JAMES LAWRENCE JR. (1813–1814), lived only fifteen months and was said to have been buried near his father under the old monument. Julia moved to Newport and lived quietly there, never remarrying.

Her interment at Trinity was a minor news item in 1865, but no one mentioned exactly *where* she was interred; if hers was an in-ground burial, it would have been the last such burial at the churchyard. Burial beneath that monument would have been difficult, illegal, and likely not particularly close to her husband's actual burial spot. The original monument stood

An article from 1813 stated that one who viewed Ludlow's remains in Salem, Massachusetts, "recognized a ring on the finger of the deceased, it being the same she had given as a token of respect to Charles Nathaniel, a Jew, who was lately interred in Halifax...near Ludlow." This suggested that body may not have been Ludlow's at all.* Records are unclear about whether Ludlow was buried next to Lawrence or elsewhere in the churchyard.

* From the Lawrence file, quoting *Acadian Recorder*, September 11, 1813.

in the southwest corner of the churchyard, and there is no record of a removal, so Captain Lawrence's body was more likely somewhere in section 1-D.[20]

Some references to Captain Lawrence's burial assume that he was placed in a vault, not buried in the ground, but there's no clear evidence in the records. One funeral report states only that Lawrence and Ludlow were "consigned to the ground," which doesn't rule out a vault.[21]

So, Captain and Mrs. Lawrence's burial spots—and even the nature of their interments—remain mysteries.

## Views Through the Fence

Visible through the fence from Broadway is a grim face topping a marker for Andrew Mills (circa 1705–1749, A6), whose stone denotes him as the "Purser of his Majestys Ship *Greyhound*." The *Greyhound* was a privateer, a ship that engaged in piracy for the Crown. In 1743, before shipping out under Captain Jeffery (see page 124), Mills made out a will, stating that he

Waghorne, the newly identified Stephens, and Mills. The larger marker behind theirs, officially unknown, has been identified as that of Grace Lyde.

was "in bodily health, but considering the dangers of the seas," which was standard language in sailors' wills.

Mills's headstone is located in a cluster of markers that are in varying states of decay. On the far left of the cluster, featuring a death's head with an awful lot of teeth, is the largely buried stone of JOHN WAGHORNE (CIRCA 1692–1745, A4), a constable who made his living by Japanning, a type of lacquering.[22]

The illegible limestone marker between Waghorne's and Mills's could not be identified in the 1980s, but it's for royal artillery soldier JAMES STEPHENS (DIED 1767, A5).[23] It once had an epitaph along the lines of:

> *After faithful service rendered to his king and country, amid scenes of hardship and danger, in Europe and America, died here, of a fever in the year 1767.*

A writer in 1856 said, "[The Stephens stone] has a blurred appearance. The letters have lost all their sharpness. The entire surface of the stone is roughened, very much as sugar is when partially dissolved. In fact, it looks mean, coarse, and stingy."[24] He then compared it to the older, still-sharp sandstone markers for Waghorne and Mills.

The writer would be gratified today: the Waghorne and Mills sandstone markers are still legible, but his article is the only way the Stephens marker can be identified.

## GENERAL BRADSTREET'S ROWDY FUNERAL

"No characters, madam, are free from blemish. The greatest and almost the only one in his was an unbecoming resentment against his family." So wrote Phillip Schuyler in a letter to Mary Bradstreet, informing her of the death of her husband, GENERAL JOHN BRADSTREET (CIRCA 1714–1774). The good news was that Schuyler had persuaded Bradstreet to throw out his original will in favor of one that provided for his estranged wife and daughters, but Schuyler couldn't say Bradstreet had been happy about it. The new will, of course, also left a great deal to the Schuylers, including a bequeathment to teenage Peggy, who'd nursed Bradstreet in his last illness until he died in her arms. Bradstreet, Schuyler's former commander, had helped build his fortune and reputation, both of which would prove valuable in the Revolution.

General Bradstreet was one of the first brilliant military tacticians in the colonies and a veteran of several British campaigns, as well as several schemes to bring himself fame and fortune. An eccentric who made both friends and enemies easily, he was filled with ideas but not known for great judgement. A biography by William Godfrey was aptly titled *An Irregular Regular*. Since Bradstreet was a friend of people such as Schuyler and John Morin Scott, it's quite possible that he would have joined the American side in the Revolution, but he died of dropsy just before it began. Letters Schuyler wrote back to England about Bradstreet's estate refer to the "dark aspect" cast by the controversy with "the mother country."

According to a letter in the Trinity Archives, Bradstreet's military funeral at Trinity was a riotous affair costing £400 (roughly two years' salary for a laborer). Mourners went through ninety bottles of wine and trashed the church so thoroughly that Schuyler was fined £12 for broken windows, broken pews, and cleaning fees.[25] In modern vernacular: the mourners, likely including the Schuyler sisters, partied hard and trashed the place.

Schuyler's own letters say that Bradstreet was buried under the chancel of the first church (two years before it burned). But as of 1911, descendants of Bradstreet believed that an illegible table grave adjacent to the fence of the Lawrence monument—likely the otherwise-unidentified C7—was a monument for the general. It was said that several family members had stones nearby it, though by 1897, the only one still legible was that of JOHN CHARLES EVANS (CIRCA 1738–1793, B2), Bradstreet's son-in-law.

## JARVIS-PECK

Among the graves seen from the path is a newer marker (D4) above the Jarvis-Peck vault, added in 1938 through the work of ELLEN ANDERSON JARVIS (1874–1957), a missionary in China and the Philippines who herself was the last to be interred in the vault. Only a couple of interments within it are identified for sure, but sixteen coffins were inside as of 1868.

Behind it is a ledger stone carved by Uzal Ward for MARY WRAGG (CIRCA 1748–1759, C3).[26] Mary's father, James Wragg, placed advertisements in 1750s newspapers advertising that he was available to teach night school classes: "Writing, arithmetick, merchant accounts, navigation, surveying, gauging, dialing and astronomy, with the use of globes."[27] This was all done

## SLAVERY IN NEW YORK

In the 1700s, slavery was more common in New York than in any other major American city except for Charleston, South Carolina. Though records are sometimes unclear, by some estimates, half of the white population enslaved people before the Revolution. Enslaved people worked in a variety of jobs, both skilled and unskilled.

It would be dismissive to say that slavery in New York was "milder" than it was in the South, though New Yorkers of the day often told themselves as much. John Jay said as much explicitly in 1788: "The treatment which slaves in general meet with in this State is very little different from that of other servants."* Certainly the culture of slavery wouldn't have *looked* the same to an observer as it did in the cotton states or on the islands. And threats to sell enslaved people to other enslavers in the South were considered highly effective. In New York, enslaved people had certain legal protections that they wouldn't have had in the South and often seem to have had some spending money, leisure time, and places of entertainment that catered to them. Newspaper advertisements relating to them refer to individual fashion senses and habits of drinking or smoking.

Though some aspects of eighteenth-century New York are relatable to us today, it was a different world that doesn't truly correlate or "hold up a mirror" to our own. Slavery was such a fact of life that few seem to have questioned it; even people who were opposed to slavery in principle tended not to make much noise about it. New Yorkers couldn't have avoided buying goods or using services that involved slave labor. In a world of indentured servants and bound apprentices, it may simply not have seemed as shocking as we expect. But the enslaved people didn't have the choices that servants and apprentices did, and there was usually no expiration date to their service.

But somehow, the institution never became as central to New York's sense of identity as it did the southern states; one prominent Georgia politician even moved to New York in 1799

* John Jay letter, June 1788.

because it was safer to hold antislavery views there (page 164). Things changed relatively quickly in New York—at least compared to some places—after the Revolution. A Manumission Society was formed, and freeing people who were once enslaved became something of a trend. A law was passed by the end of the century that gradually phased slavery out.

How are we to think of the people interred here who owned other human beings? Is it fair to judge people of previous eras by modern standards? If not, shouldn't we at least draw a line at slavery? Should we credit people if they eventually freed the people they enslaved? Are we being too generous with ourselves if we assume we wouldn't have held the same beliefs if we had been raised in the world they had?

The answers are beyond the scope of this book, but these are important issues to consider.

in a house owned by "Mr. Peck," presumably the Benjamin Peck who built the adjacent vault. Mary's epitaph reads:

*Her Days Whear short as ye Winter Sun*
*from Dust she came to Heaven Return*

*Beneath*
*This Child asleeping Lies*
*to Earth Whose ashes Lent*
*More Glorious shall hearafter Rise*
*tho not more Innocent*
*When archangles Trump shall Blow*
*and Souls & Bodyes Joyn*
*What Crowds will wish their lives Below*
*had been as short as thine*

The portion beginning with the word *beneath* is taken from *Poems on Several Occasions* by Samuel Wesley the Younger, written around 1730. In 1896, John Flavel Mines noted, "It is noticeable in connection with this inscription that our ancestors were not always gifted in the art of spelling."[28] Spelling was *not* something Wragg offered to teach.

# Section S1-B

Section 1B is full of larger unidentified markers. Two of the most legible graves (modern restorations) in the section are those of Abraham Child (died 1817, G1) and Francis Child Sr. (circa 1747–1808, G2). Abraham was a tailor and likely the same Abraham Child who sold a servant named Rose Butler to the Morris family. Her story was far better recorded than his.

Born in late 1799, Rose would have been among the first Black women born under the gradual emancipation law that was enacted in New York that year. But the law required twenty-five years of indentured servitude before a person was actually granted their freedom. In 1809, Rose's indenture was sold to Child, and a few years later, he sold what remained of it to the Morris family.

In 1817, Rose was accused of attempting to seal the Morris family in their house and burn it down, an attempt that was thwarted before anyone was hurt. She expressed no remorse but claimed that two white men had talked her into the deed. The fact that the house *did* burn down while she was in jail seems to back this up. But Rose refused to name names. Notes from her trial show the extent to which society expected indentured servants to love and obey their "owners." A judge said, "It is remarkable that Rose Butler has shown no marks of contrition…but has declared and expressed her resentment against her mistress ever since.…She is a person of extraordinary natural depravity."[29]

Modern readers will also note the long "S," which resembled a lowercase "f," making it appear to say Wragg's "days were fhort." The rules for using the long "S" were so varied over the centuries that one could almost say they were arbitrary; the long "S" was going out of fashion by 1800 but appears on several gravestones at Trinity and St. Paul's. Joseph Penn's marker in S1-B, pictured, uses it several times, as well as the archaic printer's abbreviation "ye" for "the" (which was pronounced "the.")

The sentencing judge said to Rose, "I understand you are quite intelligent…yet it is necessary that you be cut off from society." She was hanged and buried in a potter's field some distance north. Nine years later, slavery officially ended in New York, and that same year, the potter's field where Rose was buried became Washington Square Park. A particular elm tree in the park, over three hundred years old and thought to be the oldest tree in Manhattan, is known today as the Hangman's Tree. Though there's no evidence that it was actually used for hangings, it's likely that a few of the people who crowded the grounds for the execution of Rose Butler tried to climb it for a better view.

## Lost Markers in S1-A and S1-B

One now-missing marker that was said to be in this section was an upright marble slab for Witkamus de Marisco (1720–1765); it had a Latin motto that translated to "by his father's mother's side he was most nobly born." Marisco was William Marsh, a county clerk from Albany who was said to have dictated what the stone would say in his will.[30]

An 1847 article said that near Lawrence's monument was a stone for Henry Lane. Matching Marsh's self-importance, Lane's stone identified him as "a merchant, and son of Thomas Lane of London, knight and alderman." The article said, "His friends seem to have a high opinion of Henry's standing and connections and to have been anxious to impress you with the idea that no common dust was at your feet.…Snobs are to be found everywhere."[31] Both Marsh's and Lane's stones were gone or illegible by 1897.

More intriguing is the large marble monument (C6) in the center of S1-A, which is officially unidentified but is, beyond a reasonable doubt, the remains of a memorial for Grace Lyde (1778–1820).[32] An 1839 reference to Lyde's marker called it "a handsome monument, some three feet square, and of proportional height, open at the four sides, containing a marble urn."[33] An article from 1855 noted that the handsome Lyde monument was crumbling and described it being "in easy view from Broadway and near the fence."[34]

Most telling of all, an 1886 book on stonework said Grace's monument was "near Broadway, about halfway between the church and Rector Street, in the shape of a square marble monument with an inclined top now about

## Epitaphs

This common epitaph appears on graves at both Trinity and St. Paul's:

*Afflictions sore long time I bore*
*Physicians aid proved vain*
*Till God alone did hear my moan*
*And ease me of my pain*

The verse was well-known enough to be referenced in Dickens's *David Copperfield*; David notes it on a tablet in his childhood church and wonders how the doctors liked to be reminded that their aid had proved vain every week. Even before Dickens, writers who referred to the verse assumed their readers would be familiar with it. As early as 1778, essayist Vicesimus Knox said that parish clerks had provided it as an epitaph on at least one grave in nearly every English churchyard.*

It's only one of many epitaphs seen at Trinity and St. Paul's that are also seen in a number of other graveyards. Some are seen on dozens of graves, with minor variations, others on just a couple. Many came from hymns and poems, and some were probably original creations that simply spread from churchyard to churchyard.

How did these verses spread? Even among those that came from famous sources, how did so many people pick the same few lines as epitaphs? There were a few collections of epitaphs published, and one would imagine that stone carvers had a book of suggested inscriptions at the ready. But no document published seems to cover nearly all of the common verses.

Most likely, epitaphs spread like folk songs or nursery rhymes; people would memorize a verse they'd seen on a grave and later put it on others, with variations either from a lapse of memory or to fit new circumstances.

By the time burials were stopped at Trinity in the 1820s, maudlin epitaphs were out of style and frequently pointed out as embarrassing. One 1846 writer—likely Walt Whitman—wrote, "These 'uncouth rhymes,' the reader will remember, have a deep meaning and applicability to the near relatives and friends of those buried there, though to the critical stranger's eye they appear worse than indifferent as literary compositions."†

* Vicesimus Knox, "On Monumental Inscriptions," in *Essays Moral and Literary* (1785).
† "Brooklynite," *BDE.*

Grace Lyde's marker and an unidentified box grave.

four feet high." According to that source, "Originally this was twelve feet high, supported on polished columns, with an open space underneath, in the center of which was an urn." This monument, the book said, was illegible by 1860, and in danger of falling around 1880, when it was taken down, and "all that could be used was put up in its present shape."[35]

Grace was the wife of broker Edward Lyde, who died after burials were stopped at Trinity, and was interred in a vault at St. Mark's in the Bowery. Records show the Lydes were closely tied the family of David Ogden (page 51).

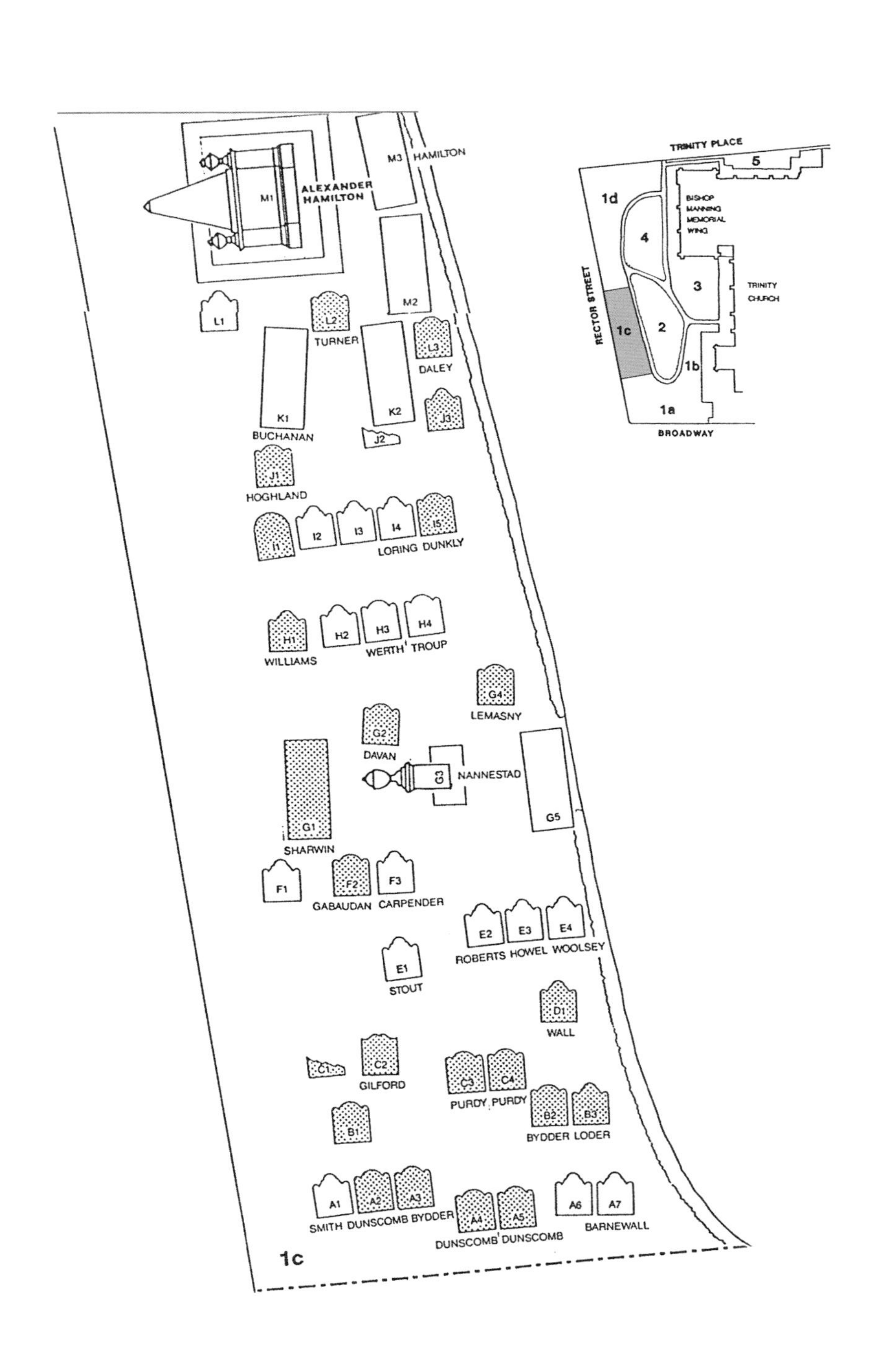

M3 HAMILTON
M1 ALEXANDER HAMILTON
M2
L1
L2 TURNER
L3 DALEY
K1 BUCHANAN
K2
J2
J3
J1 HOGHLAND
I1
I2
I3
I4 LORING
I5 DUNKLY
H1 WILLIAMS
H2
H3 WERTH
H4 TROUP
G4 LEMASNY
G2 DAVAN
G3 NANNESTAD
G5
G1 SHARWIN
F1
F2 GABAUDAN
F3 CARPENDER
E2 ROBERTS
E3 HOWEL
E4 WOOLSEY
E1 STOUT
D1 WALL
C1
C2 GILFORD
C3 PURDY
C4 PURDY
B2 BYDDER
B3 LODER
B1
A1 SMITH
A2 DUNSCOMB
A3 BYDDER
A4 DUNSCOMB
A5 DUNSCOMB
A6
A7 BARNEWALL
1c
TRINITY PLACE
5
1d
4
BISHOP MANNING MEMORIAL WING
RECTOR STREET
3
TRINITY CHURCH
1c
2
1b
1a
BROADWAY

# SECTION S1-C

At the edge of Section S1-C are two white markers, the larger of which is now illegible but is known to be for Elizabeth Barnewall (circa 1859–1801, A7).[36] She died of tuberculosis during an autumn in which her husband, a merchant, was taking out advertisements offering lemons for sale.[37]

Among the legible graves in the area is one for cartman James Purdy (circa 1739–1794, C3):

*As you go by remember me*
*As you are now so once was I*
*As I am now so much you be*
*Assuredly you all shall die*
*Both rich and poor, the old and young*
*Your time on Earth will not be long.*

Though the sentiments in each line are common for epitaphs of the era, the ABABCC rhyme scheme marks this as an unusual variation.

The eastern portion of the section is dominated by the tall marble monument, completely illegible today, for Lars Nannestad (1757–1807, G3). The inscription on the back read, in Danish:

*Underneath lay the remains of Lars Nannestad, his Danish majesty's weighter and post-master in the island of St. Thomas, assessor in the burgher-council, church warden, and guardian of the poor at the same place. He was born on the 6 June, 1757, at Lille Nestved; married, in the year 1789, to Anna Maria Elizabeth Windberg, and arrived with her at New York on the 31st Day of May, 1807, for the benefit of declining health, and was the 24th day of July, same year, called to a better life, aged 49 years and some days. The surviving and disconsolate widow has erected this monument as a grateful remembrance of a most affectionate husband.*[38]

Lars most likely left St. Thomas, in what was then known as the Danish West Indies, ahead of an expected British takeover. England was fighting to keep the Danish from aligning with Napoleon and invaded the islands in December 1807.

## THE SHARWINS AND ELIZABETH

Behind Lars's stone is a box grave for saddler RICHARD SHARWIN (1739–1783, G1). In January 1775, Richard was in Boston and joined with a group of drunken British soldiers when they attacked the town, a miniature riot for which he and several officers were briefly detained. He left with the British troops when they moved on to New York.

He had managed to maintain a semblance of neutrality through the war, during which his services making saddles were in great demand. In their book *Espionage and Enslavement in the Revolution*, Claire Bellerjeau and Tiffany Yecke Brooks note that Sharwin's death in 1783, just as the war ended, was "as conveniently timed as such unfortunate events can be," as demand for his business had plummeted.[39] An obituary called him "one of the most eminent saddlers in America" and noted that "he has made a pretty fortune with an unblemished character. He was a pleasant, generous man, and always much esteemed by a very extensive acquaintance."[40]

The events his death set in motion are what kept his name alive—at least as a footnote. His widow, Ann, used the money he left her to buy an enslaved woman named Elizabeth (known as "Liss") from Robert Townsend, who had been a member of Washington's Culper Spy Ring. Townsend's parents had enslaved Liss in New England, but she had escaped with British officers to New York some time before, only to find herself enslaved by one of them. That officer planned to move to Canada, and Liss didn't want to go there. Learning that young Robert was in New York, she went to his shop and asked him to repurchase her. He agreed (his financial records mention buying her tea) and later sold her to Ann Sharwin.

This sale was unusual; records stated that Liss knew Ann and "consented" to live with her. There was even an agreement that if Ann ever left New York or wished to sell Liss, Robert would repurchase her.

But when Ann's next marriage—to one Alexander Robertson—broke up (for which Liss was blamed), Liss was secretly sold to a man in Charleston, while her baby remained with Robertson.

Only days after the sale, the antislavery New York Manumission Society was formed, and Robert Townsend joined. When he learned what had happened following Ann's divorce, he took the child from Robertson and worked diligently until he found Liss, whom he repurchased and freed. She appeared in the 1790 census as "Free Elizabeth" and obtained her formal manumission in 1803.

Though it remains strictly speculation, it's been suggested that Liss assisted Townsend in his spy work.

West of the towering Nannestad grave are a couple rows of smaller stones. Among them, near the fence, is a mostly broken stone topped by a freemason symbol for THOMAS WILLIAMS (1751–1804) AND ANNA WILLIAMS (DIED 1800, H1), which used to contain the common epitaph beginning with "afflictions sore long time I bore" (see page 31).

Closer to the path is one of the more intricately carved markers in the section: CAPTAIN JOHN DALEY (CIRCA 1740–1774, L3), who is said to have died on a voyage from New England to New York. Clustered around it are three box tombs just east of the Hamilton plot; the one closest to Rector Street is for merchant JOHN BUCHANAN (CIRCA 1760–1812, K1).

## AARON BURR

Though he is buried in New Jersey, Aaron Burr (1756–1836) seems to almost haunt the lives of people interred at Trinity and St. Paul's.

Burr was in law school when he joined the Continental army. A story that he tried to recover the body of General Montgomery (page 252) after the invasion of Quebec may not have been true, but it made Burr a legend in his own time. He married Theodosia Provost, who was ten years his senior and the widow of a British officer.

His first act as a politician in the state assembly was to introduce a bill ending slavery in the state. The bill failed, and Burr didn't free the handful of people he enslaved himself, but it's worth noting that he was ahead of his time on many issues.

Burr tied with Jefferson in the presidential election of 1800, becoming vice president when the executive office went to his rival (in those days, the runner-up in the election

Burr and his wife, Theodosia. *Frick Art Reference Library.*

was vice president). But Jefferson could never stand him, and Burr ended up running for governor of New York in 1804 while still in office as vice president. It was rumored that as governor he'd support an effort to split New York off from the union, and Burr didn't do much to dispel the idea. But he lost the election, partly because of the efforts of his political rival Alexander Hamilton (page 40) and gossip-mongering journalist James Cheetham (page 177).

After Burr killed Hamilton in a duel (page 40), his political career was essentially over, but his ambition was unquenched. He spent decades involved in schemes, legal shenanigans and wild ventures.

At the age of seventy-seven, he married the widow Eliza Jumel; she was nearly twenty years his junior and had been raised in a brothel, but she married into high society. They were separated after four months, and Madame Jumel engaged Alexander Hamilton Jr. as a divorce lawyer. Burr died in a boardinghouse the day the divorce was finalized.

In his will, Burr acknowledged two secret daughters whom he'd fathered by different mothers in his seventies, and they were likely only two of many. In 2018, DNA tests indicated that he also fathered two children by Mary Emmons, an East Indian–Haitian servant. The oldest of these two, Louisa, was born the same year as Burr's daughter with Theodosia (Theodosia Burr Alston, who died at sea in 1813). The younger, John Pierre, was fathered while Burr's wife, Theodosia, was dying. He grew up to be a prominent part of the Underground Railroad in Philadelphia.*

Theodosia Prevost Burr died in 1794 and is sometimes said to have been buried at St. John's Burying Ground, but that would have been a very early burial there, and records are unclear. Her first wedding took place at Trinity, and she may be interred here or at St. Paul's.

* "Aaron Burr—Villain of Hamilton—Had a Secret Family of Color; New Research Shows," *Washington Post*, August 24, 2019.

# THE HAMILTON PLOT

ALEXANDER HAMILTON (CIRCA 1755–1804, M1) was younger than most of the other founding fathers and came from a vastly different background. While many were born into wealthy families, Alexander was raised in the West Indies by a mother who had been jailed for adultery. He was abandoned by his father, cheated out of an inheritance, and always on the brink of ruin in his youth.

When he arrived in the United States to study law, Hamilton knew that fighting in a war was the most reliable way to make a name for himself. His brilliant mind gained him a role as Washington's aide-de-camp, a job he accepted despite his reckless thirst to prove himself in combat.

After the war, he wrote many of the *Federalist Papers*, arguing for the ratification of the new Constitution. Then he served as Washington's secretary of the treasury, engineering the financial system behind the early government. He did all of this against a backdrop of tangled love affairs, personal grudges, the birth of party politics, and the growth of a great city.

While Hamilton was veritably obsessed with duels and *nearly* fought several, he avoiding actually fighting in one until 1804. That year, word went around that Hamilton had alluded to a "still more despicable" thing that could be said of Vice President Burr than what James Cheetham (page 177) was publishing, and Burr demanded an explanation. After a series of letters and challenges, a duel was arranged. Hamilton told several people he planned to fire in the air, but Burr shot to kill, and Hamilton was fatally wounded.

His funeral was a huge affair, with a eulogy given by Governor Morris, and later, a monument was placed on his grave by the Society of the Cincinnati, a fraternal organization for Revolutionary officers. Ron Chernow published a massive biography in 2004, and it served as the inspiration for Lin Manuel Miranda's smash hit musical *Hamilton* in 2015.

Three years before the Burr-Hamilton duel, Hamilton's son PHILLIP HAMILTON (1782–1801) was killed in a duel with lawyer George Eacker (page 231), who challenged the teenage Phillip over his obnoxious behavior with his friend Stephen Price (pages 72, 86, 214 and 232) in a theater. Phillip was going through a wild stage; Robert Troup had described Phillip as "a sad rake," and Alexander had recently instituted a strict schedule to keep his son out of trouble. He affectionately referred to Phillip as being "naughty" in letters.

The exact location of Phillip's burial is not known, though it's reasonable to assume he was buried near his father. A number of late nineteenth-

*Above*: The Hamilton plot (and a shoe store that was not entirely confident) in 2018.

*Left*: Eliza Hamilton, from a 1781 portrait. *New York Public Library.*

century articles stated that Phillip's remains were located under the Hamilton monument, though none were written by people who really would have been in a position to know.

By the middle of the nineteenth century, newspapers were running articles marveling that ELIZA SCHUYLER HAMILTON (1757–1854, M3), Alexander's widow, was still alive.

Born to one of the most powerful families in New York, Eliza spent her later years collecting her husband's papers and working to protect the legacy of "My Hamilton," as she called him. She also engaged in charity work, including the founding of the city's first private orphanage.

In her eighties, she made regular trips to the law office where George Templeton Strong (page 73) worked. On a "savagely cold" New Year's Day in 1840, he noted, "Old Lady Hamilton said it was a mere trifle, nothing at all to the winter of 1780." When Eliza was in her nineties, Strong wrote, "I don't believe that old lady has the slightest intention of ever going to a better world: such a specimen of juvenile antediluvianism I never encountered."[41]

By the time of Eliza's death, only vault interments had been allowed at Trinity for more than thirty years. But an exception seems to have been made for Eliza, who was given an in-ground burial. (The fact that Trinity was fighting against the extension of a road through the churchyard at the time may have played a role—see page 112.) At her request, Eliza was given the simplest funeral possible, but her mahogany coffin was placed in the church for spectators to see before she was laid to rest.[42]

## THE LOST "MY MOTHER" GRAVE

Nearly every nineteenth-century account of Trinity referrs to one monument that gave no name for its occupant. It read only:

> *My Mother!*
> *Til the trumpet shall sound*
> *And the dead shall rise*

This simple epitaph became famous. In 1829, the *New York American* said it was "so singularly and affectingly beautiful, we cannot forbear to record it, and the emotions it awakened in the bosom of a stranger."[43] McDonald Clark wrote a lengthy poem about it. Walt Whitman referred to it in his novel

Box grave that was likely the lost "My Mother" monument.

*Jack Engle* and called it "the manifestation of a most sweet motive!"[44] For a time, it was mentioned in articles as often as the Hamilton and Lawrence graves—and usually inspired much longer descriptions.

As famous as the "My Mother" marker was, its exact location was lost when its inscription faded. But the various descriptions of it make it traceable. The 1829 article called it "an oblong masonry, surmounted by a slab stone." Several mentioned that it was near Alexander Hamilton's marker, and an 1880 book, written after Eliza had been interred, said it was "Just below the grave of Mrs. Hamilton" and close to the tombs of Joseph Aquiller (died 1803) and Buchanan.[45] It was almost certainly, therefore, the unidentified box grave marked M2 on the map.

Aquiller, perhaps, is the owner of the other unidentified box grave in the area (K2), though no one by that name ever seems to have existed at all (the 1880 book was rather typo-prone).

There was also a grave marked "My Father" near the south door as of 1897.

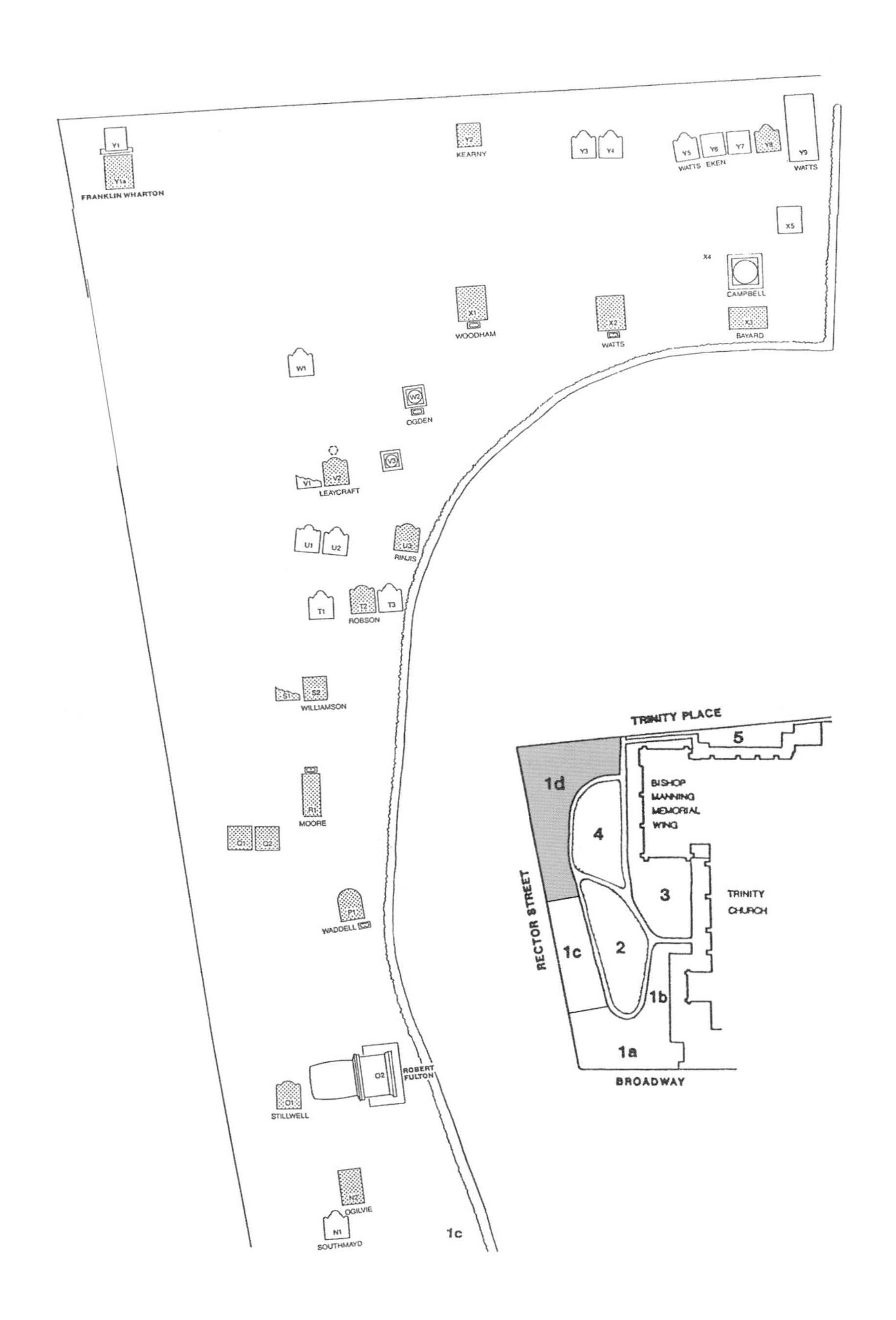

FRANKLIN WHARTON
KEARNY
WATTS
EKEN
WATTS
CAMPBELL
WOODHAM
WATTS
BAYARD
OGDEN
LEAYCRAFT
RINJIS
ROBSON
WILLIAMSON
MOORE
WADDELL
ROBERT FULTON
STILLWELL
OGILVIE
SOUTHMAYD
1c
TRINITY PLACE
BISHOP MANNING MEMORIAL WING
TRINITY CHURCH
RECTOR STREET
BROADWAY

# SECTION S1-D

Section 1 continues along the edge of Rector and Church Streets. It is home to several vaults.

Stone vaults honeycomb the ground beneath Trinity and St. Paul's. The larger ones are about the size of a one-car garage, with space for more than twenty coffins. Most are accessible by digging out a staircase to a door.

Vaults appear to have been remarkably affordable. Though the costs for vaults varied, they tended to cost around £15 in the early days and, later, $1 per square foot—in both cases, they would be roughly in the range of $1,000 today. A single in-ground burial cost about £0.03, so vaults certainly cost more, but they were nowhere near the cost of later mausoleums and large monuments.

In 1904, the church's sexton noted that sealed metal caskets were now required in vaults, "Which is very different form the old way of doing. Down in some of the vaults the [wooden] caskets are arranged on shelves, and some of them have almost crumbled away, leaving the skeleton exposed."[46]

Shelves, in fact, were the exception; in most vaults, the coffins were simply stacked on top of each other. Stories would circulate of gruesome heaps of bones inside of vaults. An inspection of each vault was made in 1868; sometimes, only coffin plates and dust were found.

Today, most of the vaults can still be used, but only cremated remains in urns are permitted, and interments are uncommon.

# ROBERT FULTON

*While we were putting off from the wharf, which was crowded with spectators, I heard a number of sarcastic remarks; this is the way, you know, in which ignorant men compliment what they call philosophers and projectors.*

—*Robert Fulton*[47]

There was a time when few inventors were more famous than ROBERT FULTON (1765–1815, 02), a dashing, sociable, and artistic man who absolutely changed the world.

After a stint making his living as a painter, a doctor advised young Fulton to travel. He arrived in Europe in 1786, and within a decade, he'd achieved a measure of fame for the inventions he developed to help dig canals. In Paris, he designed and built an early submarine, the *Nautilus*, for the government. Several government officials were excited by the early models, but Napoleon was apparently unimpressed.

In England in 1804, now working against Napoleon instead of for him, Fulton designed early naval torpedoes.

But it was back in the United States in 1807 that Fulton built *The North River Steamboat*, the first truly effective steam-powered vessel. In August of that year, he made a great show of setting off from New York City to Albany in the boat. Fulton was, by all accounts, a captivating and popular man, but no one believed he would be successful with this invention.

Dr. John W. Francis noted that even Fulton's best friends thought he'd lost his mind. "I have heard the cry of 'Crazy Fulton' issuing at times from the ignoble masses," he later wrote. "Even at the time when the auspicious moment had arrived, when his boat was now gliding on the waters, individuals were found still incredulous, who named his vast achievement the 'Marine Smoke Jack' and 'Fulton's Folly'…[but] he was working for a nation, not for himself, and the magnitude of the object absorbed all other thoughts."[48]

Fulton made the round-trip voyage to Albany, which normally would have taken over a week, in sixty-two hours.

"The morning I left New York," he wrote, "there was not perhaps thirty persons in the city who believed that the boat would ever move one mile an hour or be of the least utility....But thousands of witnesses have now seen the steam boat in rapid movement, and they believe." Though he admitted that making money was some inducement to him, he said, "I feel infinitely more pleasure in reflecting with you on the immense advantage that my country will derive from the invention."

In that instant, the age of steam began. Few inventors could take credit for changing the world so thoroughly. Fulton's elation is clear in the letters he wrote; his new invention would revolutionize travel and commerce, and his torpedoes, he believed, would soon create "Liberty of the seas; an object of infinite import to the welfare of America, and every civilized country." (torpedo victim Thomas Slidell, page 72, might disagree).

Fulton's business partner was Robert Livingston, whom he'd met and worked with in France. Livingston's niece Harriet, who had once been engaged to George Eacker (page 231), was an accomplished artist, and Fulton bonded with her over their shared loved of painting. At one point, he asked Mr. Livingston whether he should pursue Harriet romantically. Harriet was twenty-four, and Fulton was forty-two and didn't come from one of the "great families" of New York as she did. But Livingston is said to have replied that her father might object, but it was *her* opinion that mattered, not her father's. "If Harriet does not object," Livingston reportedly said, "and she seems to have a world of good sense—go ahead!"

The two were married in 1808 and had several children, though Harriet's letters indicate that she quickly got frustrated with Fulton's addiction to work, his carelessness with money, and perhaps even his lack of social pedigree.[49]

He died of pneumonia in 1815. He had saved his friend Thomas A. Emmet (page 181) from a frozen river, and his doctor believed he had contracted the fatal illness in the process.[50] By this time, Fulton's genius was so celebrated that members of the New York state government passed a resolution to wear signs of mourning for weeks.

Fulton is interred in Harriet's family vault, which was moved in the 1960s to the other side of the church (page 165). (Harriet herself was eventually buried in the town of Claverack.) He had no visible marker until this one was placed in 1901 by the Society of Mechanical Engineers.

"At the front of the quaint old burying ground," wrote *Scientific American* at the time, "run the electric cars, at the head the elevated railroad, and at the foot of Rector Street…some of the fastest vessels in the bay make their landings. What more fitting spot could be obtained for the resting place of one whose activities contributed so large a degree to the progress which is so much in evidence immediately around the historic old church?"[51]

## THE WADDELL VAULT

*The village legends say they talk;*
*Those tomb-somnambulists do walk,*
*In lanes of moonlit church-yards stalk,*
*With viewless incantation spell*
*At midnight toll the belfry bell.*

*Why past the gloom of mould'ring urns*
*From the angelic isles*
*Thy welcome shade disturb'd returns*
*And from thy portrait smiles?*

*—From "Autumn Dream," by Francis Waddell*

Just beyond Fulton's marker stands a headstone (P1) marking the family vault of CAPTAIN JOHN WADDELL (1714–1762), a shipbuilder and merchant. His wife, ANNE KIRTEN WADDELL (1716–1773), was the only woman listed among the fifty-nine founders of the New York Society Library in 1772. After her husband's death, she managed his large estate and operated a store on Dock Street selling imported goods.

A great-grandson, FRANCIS "FRANK" WADDELL (1808–1859), was once called "clever in every sense…and a shining light in our highest society."[52] Frank was a bon vivant, poet, philosopher and comedian. One story held that his eccentricities came from an accident: while walking down Pearl Street, a heavy sign fell on his head, and "to the day of his death [he] was erratic, and averse to all regular habits of life."[53]

He was the life of every party, master of every drawing room. One friend said, "Among the bucks no one was more buckish…no manner more gentlemanly, no clothes more elegant, no equipage more stylish, no horses faster and handsomer than his."[54] As Frank was always in and out of money, it's notable that none of the contemporary writings about him ever mention

*Left*: Frank Waddell, circa 1837, by John Vanderlyne. *Metropolitan Museum of Art.*

*Right*: Charlotte Coventry Waddell. *New York Public Library.*

him having a job. One story holds that he spent one night on a New York stage telling humorous stories, and thereafter, anytime he needed money, he would tell his mother he was thinking of going onto the stage again, and she'd immediately pay him not to. But it was also said, "Upon our rich nabobs, who possessed no other shining quality than money, Frank absolutely looked down."[55]

In 1843, Frank attended an event at the White House; he was an old friend of Priscilla Tyler, President John Tyler's daughter-in-law (and acting first lady before he married Julia Gardiner, page 226). Regarding portraits of the Tyler family, Priscilla noted that all of them had large noses; it was up to her, she said, to introduce a "pug nose" into the bloodline. "Not to be wondered at," Frank said. "For I remember you were always pug-naciously inclined from a child." The reporter who observed the exchange noted that it was a terrible pun.[56] Some of Frank's other published puns—and there were many—were even worse.

Though he published a few volumes of poetry, friends noted that he was not the sort to sully his muse by publishing, but more the type to keep his manuscripts "tied with blue ribbons and hidden in the secret drawer of scented boudoirs." Upon Frank's death in 1859, the *Herald* said, "He was the man to write a sonnet to a lady's eyebrows."

On his deathbed, he was heard to say, "Oh, the majesty of death!" Then he prayed the Lord's Prayer and died just after saying "amen." By then, he was known as "the last of the swells." "He should have lived in the eighteenth century," wrote one obituary, "and flourished among the courtiers who whispered soft nonsense in the ears of de Maintenon....He was the last of the old type of beaux, and he went gracefully out from a scene on which he had lingered after the prompter had rung the bell, the lights had been extinguished, and all the actors but he had made their final exits."[57]

His sister-in-law, CHARLOTTE COVENTRY WADDELL (1816–1891), hosted legendary receptions in the 1840s at the "Waddell Castle" on Fifth Avenue. According to Chauncey Depew, "for one evening in the week, all that [was] eminent in literature, journalism, the law, pulpit, medicine, science, and art... could meet in equal footing." Visitors such as Thackeray and Washington Irving sang her praises. Depew recalled that Charlotte "had the rare art of knowing when and how to bring out the best points of guests...and she could herself contribute a recitation or delineation or reminiscence worthy of the powers of the most distinguished about the board."[58] She enjoyed dressing as Marie Antoinette at costume balls. After her husband's fortune was swept away in the monetary crisis of 1857, she used her own financial acumen to rebuild the estate to greater heights than it had reached before.

When Charlotte was interred in the vault in 1891, a widely printed newspaper account said that when it was opened, "Nine coffins lay along one side. Some of these, which were placed there about one hundred and fifty years ago, had crumbled to pieces, their places being marked only by a grewsome [*sic*] heap of bones and bits of wood. The other boxes still retained their shape, but seemed ready to drop to pieces on being disturbed....It was necessary to turn the coffin endwise, so cramped was the aperture. Mrs. Waddell being the last of the older generation, hers will be the last body consigned here. The entrance to the vault will be sealed."[59]

A snarky note in the Trinity vault record book states that the bill for sealing the vault was sent to J.M. Bundy, editor of the *New York Mail and Express*.

At R1 is the Bind-Moore vault, with a small individual marker for REVEREND BENJAMIN MOORE (1748–1816), who administered communion to Alexander Hamilton on Hamilton's deathbed (though he was reluctant to do so, as Hamilton was not an Episcopalian and had participated in a sinful duel).[60] His son Clement Clarke Moore (interred in the uptown Trinity Cemetery) was the author of "'Twas the Night Before Christmas."

Another man in the Moore vault, THOMAS BARROW, was a seller of prints and artist materials who also created paintings of the ruins of Trinity Church after the fire.

Nearby are two larger markers; one (W2) is marked with a metal plaque identifying the occupant as a yellow fever victim.

## "THE PREVAILING EPIDEMIC"

No one knew that yellow fever was spread by mosquitos until the twentieth century. In early New York, the disease would shut down the city from time to time, and everyone was helpless. The 1798 epidemic was particularly deadly: from July to October that year, some 2,100 people—about 6 percent of the city's population—perished.

Among them was a promising young merchant, DAVID OGDEN (CIRCA 1769–1798, W2). His resting place is now marked by a worn monument fronted by a metal plaque that remains legible, stating that he "on the 27th of September 1798 in the 29th year of his age ~Fell a Victim~ To the then prevailing epidemic."

Watercolor of the Ogden monument, pre-restoration. *Trinity Archives.*

David was part of the firm of Morewood and Ogden, a Pearl Street mercantile firm that offered hundreds of crates of assorted merchandise, everything from fabrics and linens to picture frames and razors.[61] Thomas Morewood (page 54), his partner, left all of his New York real estate to David when he died of yellow fever, but David died only days later of the same disease.[62]

David understood his own fever risk well enough to make out a will just days before his death. He left a good deal of money to his family and set up an annual income for his wife. One of the witnesses for his will was George Eacker (page 231).[63]

## JOHN LAMB

*I won't visit him. I know him to be a Tory, and I would not visit my own father, in a similar category.*

—*attributed to John Lamb*[64]

A descendant of Lamb with the grave she believed to be his. *Trinity Archives.*

The large marker near Ogden (V3) is sometimes said to be that of GENERAL JOHN LAMB (1735–1800), though evidence is far from clear (see page 54). Lamb was a wine dealer who joined the radical Sons of Liberty early in the Revolution; there are tales of him breaking into the printing house of John Holt (page 194) after hours to print anti-British handbills.

Lamb spoke English, Dutch, French and German fluently and wrote in a style a biographer called "bold and nervous," with no fear of offending the Crown when he voiced his indignation to British rule. Though most important firsthand accounts of Sons of Liberty activities were unsigned, many are believed to have been written by Lamb.

When the war began, Lamb lost an eye at the Battle of Quebec, helped capture Fort Ticonderoga, and commanded the Second Continental Artillery at the Battle of Yorktown. Letters to Washington show that Lamb was deeply involved in squabbles about rank and seniority, as many officers were. Though the Sons of Liberty could be a rowdy bunch, Lamb appears to have taken decorum, rank, and respect very seriously.

Back home, Lamb became a vocal antifederalist, arguing against the ratification of the Constitution. But after it was adopted as the law of the land, he took an appointment from George Washington as a customs collector. When a subordinate embezzled thousands of dollars from the government, Lamb faced imprisonment. His old rival Hamilton (page 40) investigated the matter, determined that it wasn't Lamb's fault personally, and arranged for him to make amends by paying the money back. This left Lamb in financial trouble, but at least he was free. The obituaries that announced his death three years later ran alongside advertisements for the sale of his seized property.[65]

# FRANKLIN WHARTON

In the far southeast corner of the section is a lone marker—a recent military-issue headstone—for COLONEL FRANKLIN WHARTON (1767–1818, Y1), one of the first commandants of the United States Marine Corps. When his Trinity neighbor Samuel Swartwout (page 80) was arrested for treason (page 79), it was Wharton who guarded him in the barracks.[66]

In the War of 1812, Wharton directed corps operations from his Washington, D.C. office. An ambitious marine who wanted Wharton's job had him court-martialed for evacuating troops as the British burned Washington in 1814 and for not wearing a uniform. The charge for evacuating was dropped, but President Monroe ordered the army to hold a trial on the uniform charge. Though Wharton had been instrumental in standardizing marine uniforms in the first place, he argued that there was not *technically* a rule requiring them, and he was acquitted. He declined Monroe's pressure to resign.

A direct descendant of King Edward I, Wharton was said to be "possessed of ample fortune, and living far beyond his income from the government." Suffering ill health in 1818, he left D.C. for a trip to be with his family in Pennsylvania. But according to an obituary, "He reached New York very much exhausted....The best medical aid was afforded; but, alas! He could go no further!"[67]

Near the path is a plain stone (X2) with a faded plaque marking the Watts vault (the actual interments associated with the Watts statue, page 57).

The larger urn-topped marker at the edge of the section (X4) once had an epitaph for CATHERINE "KITTY" BAYARD CAMPBELL (1784–1813) and functions as a marker for the Bayard-Campbell family vault. Catherine's father, merchant WILLIAM BAYARD JR. (1761–1826), was also one of the "subscribers" behind the Tontine Coffee House at Wall and Water Streets, the center of city life at the time.

The Tontine's name came from the way it was funded: a *tontine* is an agreement in which subscribers each buy a share, and when one of them dies, their share is divided among the other shareholders. In 1792, 203 subscribers bought shares at $200 each, and each was entitled to pick a "nominee" for the tontine. Most picked young children. William Bayard bought one for his youngest daughter, MARIA BAYARD CAMPBELL (1789–1875), who would live to be among the final seven shareholders; her share was eventually estimated to be worth around $100,000.[68]

Maria was the second wife of DUNCAN P. CAMPBELL (CIRCA 1781–1861), a merchant who had first married her sister Catherine. A friend noted that Duncan spent two or three hours daily drinking mugs of "the unrivaled old beer" in The Grotto at 114 Cedar Street from 1840 until his death, walking there by the same exact route from his home every day.[69]

## LOST MARKERS IN S-1D

The idea that the monument at V3 was Lamb's comes from a letter Trinity received in 1937, stating that *Lossing's Pictorial Field Book to the Revolution* said Lamb's was an urn-topped marker in the southwest corner. Two other urn-topped markers there were still legible, so it was guessed that the illegible V3 must be Lamb's. But Lossing's book, in fact, said no such thing. Indeed, Trinity's files indicate that they weren't confident he was ever buried here at all. Even if he was, it was unlikely that he'd have a large marker, given that he died destitute. Press reports don't mention a burial place, and there is not a record of him in the burial registry.

An 1850 biography says Lamb was buried at Trinity, and vestryman Anthony J. Bleecker confirmed it in 1854.[70] But Bleecker was only seven months old when Lamb died, and, in any case, claimed that he was in the north churchyard (possibly for political reasons—see page 112).

The 1897 transcriptions of gravestones show that THOMAS MOREWOOD (DIED 1798), David Ogden's business partner (page 51), once had a gravestone near David's that had the exact same epitaph, noting that he "fell a victim to the then-prevailing epidemic."[71] No legible marker is attributed to Morewood now. It would make sense if the V3 marker was in fact built as a twin monument for Ogden's partner, who died of the same disease in the same week. The dome atop V3 shows clear evidence of a long-ago repair; perhaps it was once an urn matching David's, but when it broke, the remains were plastered back in a more stable upside-down position.

Other graves were known to have existed in the section once but are no longer present (or are at least not legible). These include one for midshipman BENJAMIN CARPENTER (1800–1820), which was said to be a marble stone near Wharton's marker. It read:

The Ogden marker and its unidentified counterpart. Though often attributed to John Lamb, it was possibly a matching monument to Ogden's for his business partner Thomas Morewood.

> *This humble tribute is sacred to the memory of all that can be lost in a son and a brother. Mid. Benjamin Carpenter of the US Navy. He was drowned on the 25th of May, 1820. Aged 19 years, 11 months, and 25 days.*[72]

The original Lawrence monument appears to have been in this section, and there was a marker here for Civil War hero Philip Kearny before his remains were moved from the Watts vault to Arlington. In surviving illustrations, it looks like a box grave.

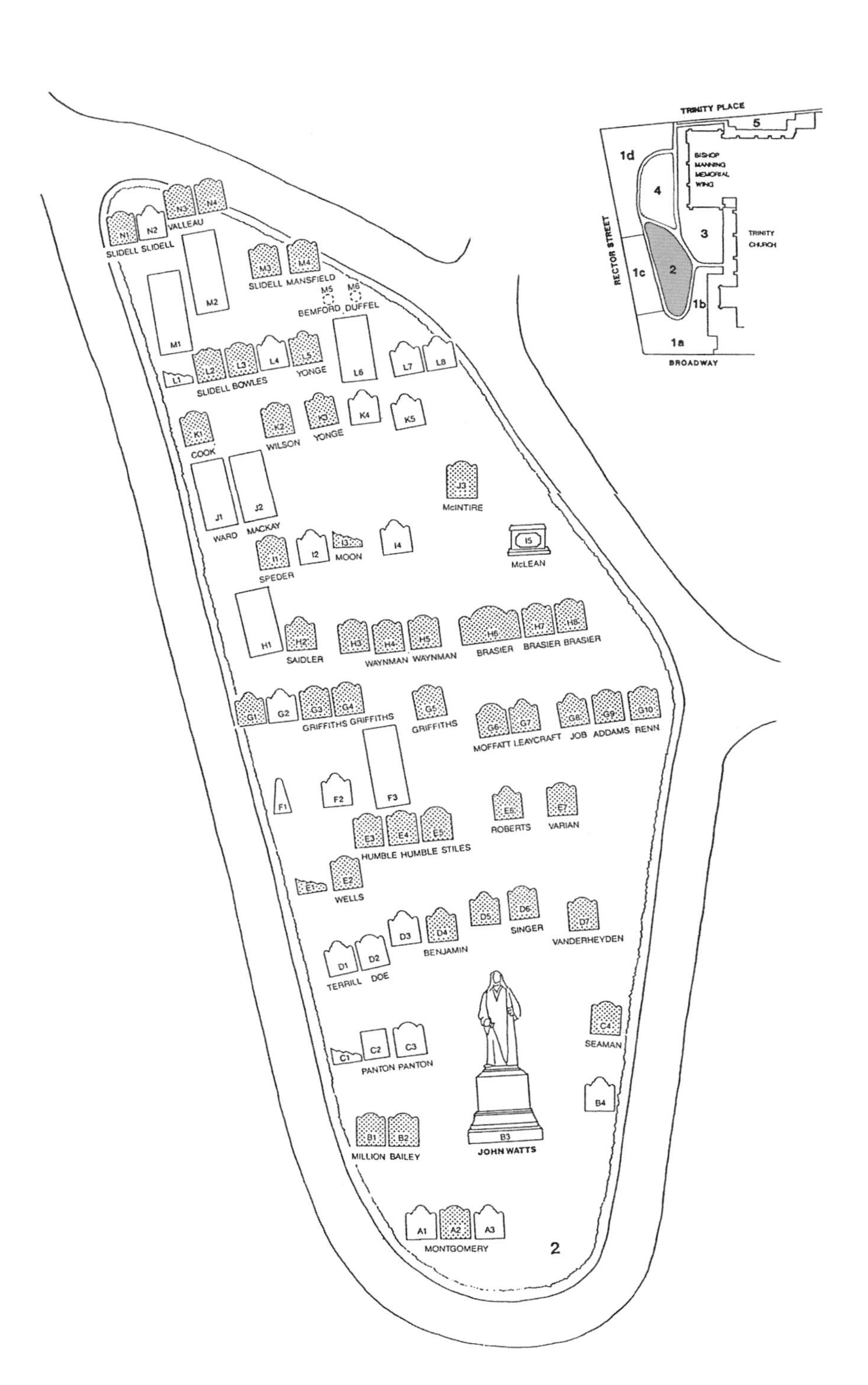

SLIDELL SLIDELL VALLEAU
SLIDELL MANSFIELD
BEMFORD DUFFEL
SLIDELL BOWLES
YONGE
COOK
WILSON
YONGE
McINTIRE
WARD MACKAY
MOON
SPEDER
McLEAN
SAIDLER
WAYNMAN WAYNMAN
BRASIER BRASIER BRASIER
GRIFFITHS GRIFFITHS
GRIFFITHS
MOFFATT LEAYCRAFT
JOB ADDAMS RENN
HUMBLE HUMBLE STILES
ROBERTS
VARIAN
WELLS
SINGER
VANDERHEYDEN
BENJAMIN
TERRILL DOE
SEAMAN
PANTON PANTON
MILLION BAILEY
JOHN WATTS
MONTGOMERY
2
TRINITY PLACE
BISHOP MANNING MEMORIAL WING
TRINITY CHURCH
RECTOR STREET
BROADWAY

# SECTION S2

Section S2 is dominated by the statue of JOHN WATTS JR. (1749–1836, B3), though the actual Watts vault is located in 1D (page 53). Watts was the only New Yorker to hold an office with both the British *and* American governments. As a young man, he became the last royal recorder of New York City. After the Revolution, he held a variety of political jobs, including representing New York in Congress. The statue was commissioned in 1893 by his grandson.

Near the statue, in the eastern tip of the section, is a remarkably crisp stone for CAPTAIN WILLIAM STONE MONTGOMERY, ESQUIRE (CIRCA 1754–1778, A2), which notes his service in "His Majesty's Ninth Regiment Infantry." William was a teenager when he joined the British army and was soon described as "an officer of great merit." He was wounded in the leg at the Battle of Fort Ann in 1777, which, though a British victory, kept a portion of the British army from reaching Saratoga, allowing for an American victory there. Montgomery was taken prisoner and died of his wounds in New York the next year.[73]

Watts's father, a Loyalist who went to England before the Revolution and never returned, famously described law as a "system of confounding other people and picking their pockets, which most of the profession understand pretty well."*

* Watts, letter to William Baker, January 22, 1762.

*Left*: The Watts statue, some distance from his family vault.

*Below*: The Griffiths graves, with a soul effigy, cherub and death's head.

Walking along the left (south) side of the section, there is an unidentified triangular marker (F1). Behind it are the graves of three brothers who died over the course of half a century; they aren't arranged in chronological order, but from the three stones, one can trace the evolution of monument design.

On the right is the marker of infant WILLIAM GRIFFITHS (DIED 1746, G5), whose stone features a winged "death's head" and this epitaph:

> *Farewel* [sic] *Dear Babe, till we Do Meet*
> *Within the Gate of Zion's Street.*

On the left is a marker for ANTHONY GRIFFITHS (1745–1788, G3) which features the "soul effigy" style that eclipsed skulls in popularity over the course of the 1700s. In the center, there is a more innovative three-dimensional cherub face for JOSEPH GRIFFITHS (1754–1796, G4). Anthony and Joseph were ship chandlers who also sold tea and other goods.[74]

It is a remarkable and perhaps satisfying twist that we often know nothing of the personalities of people interred here but *do* know a bit about the personalities of their servants and enslaved laborers. In many cases, these insights come from advertisements soliciting their capture. Anthony once had a ship called the *Speedwell*, from which a well-dressed teenage apprentice named Jonathan Friendchild ran away in 1775. Besides an exact list of the clothes he was wearing and those he had stolen, Friendchild was described in advertisements soliciting his capture as being "five feet three inches, lusty."

Beyond the Griffiths family plot is a marker for hardware and dry goods dealer JAMES SAIDLER (CIRCA 1751–1803, H2) with a verbose epitaph that is broken away at the bottom. It read:

> *THIS MARBLE designed with unambitious purpose and chiefly to preserve in remembrance of his excellent Disposition and amiable Qualities is sacred to the Memory of JAMES SAIDLER who departed this life July 29th, 1803, aged 52 years*

The inscription seems ironic now, intended as it is to "preserve in remembrance" a man whose name is no longer on the stone.

Saidler checked out nearly one hundred books from the New York Society Library; his records there show a love of travel and theater books, fairy tales and, particularly, Thomas Holcroft's satirical novel *The Adventures of Hugh Trevor*, which criticized organized religion, organized society, the legal system, and so much more that Holcroft was arrested in England for high treason. Saidler checked it out multiple times.[75]

A little bit behind Saidler's stone are box tomb markers for two southern men who died weeks apart. On the left is COLONEL JOHN WARD (CIRCA 1766–1816, J1) of South Carolina, who served as the mayor of Charleston and as president of the South Carolina State Senate.

A militia captain, Ward offered the soldiers in his command for service during the War of 1812, but no action came to Charleston. Family reminiscences portray him as a favorite of children who was known far and wide for the Christmas parties he threw. As a politician, he was described as a pleasant speaker "with a penetrating look…dignified when in the chair but a little prone to levity when out of it."[76]

But as a politician, his name is also attached to many bills "for the keeping [of slaves] in due subordination." These new rules included ordering more effective "slave patrols," restricting emancipation and blocking people of color from religious meetings between dusk and dawn. Meeting behind a locked door was punishable by up to twenty lashes.[77] Family stories spoke of his "faithful" enslaved people, though his need for such laws—and his many advertisements seeking the capture of runaways—tells another story.

A family history states, "On the other side [of Ward's grave] is the grave of his overseer, who was so attached to the colonel that when he was dying, he asked to be taken to New York and buried there."* (This burial could not be confirmed.)

* Margaret Armstrong, *Five Generations* (Harper and Bros., 1930).

The box grave to the right of Ward's is for ROBERT MACKAY (1772–1816, J2). Mackay was a Savannah importer who happened to die in his bed while he was in New York. His voluminous letters to his wife provide a vivid portrait of his life and times, though modern readers may wish it gave more information about Hannah and Hero, two enslaved people who traveled with Mackay to England. Mackay's letters home often contained messages from Hannah to her family; Hannah's husband is referred to as being able to write. Hero, a footman, is spoken of as a young man who enjoyed the theater.[78] The stone was recut around the 1940s.

## THE SLIDELL FAMILY: PART 1

At the top (west) edge of the section are two unidentified box graves, a John Zuricher–carved soul effigy headstone for MARGARET BOWLES (1772, L3) and several markers for the Slidell family.

A brown stone (N1) commemorates ELIZABETH SLIDELL, "aged about 86 years," and her husband, JOSHUA SLIDELL:

> *A native of Old England, The Tallow Chandler &c. Erected by his son John in memory of his parents.*

The Tallow Chandlers Company is an organization of tallow candle makers that dates to medieval times; its London Tallow Chandlers Hall was built in the 1600s and still stands. The marker may be only a memorial, not a marker for their actual burial place, as Joshua and Elizabeth's actual burial place is not clear.

Their son JOHN SLIDELL SR. (1731–1805) was also a soap and candle maker; he married JANE ASHFORD SLIDELL (1738–1814) in 1764. There is no legible stone for the two of them, but records place both in the churchyard. There is an excellent stone (M3) for three of their daughters, JANE SLIDELL (1765–1770), ELIZABETH SLIDELL (1767–1770) and MARY SLIDELL (1769–1770), with a stylized cherub's face that appears to be reading the epitaphs below. Preservationist Miriam Silverman called it "the primary example of a children's stone in New York" and attributed it to Thomas Brown, a stonecutter who worked in New York from 1770 to 1775.[79] The three girls died within two weeks of each other; later that year, John Sr. sought to sell a teenage enslaved person whom he noted had already had smallpox and measles, which may provide a clue as to how the girls died.[80]

Below an unidentified box grave is a broken stone (L2) for a son of John Sr. and Jane who died of smallpox, JAMES SLIDELL (1774–1779), though the stone gives his year of death as "17779."[81] Silverman attributed the crudity of his stone, compared to that of the three girls, to British occupation in 1779. Many of the best stonecutters had fled.

Thomas Browne's masterful soul effigy for the Slidell sisters.

One grandson of John and Jane has a marker here: THOMAS SLIDELL (DIED 1806, N2). His stone notes that he "after an illness of 5 days was snatched from the fond embrace of his disconsolate parents." Below it is a barely legible epitaph:

*The work of God, that beauteous clay which here*
*In infant charms so lovely could appear*
*As tho' in nature's nicest model cast*
*Exactly Polish'd wrought too fine to last*
*The same powerful hand again shall rise*
*To Bloom more gay more lovely in the sky*

The lines are from a poem titled "Thought on the Grave of a Child." The author is unknown, but it was published by Quaker poet Milcah

## How Many People Are Buried at Trinity Churchyard?

Many of the burial records for Trinity Churchyard were destroyed in the 1776 fire, and records from the decades after are not complete. As such, it's impossible to know how many burials took place in the grounds. Estimates have varied wildly.

In 1846, one politician noted, "The number of persons buried in this yard down to 1822 cannot be computed, but it is almost beyond belief."* Popular estimates in 1822 had suggested up to 110,000 total interments had taken place there over the years.†

Of course, all the burials wouldn't *still* have been there. It was well known that many bodies in the churchyards were barely cold before grave robbers hauled them out to serve as medical cadavers (page 98). Other bodies had simply been displaced by the process of digging new graves. As one man later recalled, "Trinity Churchyard...got so full that when digging a new grave the coffins of occupants of adjoining graves would be knocked to pieces, their bones falling beneath the digger's spade, and soon finding themselves tossed into a pit in one corner of the yard, known as 'the bone hole' where they often lay exposed."‡ An 1822 writer noted that "a charnel house has been found necessary, to clear off the remains disinterred, for new occupants."§ (A charnel house had been built in 1787, and there may have been an earlier one.)

Long after burials stopped, estimates for how many had been interred there continued to climb, often to double the estimate from the 1820s or even beyond. In the 1840s, one newspaper noted, "They say that three hundred thousand persons have been buried in this churchyard. If the Resurrection of the dead is to be in very truth a *material* resurrection (which we do not believe), what a 'getting up' there will be around Trinity!"¶

But it's worth noting that these growing estimates aren't necessarily based on data and usually came up in political debates. People who thought cemeteries were health hazards would claim as many interments as they could—as would people who felt that cemeteries needed to be protected from new roads and buildings. No one has ever come up with a truly reliable estimate.

---

* Documents of the Assembly.
† "To the Mayor...," *NYAm*, August 21, 1822.
‡ "Early New York," *NYP*, reprinted in *Democrat and Chronicle*, October 1, 1882.
§ "Public Cemeteries," *NYS*, August 20, 1822.
¶ *Sunday Dispatch*, December 7, 1845.

Martha Moore in a volume of poems that were mostly written by women she knew.

The winding Slidell family saga would continue with their family vault in a section nearby (page 71).

Next to Thomas Slidell's stone is a marker for Theodore Burke Valleau (1791–1806, N3). Theo was only thirteen at the time of Alexander Hamilton's fatal duel, but his signature appears on his will as a witness; he's said to have been a clerk in the office. He died two years later. His inscription is largely broken, but the apparently original epitaph read:

*Ah! Dear departed son*
*thy afflicted parents greatest hope & comfort*
*Early art thou snatched from hence*
*to join the blissful throng of heaven*
*known*
*thou wast to few, but by those few*
*known*
*To be of soul angelic*[82]

In the middle of the section are several markers for the Brasier family. The most notable is that of George Brasier (circa 1716–1772, H8), which was carved by John Zuricher and features a lengthy epitaph. Though around half of the marker appears to now be underground, cutting off the text after the line ending in *mourn*, the same lines appear on a 1790s marker in South Carolina, so we can assume the full text would read:

*From Pains, from Sorrow, and from Care set free,*
*Rest here secure in thine Integrity.*
*Tho all thy Life in Virtuous Deeds was spent*
*Yet from Affliction thou was not exempt.*
*But here a safe Asylum thou shalt find*
*From all that could disturb thy anxious Mind.*
*Thy loving* [Husband] *in silent Sorrow mourn*
*And all thy Friends in grief weep o'er thy Tomb.*
*Then rest my Love, while I in vain deplore*

*Thy sudden Fate, and grieve thou art no more.*
*Oh! May thy gentle Spirit wing its Way*
*To blissful Regions of unfading Day.*

The larger white marker behind Brasier's is for ELIZABETH SWAIN MCLEAN (DIED 1793, I5), who married shipmaster Charles Mclean in 1779; Charles is mentioned on this stone (an 1869 replacement of the original) but also has a marker in the next section, directly across the path (page 67).

## LOST MARKERS IN S2

Older sources mention markers in this area for CAPTAIN JOHN GRIFFITHS (1716–CIRCA 1783) and his wife, JANE GRIFFITHS (CIRCA 1720–1789). These may have been two of the various unidentified gravestones near the other Griffiths' stones.

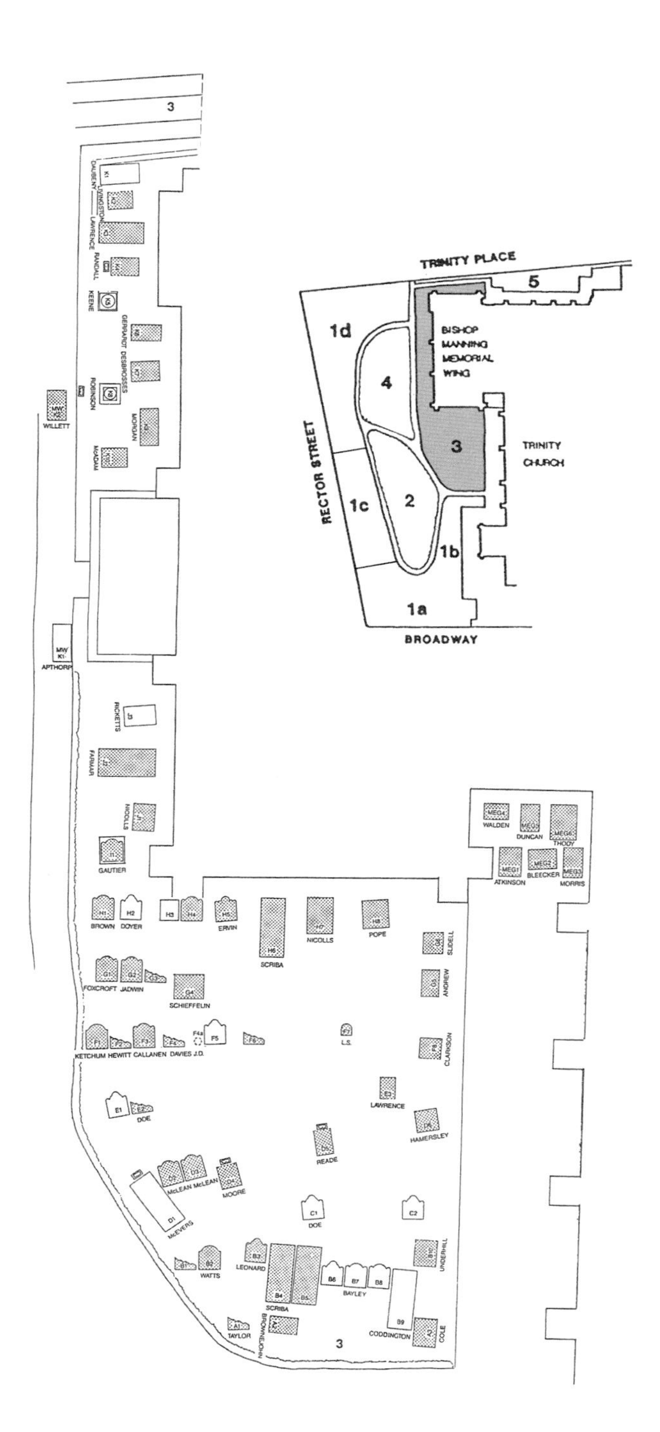
TRINITY PLACE
5
1d
BISHOP MANNING MEMORIAL WING
4
3
TRINITY CHURCH
RECTOR STREET
1c
2
1b
1a
BROADWAY
3
DAUBENY
LIVINGSTON
LAWRENCE
RANDALL
KEENE
GERHARDT
DESBROSSES
ROBINSON
MORGAN
WILLETT
APTHORP
RICKETTS
FARMAR
NICOLLS
GAUTIER
WALDEN
DUNCAN
THODY
ATKINSON
BLEECKER
MORRIS
BROWN
DOYER
ERVIN
SCRIBA
NICOLLS
POPE
SLIDELL
ANDREW
FOXCROFT
JADWIN
SCHIEFFELIN
KETCHUM HEWITT CALLANEN DAVIES J.D.
L.S.
CLARKSON
LAWRENCE
HAMERSLEY
DOE
READE
McLEAN McLEAN
MOORE
McEVERS
DOE
WATTS
LEONARD
UNDERHILL
SCRIBA
BAYLEY
TAYLOR
BROWNEJOHN
CODDINGTON
COLE
3

# SECTION S3

Section S3 is largely composed of underground vaults. Many of the names on the vault markers are familiar as those of the "old families" of New York, which diarist Strong (page 73) described in the mid-1800s as "names that retain some slight coppery smell."

Recently, a new ramp was added, which necessitated remaking some tablets marking the spots of vaults, as the ramp went over the original markers.

One of the new tablets visible on the top of the ramp reads "Matthew L. Davis Sepulchre 1818." MATTHEW DAVIS (1773–1850) was Aaron Burr's biographer and confidant.

## MATTHEW L. DAVIS: BURR'S LAST FRIEND

*If a thought is clear, why not give it clearly? If it is vague and dubious, why give it at all?*

—*Matthew L. Davis*[83]

A reporter described Matthew Livingston Davis as "not malicious, but... extremely mischievous" and related a tale of how Davis had used all of his dirtiest tricks to get a friend nominated for a city office.[84] When congratulated on his success, Davis said, "I'll show you a trick better....I am now going

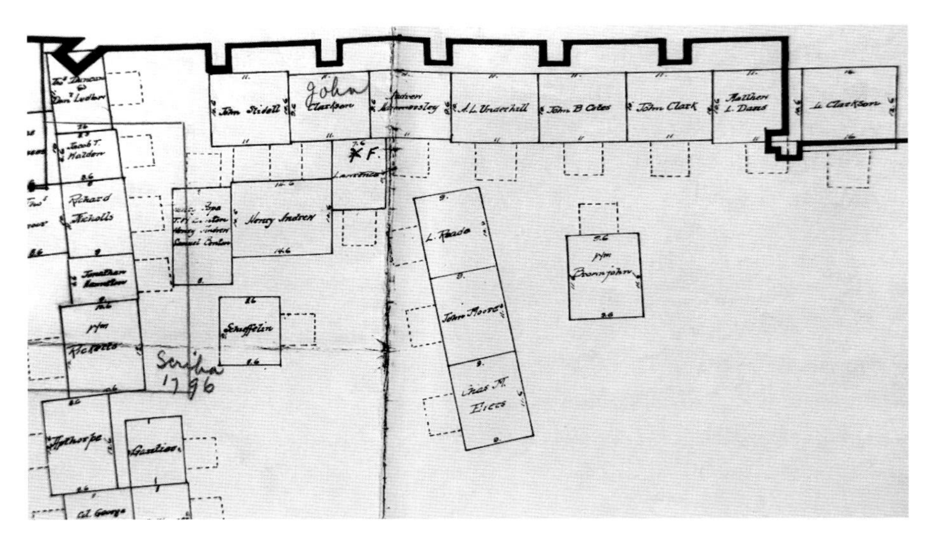


A map of the subterranean vaults in S3.

to work to defeat him." He proceeded to do just that "without any other apparent motive than his love for fun."[85]

His *New York Atlas* obituary said, "It was in the midst of the hurly burly scenes of life—scenes that would discomfit most other men—that [Mr. Davis] enjoyed the greater amount of happiness."[86] One historian said Davis was "a man who could never resist a shady deal or a dishonest dollar, a man whose political acumen was constantly available for sale."[87] He drifted in and out of politics, journalism, and trouble all his life.

He was, in short, just the sort of man who would be Aaron Burr's best friend.

Davis ran newspapers that supported Burr and his Democratic-Republican faction of New York politics in the 1790s. Over time, he became Burr's trusted confidant and accompanied him to the duel against Hamilton. Davis had already threatened to shoot James Cheetham, a journalist who insulted Burr (page 177), and after the Hamilton duel, he went to jail rather than testify about it.

For a time, Davis lived in Washington, D.C., writing for New York papers under the name the "Spy in Washington" and stirring up scandals among politicians who described him as "brooding calumny, black, base, and foul…a scoundrel, liar and coward." In 1838, Davis reported on a rifle duel between congressmen Jonathan Cilley and William Graves, coolly telling the particulars and breaking mid-column to note, "While I am writing, I am interrupted by a man entering my room and informing me that the body of Mr. Cilley has just been conveyed to his lodgings."[88] Other journalists noted the irony that the duel arose from remarks in an article by Davis, "the pimp of Aaron Burr," himself.[89]

Davis tried hard to clean up Burr's image. In the introduction to his Burr biography, he wrote, "There was a mass of letters…indicating no very strict morality in some of [Burr's] female correspondents.…[Burr] prohibited the destruction of any part of them during his lifetime [but] as soon as Col. Burr's decease was known, with my own hands I committed to the fire all such correspondence."

When Davis died, it seemed like everyone had a favorite Matthew Davis story to share. Even those who couldn't stand him realized they had a soft spot for "the old boy in specs" who had been a character in the city as long as most could remember.

## John B. Coles

West of Davis's marker is the vault of John B. Coles (1760–1827), one of the heroes of the yellow fever outbreak of 1798. Besides raising a remarkable amount of money for relief, Coles joined with Aaron Burr, John Watts (page 57) and others to form the Manhattan Company, whose stated purpose was to raise money to provide cleaner water to the city in the hopes of preventing further outbreaks. Clean water may not have actually helped with yellow fever, but it was still a good idea.

Burr sneakily inserted a bit into the company's charter that allowed it to use excess funds to become a bank. Soon, the company was far better known as the Bank of the Manhattan Company, which competed with Hamilton's bank and provided funds Burr used to help his party win the election in 1800. (Eventually, it became Chase Manhattan Bank.) Coles and John Barker Church became the bank's token Federalists, opposed to much of what Burr was doing, though they remained on the board of the bank.

A flour merchant by trade, among his other ventures, Coles built a bridge over the Harlem River, was on the committee that laid out the streets above Union Square, and was noted for his wine cellar. Early in life, he enslaved a woman named Peggy, though manumission records show that he freed her in 1804 and later was a member of the committee chaired by Matthew Clarkson (page 70) to oppose the expansion of slavery into new states.

# MATTHEW CLARKSON

> [Clarkson] *said to me on Thursday, just after our friend* [Alexander Hamilton] *had expired: "If we were truly brave we should not accept a challenge; but we are all cowards."…There is no braver man living* [than Clarkson], *and yet I doubt whether he would so far brave the public opinion as to refuse a challenge.*
>
> —*Gouverneur Morris's diary, July 1804*

In the John Clarkson vault (F8) is GENERAL MATTHEW CLARKSON (1758–1825), who was only a teenager when he joined the Continental army. He survived the famous winter at Valley Forge, was present when Cornwallis surrendered, and served as assistant to the secretary of war from 1781 to 1783, when he was in his early twenties. Afterward, he worked as a merchant and was connected to countless philanthropic organizations, including the founding of a free school for Black students in 1786.

Matthew Clarkson, from a Gilbert Stuart portrait. *New York Public Library.*

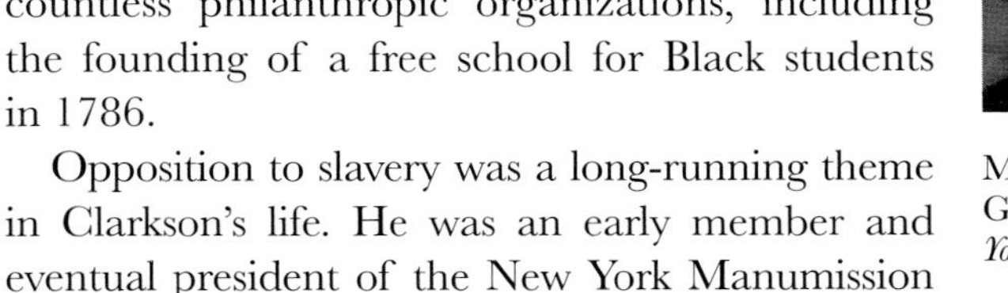

Opposition to slavery was a long-running theme in Clarkson's life. He was an early member and eventual president of the New York Manumission Society and introduced one of the many early bills to end slavery in New York.

In 1819, he was chair of a meeting, witnessed by thousands, to oppose the expansion of slavery into any new territories. The first resolution the group adopted stated that "the existence of slavery in the United States is, in the opinion of this meeting, a great political as well as moral evil."[90] Clarkson opposed Congress's eventual capitulation to slave states, in which they allowed the institution in new states added to the Union south of Missouri.

When the last enslaved people in New York became free, two years after his death, a portrait of Clarkson was prominently displayed in the celebrations at Zion Church.[91] But lest we think that his work and the end of slavery ended the racial problem in New York, *Harper's Weekly* carried an illustration of a Black man being lynched on his namesake Clarkson Street during the antidraft riots of 1863, when diarist George Templeton Strong (page 73) wrote, "Jefferson Davis rules New York today."[92]

In 1839, the original vault was wrecked by the construction of the new church, and the contents were moved to a new vault. A note from the time

2nd Pile.
No. 1 Ground, Belinda Clarkson – ✓
2 next, William S. Clarkson – ✓
3 Top, M. Clarkson – ✓

3rd Pile.
No. 1 Ground, Nancy Brown –
2 Next, Eliza Clarkson – ✓
3 next ~~Tops~~, Freeman Clarkson – ✓
4 next – Mary Clarkson –
5 top – Freeman Clarkson of the Pile

Detail of an 1839 report from the Clarkson vault, found among John Jay papers. *Trinity Archives.*

enumerates the contents of the old vault in five "piles" of coffins, the last of which included a box containing eight unidentified skulls. Most of the twenty coffins were identified as belonging to members of Clarkson's extended family, but there was one for a person named NANCY BROWN, whose date of death and connection to the family appear to be a mystery.

## THE SLIDELL FAMILY: PART 2

> *When I had got clear, I turned to look at the* "Lucy" [Lusitania] *in her last agony.... She took another move and reared almost perpendicular, with her stern in the air, as the* Titanic *is said to have done before she plunged to the bottom.*
>
> —*Thomas Slidell, 1915*

A vault adjacent to Clarkson's, ironically, is one with ties to the Confederacy.

One son of John and Jane Slidell (page 61), JOHN SLIDELL JR. (1772–1816), went into the family business of soap and candle making. His eldest son, John Slidell III, attempted to take on the family business of soap and candle making for a time. But after he was caught having an affair with the wife of theatrical manager Stephen Price (page 86), Price challenged him to a duel. In the ensuing battle, Slidell shot Price in the leg. This damaged Slidell's reputation enough in New York that he moved to New Orleans, where he eventually became a senator and vocal advocate for seceding from the Union to preserve slavery. When he became the Confederate minister to France, Union papers made light of his long-ago duel with Price and of the fact that he had been a New York soap boiler in his youth, though he now claimed to be a Southern aristocrat and called Northerners "a herd of vulgar, peddling traders."[93]

Indeed, he was said to be very sensitive to remarks about his background in the soap and candle trade; when a woman joked that his travels must take him to Greece (because he used to make grease) and that he was dipped, not molded, into high society, it was said that he never got over it.[94] Diarist Strong (page 73) called his 1871 death "no great loss to mankind"; he was buried overseas.

This vault was probably built upon Slidell Jr.'s death; the old marker said "1816." But the date of his interment here is uncertain. Indeed, there's much confusion about who, exactly, is in this vault. In the early 1830s, a new "John Slidell" vault was built at St. Mark's in the Bowery, but throughout the 1830s, there were records of petitions to have family bodies moved from there *to* the vault in Trinity. A 1950s search for the body of Slidell Jr.'s son-in-law, Commodore Matthew Perry, in the St. Mark's vault found nine coffins there (though Perry had been moved to a new family plot in Rhode Island). An inspection here in 1944 found only three coffins, likely those of children. But who was here, who was moved and who was moved back is impossible to know.

One certain interment here is that of a great-great-grandson of John Jr., THOMAS SLIDELL (1873–1946), who became an artist, lawyer and newspaperman. In 1915, he was speaking with Chicago publisher H.S. Stone in the smoking room of the RMS *Lusitania* when it was hit by a torpedo, an event that led to America's entry into World War I. Both Slidell and Stone said "Torpedo!" at the same time and ran for the deck. While Stone didn't survive (he was interred at Graceland Cemetery in Chicago), Slidell lived to give a firsthand account of the affair for the *New York Times.* He had been traveling with Alfred Vanderbilt and watched as the mogul gave up his life vest.[95] Two years before Thomas died in Paris, he arranged for his ashes to be interred in the family vault here. His son JOHN RODGERS SLIDELL (1908–1986) was interred here as well.

Beyond Slidell are a cluster of small markers for vaults that are underneath the church. Among them is that of merchant Anthony Lispenard Bleecker (1741–1816). The Bleeckers were an old New York family; some told stories of the day Anthony came home and announced he'd bought 160 acres of land where his namesake street now runs "out in the country" in Greenwich Village. The family thought he was wasting his money.[96]

His grandson Anthony J. Bleecker (1799–1884) was thought to be the last interment at one point, but it has recently been renovated to receive ashes of future generations. Anthony J., besides being an auctioneer, was a Shakespeare scholar; one great actor of the day said that Bleecker had forgotten more about Shakespeare than he himself ever knew.[97]

## The Secret Diaries of the Brownejohn Vault

> *Pending our conference* [with Secretary of War Stanton], *the long, lean figure of Uncle Abraham suddenly appeared at the door.…Lincoln uttered no word, but beckoned Stanton in a ghostly manner with one sepulchral forefinger, and they disappeared together for a few minutes.… We saw Abe Lincoln in the telegraph room as we entered the office, waiting for dispatches, and no doubt, sickening with anxiety—poor old codger! But it's shameful so to designate a man who has so well filled so great a place during times so trying.*
>
> *—George Templeton Strong, May 8, 1864*

In the middle of the section is a marker for the vault of William Brownejohn (died 1785, A2). It's dated 1841, though there are references to the family vault existing already when Mary Brownejohn (died 1785) died decades earlier.[98] William advertised both medicines and spices for sale (and for the return of runaway enslaved people named Jack and Brutus). There is a story that he melted lead from his windows to make bullets for Washington's army.[99]

A great-grandson of William and Mary interred in the vault is George Templeton Strong (1820–1875), a musician and lawyer. One historian called his massive diary "the best diary—in both historic and literary terms—ever written by an American."[100] Though Strong seemed too bored by his legal work to mention it much, he wrote of both great national events and solitary nights when he stayed home and "smoked volcanically" with wit, insight and literary flash. While so many in Trinity Churchyard left nothing written behind, Strong left over four million words.

George Templeton Strong, circa 1861, by Mathew Brady. *Library of Congress.*

One of the fun things about the diary is that Strong could be a bit of a jerk. Though well liked in the city, he was judgmental and critical of everyone and everything, including himself, and since he never meant the diaries to be read, he was free to speak his mind in them. His detachment can be highly amusing. When he first attended a meeting of the New York Historical Society, he watched as several old men, under the direction of Albert Gallatin (page 162), got all excited about unveiling a war relic that turned out to be an old button. Strong was embarrassed for all of them and left early.

Elsewhere, he said that Edwin Booth overdid it a bit as Hamlet, called one of the "freaks" at Barnum's Museum "a real prodigy of hideousness" and gritted his teeth as Eliza Hamilton asked for yet another alteration to her will. Attending services at St. Paul's in 1841, he said that the organist had "periodical fits of insanity and absurdity, during the prevalence of which he plays with as much judgement as a horse." Even the bar exam bored him: "Such a farce…such an asinine set of candidates and such prodigiously uncomfortable timber benches I never met with before."

Strong battled bouts of the "blues" throughout his life. He once wrote that he had "drifted through nearly [my] whole life without praiseworthy service…a 'respectable' and decorous dunce and drone." But he found purpose in life with the dawning of the Civil War and became a leading member of the Sanitary Commission, working for the welfare and care of soldiers. He worried at first that Abraham Lincoln's "only special gift is fertility of smutty stories" but recorded his joy at every small step toward the end of slavery ("John Brown *is* a-marching on, with seven league boots!") and said that people who disapproved of the Emancipation Proclamation "ought to be dead and buried but persist in manifesting themselves like vampires."

When Lincoln was assassinated, Strong recorded the shocked, confused, and vengeful mood in the city as scattered bits of news came in and wrote of the Trinity Church vestry meeting that day, at which Gouverneur Ogden, "whom I have always thought cold hearted and selfish," broke down in tears. He traveled to Washington for Lincoln's funeral and wrote of his "last glimpse of the honest face of our great and good president" (though, true to form, he didn't think much of the "vile and vulgar" service itself).[101]

Struck ill in 1875, Strong wrote as long as he could. In his final entry, he kept up his sense of humor, saying that his liver troubles left him "as weak as a sea anemone at low water." President Grant and J.J. Astor were among the mourners at his Trinity Church funeral a month later.

Walking along the narrow strip that separates the sidewalk from the church is a framed gravestone with a soul effigy and the archaic spelling "Here Lyes." It marks the vault of the Gautier family, who were Huguenots who fled France to settle in New York.

ANDREW GAUTIER (1720–1783) once saved Trinity Church from destruction.[102] In 1750, when a fire broke out nearby, most assumed that the church was lost. Andrew climbed the steeple himself and put out the flames with his hat.[103] After he was given a reward in coins, he had them melted down and commissioned silversmith Adrian Bancker to mold them into a bowl with an engraved illustration showing the fire.

Later, he was the craftsman who oversaw the construction of St. Paul's.

The bowl Gautier made with his reward money. *Trinity Archives.*

# HUGH WILLIAMSON

> *The relative places of fifty thousand stars have been determined by the help of telescopes....Five millions of worlds, all inhabited by rational beings! How do we seem to dwindle into littleness?...All those worlds, and every one of their inhabitants, are under the constant care of the Divine Being. Not one of them is neglected.*
>
> —*Hugh Williamson, 1769*

Embedded in the sidewalk is a marker for the Anthorp vault (K1), which contains the remains of HUGH WILLIAMSON (1735–1819), a scientist, surgeon, and statesman who studied everything from the movements of Venus to the powers of electric eels. He and Alexander Hamilton (page 40) are the only Trinity residents to have signed the United States Constitution.

Embarking for Europe to further his studies in 1773, he happened to witness the Boston Tea Party, in which angry colonists dumped English tea into Boston Harbor, and brought the first news of the event to England. At least one member of Parliament swore that Williamson telling them the dangers of impeding revolt was their first warning of the Revolution.

Benjamin Franklin, who had previously called Williamson a "detestable skunk," became a friend in London, and Williamson acted as a courier between him and the Continental Congress. They later did electrical experiments together, though they seem to have remained what we now call "frenemies."

When independence was declared, Williamson returned home and served as a surgeon for Washington's army, promoting innovative preventative medical techniques, such as vaccinations against smallpox, that made a huge difference in the war effort.

In 1787, North Carolina made Williamson a delegate to the Constitutional Convention, and he lodged with Hamilton during the proceedings. Unlike his friend Jefferson, Williamson lived by his antislavery principles, never enslaving anyone himself and arguing for its prohibition in the Constitution. In the end, he favored compromise and is credited with suggesting the now-odious rule that enslaved people were counted as three-fifths of a person in the population. But Abraham Lincoln would cite Williamson's arguments in his famous "Cooper Union Speech" in New York as evidence that the founders had intended to place slavery on a road to extinction.

After a stint in Congress, Williamson retired from public life and settled in New York, where he wrote studies about whatever interested him, arguing, among much else, that Natives were not a "new inferior race" but had migrated to North America from Asia, that snakes really do "charm" prey into their mouths, and that a canal should connect Lake Erie to the Hudson. Not all of his scientific theories hold up, but many are fascinating to read. He was the subject of a 2010 biography by George Sheldon.

Alongside the southwest portion of the church, which is the relatively new Manning Wing, Section S3 continues with a narrow patch of graves, containing a few flat vault markers and two larger monuments. The Manning Wing's construction in the 1960s covered a space that was previously a grassy field full of small vault markers. Several vaults were moved to N7 during construction (page 161); others remained in place here, though their markers were sometimes moved slightly.

The first of the two taller markers, topped by a stone urn, is for John Robinson (died 1821) (K8). Few details of it—or him—are known. Now illegible, the marker once read, "Sacred to the Memory of John Robinson, Died Aug 14th, 1821, in the 67th year of his age." The 1868 vault report said

The Eleonora Keene and John Robinson markers.

it contained three decayed coffins; a report in 1964 found it empty with "no sign of any burial whatsoever."

In front of it is the vault of Marinus Willet (K2), a member of the Sons of Liberty, though he appears to have been moved to the New York City Marble Cemetery.

The other large marker is a monument to ELEONORA MARTIN KEENE (1787–1807) (K5), whose vault is located nearby. Though now illegible, it once read, "In memory of Eleonora Keene wife of Richard R. Keene of New Orleans this monument erected by her husband she was born at Baltimore Oct 6th 1786 died at N.Y. Nov 16th 1807."[104]

## ELEONORA KEENE

> *I betook myself again to my room and disclosed to Miss O my intention to escape.... This lady, compassionating my situation, determined to serve me at every hazard. As soon as it became dark, with fluttering hearts and trembling steps we gained the street door and seized upon the bolt. The door was locked and the key taken out! We determined to persevere.*
>
> —*Eleonora Martin Keene*

The granddaughter of Captain Cresap (page 155) and the daughter of Luther Martin, a delegate to the Constitutional Convention who refused to sign the document, Eleonora grew up in Maryland but attended boarding schools in New York. As a teenager, she fell under the spell of her father's dashing young law clerk, Richard Raynal Keene.

Over the course of his life, Richard attempted to negotiate ransoms for American sailors who had been kidnapped by pirates in the Barbary War, tried to buy most of Cuba, and fought for Napoleon, among other adventures. In 1798, young Keene even wrote to George Washington, asking for money to fund some now-forgotten scheme (Washington politely declined).

Though Eleonora's father disapproved (she was fifteen and Richard was twenty-two), Eleonora was smitten with him. Her friends helped her carry on an affair for months—one older married woman counseled her that she should listen only to her own mind, not her father's, when deciding who to marry. She and Richard eloped in 1802.

Luther accused Richard of "poisoning the mind and perverting the principles" of his daughter in a series of letters that he published as a

Eleonora Martin Keene (or possibly her sister Maria) in 1802, by Charles Balthazar Julien Févret de Saint-Mémin. *National Portrait Gallery.*

pamphlet entitled *Modern Gratitude.*[105] Richard responded with letters of his own about his father-in-law's "deplorable phrensies." Between various publications, the two men went on for hundreds of pages attacking each other.

Mixed into the pages is one letter by Eleonora herself, a voice largely ignored in the fights about her. In it, she comes off as a young woman thrilled by drama, eager for excitement, and likely desperate to break away from her old-fashioned, alcoholic father.

She gave birth to a son, Luther (1803–1828), a year after the wedding, and the young couple moved to New Orleans, where Richard was made the first attorney general of Louisiana Territory. In 1804, he fought a duel with John Ward Gurley, the man who took his place. Both survived, though Gurley died in another duel not long after.

Perhaps inevitably for a man given to wild schemes and duels, Richard fell into the orbit of Aaron Burr. In 1807, Burr embarked on a strange conspiracy to form, colonize and rule an entirely new country in the southwestern states and territories. Historians still aren't sure quite what Burr's plans were or how far he got, but he was arrested for treason, and Keene was arrested with him.

Luther Martin, the father-in-law who'd attacked Keene so viciously, now defended him and Burr in court and explained to those who were surprised that the only thing Richard and Eleonora had done wrong was to go against his personal wishes. All appeared to be forgiven now; it may have helped that Eleonora had named their son after him, but Martin also perhaps gained some sympathy for the young lovers when he himself fell in love with Burr's daughter, Theodosia (who was thirty-five years his junior, already married, and, by all accounts, completely uninterested in him). Years later, a Baltimore judge recalled being invited by Eleonora to dine with her and Richard at Burr's residence in Virginia, where he watched Burr flirt with every woman present.[106]

Eleonora's cause of death is not known, though her mother died of cancer, and her father noted in 1802 that "she could not walk a few squares without complaining of a pain in her breast."[107] In July 1807, in the middle of Burr's trial, she went to New York feeling ill and died there while waiting for Richard to join her. A Baltimore paper said, "She was one of the most accomplished of her sex, and promised, had she lived, to have been one of its brightest ornaments. Those who had the pleasure of her correspondence will ever remember the strength of judgement, correctness of sentiment, and energy as well as elegance of diction displayed by her."[108]

She was interred in a lead coffin; it was the only one present when the vault was inspected in 1868. Luther Martin was interred at the now-defunct St. John's Burying Ground, and Richard was buried in St. Louis when he died there in 1839.

It's hard to know how we should think of Eleonora today. From a modern perspective, she seems like an underage victim swept up in the whirlwind of a charming rogue, but she would have rejected such a description and thought of herself as taking control of her life by eloping with Richard. Most of her contemporaries would have taken a similar view.

Very close to the Keene vault is a flat stone marking the John R. Livingston vault (K3), which happens to contain the remains of another man tried for his role in the same "Burr conspiracy" as Richard Keene.

Merchant Samuel Swartwout (1783–1856) was acquitted of involvement in Burr's Southwest Plot and later challenged the witness who first reported Burr's scheme to authorities, General James Wilkinson, to a duel. Wilkinson declined, so Swartwout published a letter stating, "I have only to pronounce and publish you to the world as a COWARD and POLTROON.…You should have been BRAVE and died like a man. You should have considered that there is some small merit even in a VILLAIN's bravery."[109] In his dealings with Burr and Swartwout, Wilkinson had falsified evidence and lied through his teeth to minimize his own role in the plot. His being caught doing so was probably a factor in Burr being acquitted.

At the time, no one realized Wilkinson was working as a spy for Spain; he'd tried to have explorers Lewis and Clark killed before their expedition could aid western expansion into territory Spain still wanted for itself. Even without knowing of this, General Andrew Jackson hated Wilkinson and loved Swartwout for antagonizing him. As president, Jackson made Swartwout the collector of customs for the Port of New York, a job he held from 1830 to 1838, during which time he apparently embezzled over $1 million.

After Swartwout's death, an obituary read "By general consent, his faults were seldom alluded to, and now that he is dead they will be buried in the grave."[110] But people continued to use "swartwouted" as a synonym for "embezzled" for years.

Lawyer JOHN R. LIVINGSTON (1803–1871), a cousin of Swartwout's wife, was interred in the vault in 1871. Diarist George Templeton Strong (page 73) served as a pallbearer, and wrote "Poor Livingston has gone where tradesmen cease from calling and the checkbook is at rest. He will have no more trouble with atrophied bank accounts and hypertrophied bills. This is a grand and solemn thought which goes far to reconcile one to the inevitable." [111]

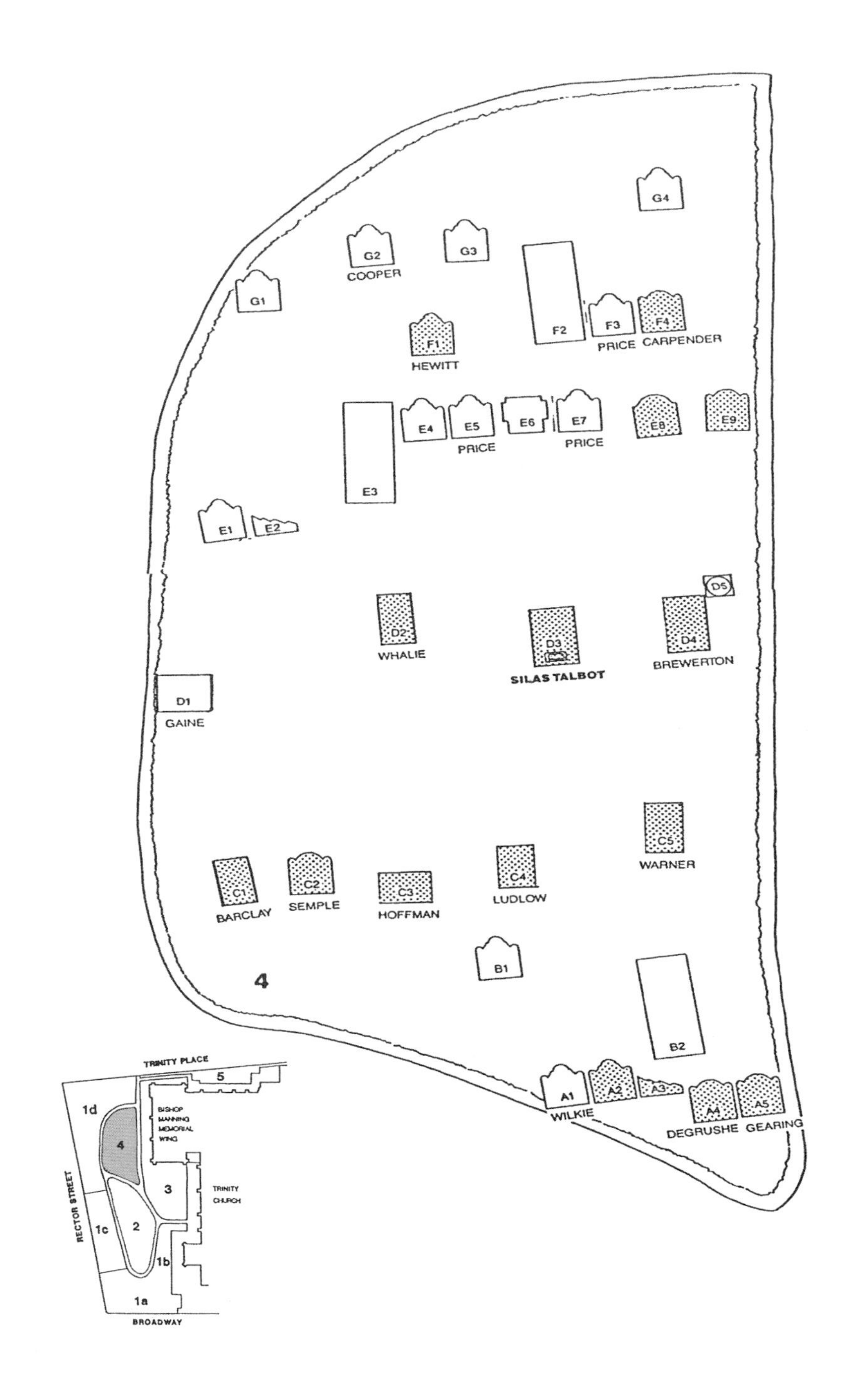
G4
G2
COOPER
G3
G1
F2
F3
F4
PRICE
CARPENDER
F1
HEWITT
E4
E5
PRICE
E6
E7
PRICE
E8
E9
E3
E1
E2
D5
D2
WHALIE
D3
SILAS TALBOT
D4
BREWERTON
D1
GAINE
C5
WARNER
C1
BARCLAY
C2
SEMPLE
C3
HOFFMAN
C4
LUDLOW
B1
4
B2
A1
WILKIE
A2
A3
A4
DEGRUSHE
A5
GEARING
TRINITY PLACE
5
1d
BISHOP
MANNING
MEMORIAL
WING
4
3
TRINITY
CHURCH
RECTOR STREET
1c
2
1b
1a
BROADWAY

# SECTION S4

## Hercules Mulligan

In the middle of this relatively sparse section is the Whalie and Mulligan vault (D2), originally built for Sarah Cooke Mulligan (1697–1777) by her son-in-law, Thomas Whaley (1715–1780), a merchant who also once served as sexton of Trinity Church. The family's best-known member today is Hercules Mulligan (1740–1825), a Revolutionary spy.

When Alexander Hamilton first came to New York, he lived with Mulligan, a tailor who was deeply involved in Revolutionary politics. Legend has it that Mulligan was the one who broke the lock to Bowling Green and led the charge to tear down the statue of King George after the Declaration of Independence was published in 1776, and he may have brought Hamilton into the cause.

He attempted to flee the city after the Battle of Long Island but was detained in New York, where the British figured they could keep an eye on him. He was arrested more than once, but a lack of evidence and his ability to talk his way out of trouble kept him free.

His shop, in fact, reportedly became a hangout for loose-tongued British officers. One evening, an officer came in for a new watch coat and bragged that "before another day," they would have Washington in their hands. As soon as the officer was gone, Mulligan sent a warning to Washington via a messenger, possibly saving his life.

Though he was once a relatively obscure figure, Mulligan rose to fame after he became a prominent character in the *Hamilton* musical, which portrays him as a spy who fed Washington far more information than he probably did. Of course, informal spies who kept good records probably wouldn't have lasted long, so few stories about Mulligan can be confirmed. Some of those that circulate today are pure fiction, and some come from anecdotes Mulligan told John Church Hamilton decades after the fact, by which time the tales may have grown taller. Historians don't find all of them reliable.[112]

This unreliability extends not just to the good stories about Mulligan but to the bad ones as well. Though J.C. Hamilton referred to the messenger Mulligan used in the affair with the British officer only as "a negro," a largely speculative 1937 biography mentioned that "[the messenger]'s name has been handed down in tradition as Cato."[113] In more recent years, some have written that the messenger was Cato Howe, a Black Revolutionary soldier from Plymouth, Massachusetts, but Howe's pension records don't appear to back this up.

Indeed, Mulligan's status in regards to slavery is murky. In 1774, his name was attached to advertisements seeking runaway white indentured servants, which suggests that he favored them as employees over enslaved labor.[114] In 1786, he was among those who signed a letter stating that he was "deeply affected by the situation of those, who although free by the laws of GOD are held in slavery by the laws of this state."[115] By that time, he was also a member of the New York Manumission Society.[116] Still, a 1790 census record does indicate an enslaved person in Mulligan's household.

His burial place is as unclear as the details of his life. Trinity's records say that he was buried in St. John's Burying Ground (page 261), while family stories state that he was interred in the Sanders vault, the family vault of his wife, Elizabeth, which is located under the church.[117] Elizabeth was interred at St. John's a year after Hercules died, but her remains were later moved to Trinity Cemetery uptown, which further confuses the matter. The Mulligan vault here functions as his "observed" grave in the same way that the third Monday in February is Washington's "observed" birthday.

Other markers in the section include one for the Nicholl vault (D3), adjacent to Mulligan's, which features a plaque for Silas Talbot (1751–1813), who is interred there. Talbot was a captain in the Continental navy, in command of a privateer ship called the *George Washington* until his capture. Following the war, he lost a fortune in the slave trade, served part of a term in Congress, and was selected by Washington to be one of the first captains of the United States Navy, in which he worked to protect American ships against French privateers.

## THE PRICE FAMILY

Among the cluster of white stone markers toward the back (west) of the section, the most legible is for merchant MICHAEL PRICE (CIRCA 1737–1821, E7), whose newspaper advertisements stated that he sold "dry goods, including Scotch snuff and pepper…with many other articles now in demand, too tedious to mention."[118] In early 1776, the Continental Congress attempted to keep the economy under control by limiting some prices, and Price and his partner were convicted of breaking the rules they imposed. They apologized, and the Congress issued a resolution that "they be restored to the favourable opinion of their country, and it is hereby recommended that they be no longer considered or treated as Enemies to the Liberties of America."[119]

But Price remained a Loyalist and fled to Canada after British occupation ended, returning to the city around 1784. One reminiscence said, "Like

The Price plot.

George the Third, whom he loved and venerated, he was crazy, and had to be watched."[120] Another recalled that before he fled, he often had British officers dine with him, and if they didn't "drink deep," he would try to flog them.[121] After the war, it is said that he managed to retain his New York property *and* receive compensation from the Crown for property that was confiscated in New Jersey, though no one knew how he managed that.[122]

Some of his inscription is faintly legible, but a portion that was transcribed in 1839 was already invisible by the end of that century:

> *Sacred to the memory of Michael Price*
> *Who departed this life May 21, 1821, in his 84th year.*
> *The gray-haired man*
> *Beside the infant sleeps.*

Nearby Michael Price's marker are several illegible markers; the same 1839 article describes there being "ten headstones in a cluster" for the Price family.[123] Seven were still legible in 1897. The marker located two to the left of Michael (E5) is known to be that of his wife, HELENA CORNELL PRICE (CIRCA 1748–1832) (E7). At F3, next to an unknown box grave, is that of a son, EDWARD PRICE (CIRCA 1793–1831). Helena and Edward died after in-ground burials were stopped, making the stones a little puzzling; the burial registry offers no clue.

One son of Michael and Helena whose grave was still legible in 1897 was grocer BENJAMIN PRICE (CIRCA 1789–1816) (LIKELY E6). Benjamin was at the theater one night when a British army officer turned around to stare at Price's fiancée, Catherine Schuyler. Price grabbed the man by the nose. Though both apologized the next day, their various friends convinced them that a duel was necessary. The officer practiced five hours a day, and when they met at the Weehawken dueling grounds, Price was killed.

Edward and Stephen Price at the Park Theatre, 1822; detail of painting by John Searle.

Years later, another officer was heard to brag that he was the one who had goaded Price and the officer into the fatal challenge. Benjamin's brother Stephen, who had vowed revenge, got wind of the bragging, went to the officer's hotel, and said, "I have come to insult you." Soon thereafter, he killed the officer in a duel. Legend has it that Michael, who had always encouraged his sons to get into duels, rewarded him with a check for $5,000.[124]

Stephen Price fought a lot of duels, including one with John Slidell Jr. (page 71), and one George Eacker (page 231), whom he'd harassed at the Park Theatre with his friend Philip Hamilton (page 40). After a career managing the Park Theater, during which he introduced the practice of bringing in "stars" to attract audiences, Stephen died in 1840, too late for an in-ground burial in the family plot at Trinity.[125]

Another son, William, was a district attorney who was said to have "Swartwouted (page 80) to France with nobody knows how much of the people's money."[126] William died by suicide at a Canal Street shooting gallery in 1846 and was interred at St. Mark's. He and Stephen were both interred at St. Mark's in the Bowery and later moved to Evergreen.[127]

## LOST MARKERS IN S4

Transcriptions show that among the illegible markers around the Price family's were markers belonging to ELIZABETH PRICE (1779–1780), HELLEN PRICE (CIRCA 1788–1790) and HELLINA PRICE (1790). One of those three could be the "infant" referred to on Michael's faded epitaph. The large cross at E6 is most likely Benjamin's marker. The 1897 transcription isn't generally in geographical order but lists Benjamin's marker in between those of his parents.

An 1839 article notes that near Michael Price's marker was a marker for a JOHN SMITH, bearing the epitaph, "Thy name will live forever."[128] It was illegible or lost by the twentieth century.

There are nineteenth-century references to a grave here for JOHN KELSO (DIED 1820), which identified him as "a pilot who unfortunately drowned." Newspaper records do state that a pilot by that name walked to the gangway of the schooner *Huntress*, jumped overboard, and perished. Captain Budd "supposed he was insane."[129] At least a portion of the marker was still legible in 1897, but its exact location is lost.

A marker in the plot for JAMES WILKIE (DIED 1805) *also* called him "a pilot who unfortunately drowned," and his death came in a remarkably similar manner.[130] A newspaper in 1805 noted that Wilkie had jumped from a cabin window "in a fit of insanity."[131] Wilkie's marker is no longer legible but identified on the map (A1).

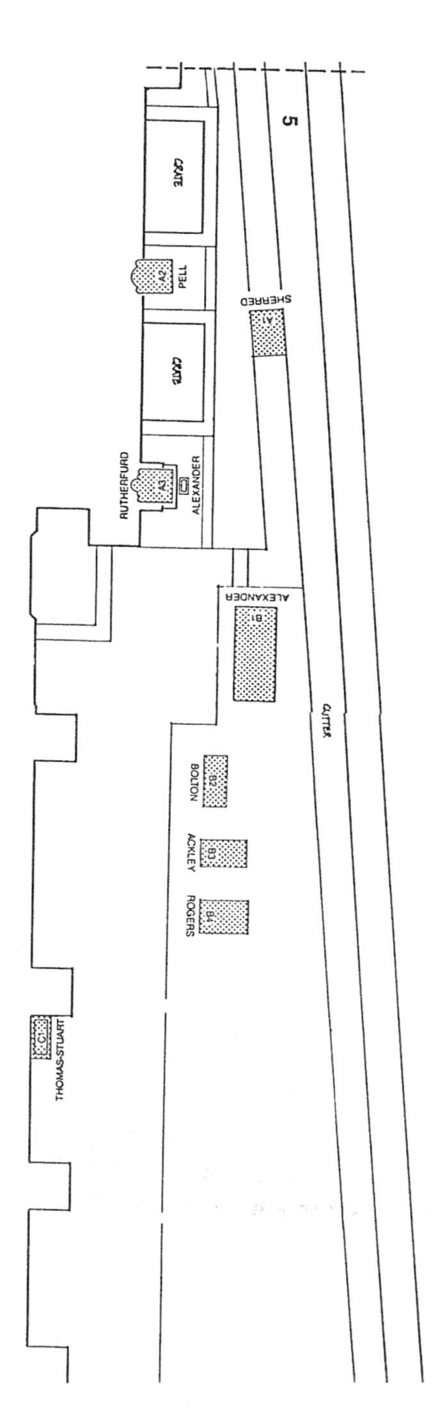
5
CRATE
PELL
A2
SHERRED
A1
CRATE
RUTHERFURD
A3
ALEXANDER
ALEXANDER
B1
GUTTER
BOLTON
B2
ACKLEY
B3
ROGERS
B4
THOMAS-STUART
C1

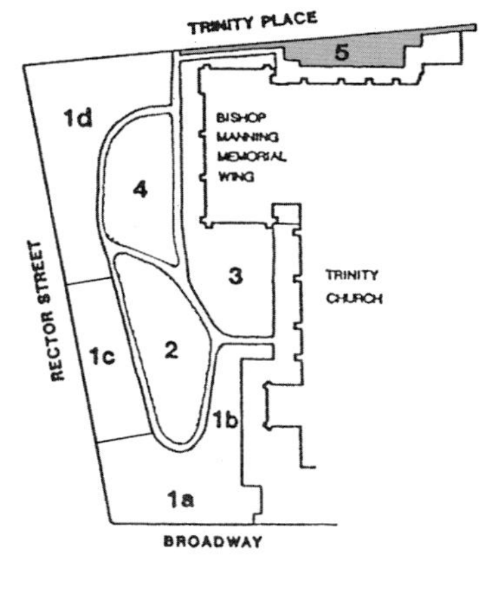
TRINITY PLACE
5
1d
BISHOP
MANNING
MEMORIAL
WING
4
3
TRINITY
CHURCH
RECTOR STREET
1c
2
1b
1a
BROADWAY

# SECTION S5

The section running along the back of the church contains several markers for vault entrances. Many markers were moved here from their original spots during the 1960s, though the vaults themselves generally remained in place.

## Ackley's Cannons

*There seems to be a speck of war in the Western Horison* [sic], *which I dare say is not displeasing to those officers of the army who are anxious to distinguish themselves. Opportunities of acquiring fame & promotion is the chief aliment upon which they can long subsist.*
*—Colonel Joseph Constant to Andrew Jackson, December 1811*

There are four known interments in the vault of Anthony Ackley (circa 1758–1805, B3), based only on nameplates found in 1964. The 1868 inspection said "four coffins nearly all decayed." In 1964, when the vault was inspected again, it was found that two cannons had been used as coffins.

There are two soldiers interred here. One is Colonel Joseph Constant (1773–1819), who, in 1803, became sheriff of New York. He later fought in the Battle of New Orleans, the climactic battle of the War of 1812 that made Andrew Jackson famous (neither army having heard that the war had ended). The other is George Marcellin (circa 1785–1810), who was described as a "promising naval officer" when he died of tuberculosis aboard the frigate *President*.[132]

The 1868 vault report says nothing about cannons, but it never mentioned anything beyond the number of coffins found and their conditions. It's possible that the cannons had been used as decorations, and during the 1868 inspection, stray rubble and bones were placed inside them.

## LORD STIRLING

*Fit persons are difficult to be found in New Jersey.*
*—Wm Alexander to Governor Franklin, January 30, 1764*

In 1729, an enslaved man named Yaff, described as "a sensible cunning fellow," wrote himself a fake transit pass and ran away from JAMES ALEXANDER (1691–1756, B1), a New York merchant. This is probably not what James had in mind when he wrote about freedom of the press and the importance of people being free to write.[133]

The Scottish-born Alexander had joined a 1715 Jacobite uprising, supporting the claims of James Edward Stuart to the throne (page 18) and fled to America when it failed. Given the anti-Catholic sentiment in New York in the era, this was a bold move. But he became a prominent attorney and even published a newspaper critical of the British government. Though he meant "slavery to tyranny" when he spoke of slavery as "abominable," his writings in the 1730s likely helped spread the developing ideas of liberty and enlightenment through the colonies. The vault was built when a son, JAMES ALEXANDER JR. (1723–1731), died of smallpox.[134]

His wife, MARY SPRATT PROVOOST ALEXANDER (1693–1760), came from a family of Dutch goldsmiths and became a major merchant herself; it was said at one time that there was seldom a ship in the harbor that didn't contain items she'd imported for sale.

James would have been heir to the title of the Earl of Stirling upon the death of his father in 1739, but he never claimed the title. Upon *his* death, though, his son WILLIAM ALEXANDER (1726–1783) filed a suit to claim it. It was granted by a Scottish court but not the House of Lords, which means the title was "disputed." But William called himself Lord Stirling for the rest of his life; even George Washington addressed him as "My Lord."

In 1822, yellow fever was reported around Rector Street, near Trinity Churchyard. Several people suggested that the noxious gasses emitting from the churchyard were spreading the disease.

In September 1822, Dr. Samuel Akerly suggested that Trinity and the other nearby cemeteries be covered in a mixture of lime, charcoal, and tanner's bark to stop the spread of disease. One Dr. Roosa was given the job, and he hired a crew to spread the mixture along Broadway and several other nearby streets, as well as the churchyards.*

Roosa reported that on September 23, he and his crew poured fifty-two casks of quicklime over Trinity and said, "The stench arising from thence was so excessive as to cause several of my labourers to cascade [vomit] freely....The smell was great in every part of the yard, but the most offensive part was in the rear, and where it adjoins Lumber Street [now Trinity Place] and Rector Street."†

Though Roosa stated that none of the workers got sick, word spread that two of them had died of yellow fever during the week they were at work. Two men *had* died, but Dr. Akerly denied that either had died of the fever. One, John Smith, had suffered from a scrotal hernia the size of a child's head. On the day Trinity was treated, Smith was not with the crew at all but was "taken with dysentery, and unable to work, and all day running from his bed to the yard." The next day, his wife gave him boneset tea, "which puked him," and then she gave him pennyroyal tea with a burnt oyster shell. The next night, he was dead, with no symptoms of fever (but any number of other possible causes of death).

Some doubted that the churchyards truly spread disease at all. Robert Hone, who would soon be mayor, stated that he was "fully of the opinion that the decomposition of vegetable matter was much more injurious than that of animal," and he doubted that "the decomposition of a dead Elephant in Broadway was as injurious as half a bushel of Cabages [*sic*]."‡ (In truth, reeking graveyards were usually only hazardous if those recently interred had died of something contagious. Otherwise, they were just terribly unpleasant.)

But even those who doubted that the churchyards were dangerous tended to agree that the time had come to close them, as they were terribly overcrowded—not to mention full of old-fashioned monuments that now seemed embarrassing. By the end of 1822, the city had forbidden burials below Canal Street, with exceptions for interment in vaults. Soon, that boundary would move farther north.

---

* *NYP*, September 14, 1822.
† *NYP*, October 3, 1822.
‡ "Interments," *The Statesman*, June 17, 1825.

In the Revolution, Lord Stirling used his own money to outfit a regiment in New Jersey and was made a general in March 1776. He was present when Washington made his famous crossing of the Delaware River and accepted the surrender of Hessian troops there. He later set up a headquarters at Valley Forge, where his parties became the stuff of legend—he was well known for his love of good food and drink. Aaron Burr wrote that Stirling was drunk "morning to morning" and said that Stirling's aide-de-camp, future president James Monroe, was mostly in charge of keeping the tankards full.[135]

This fondness of liquor would serve Stirling well; one night, General James Wilkinson (see page 80) got drunk at Lord Stirling's house and let it slip that there was a plot to oust Washington from command. When Stirling reported it, the plot fell apart.

Despite his lavish lifestyle, Lord Stirling was a brave soldier and brilliant tactician. But his lifestyle caught up with him, and he died of gout just before the war ended. Washington wrote his widow, Sarah Livingston Alexander (1725–1805), a letter, saying, "I [would suggest] every rational topic of consolation, were I not fully persuaded that the principles of Philosophy and Religion, of which you are possessed, had anticipated everything I could say on the subject."[136]

Sarah, as Lady Stirling, was treated as a peer by British officers who occupied New York. They allowed her to help herself to anything she wanted in the city, but she refused to take so much as a box of tea. She suffered financially after Lord Stirling's death, living for a time in a New York rooming house, but was noted as a prominent presence at Washington's inaugural ball.

Whether Lord Stirling is truly in the vault is a mystery itself. Initially buried at a Dutch church in Albany, he may have been moved to the family vault here after that church was demolished in 1806.[137] None of the coffin plates found when the vault was opened in 1894 confirm the presence of Lord Stirling's remains, but many plates were illegible, and no other graveyard has a better claim.

# THE NORTH CHURCHYARD

When the first Trinity Church was built, only the south churchyard was controlled by the parish; the graveyard north of the church had been a town burying ground since at least the 1680s.

In 1703, the church noted that burial fees for the north section were still being paid to the Dutch Church, and the government turned the management over to Trinity, granting the church the right "to have and to hold" the space as "a burying place for any of the inhabitants of the city." They could charge up to three shillings for burying the bodies of people over the age of twelve and eighteen pence (one and a half shillings) for those who were younger. (For comparison, the sexton was paid six shillings for digging graves in the south yard.) It's notable that the grant said the ground was to be used "for any of the inhabitants of the city" and doesn't mention race or creed (see page 178).

The gravestones here probably represent only a fraction of the actual number of burials that took place from the 1600s until 1822. Yet Section 7N appears nearly empty in old diagrams; a number of vaults and stones were moved there from the south yard in the 1960s.

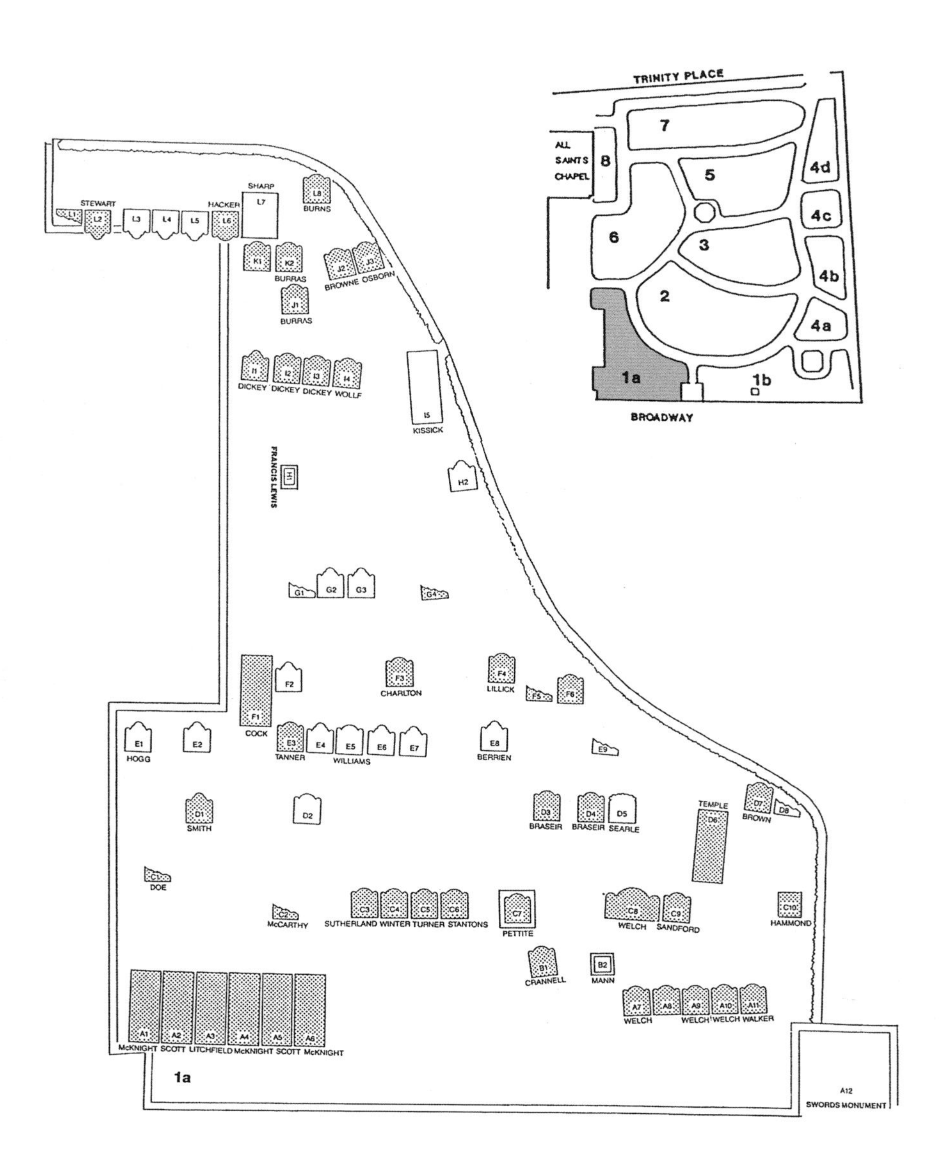
TRINITY PLACE
ALL SAINTS CHAPEL
8
7
5
4d
4c
6
3
4b
2
4a
1a
1b
BROADWAY
STEWART
L1
L2
L3
L4
L5
HACKER
L6
SHARP
L7
L8
BURNS
K1
K2
BURRAS
J2
J3
BROWNE OSBORN
J1
BURRAS
I1
I2
I3
I4
DICKEY DICKEY DICKEY WOLLF
I5
KISSICK
FRANCIS LEWIS
H1
H2
G1
G2
G3
G4
F1
COCK
F2
F3
CHARLTON
F4
LILLICK
F5
F6
E1
HOGG
E2
E3
TANNER
E4
E5
WILLIAMS
E6
E7
E8
BERRIEN
E9
D1
SMITH
D2
D3
BRASEIR
D4
BRASEIR
D5
SEARLE
TEMPLE
D6
D7
BROWN
D8
C1
DOE
C2
McCARTHY
C3
C4
C5
C6
SUTHERLAND WINTER TURNER STANTONS
C7
PETTITE
C8
WELCH
C9
SANDFORD
C10
HAMMOND
B1
CRANNELL
B2
MANN
A7
A8
A9
A10
A11
WELCH
WELCH WELCH WALKER
A1
A2
A3
A4
A5
A6
McKNIGHT SCOTT LITCHFIELD McKNIGHT SCOTT McKNIGHT
1a
A12
SWORDS MONUMENT

# SECTION N1A

The first thing one sees when entering in the north section is a row of metal ledger-style graves, all lined up next to one another, over a vault containing the families of MARY MORIN SCOTT LITCHFIELD MCKNIGHT (1753–1796, A1). The stones were recut in 1907 and remain quite legible, telling the story of a fascinating family.[138]

## JOHN MORIN SCOTT

*Great Britain must infallibly perish and that speedily.... I never loved her so much as to wish to keep her company in her ruin.*

—*John Morin Scott*[139]

When BRIGADIER GENERAL JOHN MORIN SCOTT (1730–1784, A2) held out against telling Washington to evacuate New York City in 1776, a cynic might say it was only because he owned a lot of land in Manhattan, including what is now Times Square. British occupation would be bad for him financially. But this ignores the risk he was taking fighting in a long-shot cause to start with. A successful lawyer, Scott had been risking his life, property, and reputation for years.

In 1769, he was a member of the Society of Dissenters, a group that opposed the British Parliament appointing Anglican bishops in North

The Scott-Litchfield-McKnight graves.

America, which John Adams later said was a major factor in causing the Revolution.[140] In 1775, he helped Marinus Willet (page 78) confiscate several carts of firearms from British troops who were heading to Boston.[141] One Loyalist historian lamented that "[by] foolishly engaging himself in all the politics of the republican faction with the violence and acrimony of a madman, he rendered himself despicable in the estimation of all moderate men."[142]

He became a general in Washington's army during the New York campaign but left the service to serve on the political side; he was the first secretary of state for New York, a member of the state senate, and a delegate to the Continental Congress in 1780 and 1782. He may have been more widely recognized if he'd lived long enough to retell his accomplishments later in life, but he died after a "tedious illness" in 1784, soon after the war ended.[143]

The Presbyterian John had been a harsh critic of Trinity and the growing power of the Anglican Church in life, but he was interred in the yard between the destruction of the first church and the construction of the second.

Future president John Adams rhapsodized about the lush breakfasts Scott served at his elegant home and noted that Scott was "a sensible man, but not very polite...a character [who can] sit up all night at his bottle, yet argue to admiration next day."*

* John Adams's diary, August 1774.

When the church made a show of presenting Queen Elizabeth II with 279 peppercorns as overdue rent (page 17) just a few feet from this grave, Scott may have rolled over inside it. One hopes he'd be gratified to see the more progressive, inclusive attitudes the church exhibits today.

## MARY MORIN SCOTT LITCHFIELD MCKNIGHT

At sixteen, John's daughter Mary married a British officer, COLONEL JOHN LITCHFIELD (1749–1775, A3). But she was devoted to her father's cause, not her new husband's. Colonel Litchfield died of a "rupture of a blood vessel" in July 1775, just as the war was beginning.[144] A year later, Mary was writing letters to friends referring to the "wicked designs" of "our enemy," the British.

In August 1776, General William Livingston, a friend of her father, sent word that the family should flee New York at once, and they rushed out into what Mary described as "the most violent storm I ever saw, the flashes of lightning were incessant, and one continued peal of thunder, and very dark except what light we had from the heavens, which seemed to be a blaze." Mary took over the driving of the carriage herself at one point.[145]

Her revolutionary sentiments were only expressed in private letters to friends, where war news was mixed with gossip about everyone's sweethearts. ("They will help to pass the time away if it is only in laughing at them.") But family stories say that she used her status as an officer's widow to gather intelligence.

In 1778, Mary married Dr. Charles McKnight, chief physician of the American army. She died in 1798. Obituaries called her an "amiable acquaintance" (they almost always called women "amiable") and a "bountiful benefactress" to the poor.[146]

In the same section is the marker of Mary's second husband, DR. CHARLES MCKNIGHT (1750–1791, A4). He hadn't finished medical school when he joined the army, but his zeal and talent in surgery attracted Washington's attention, and in 1777, he was appointed senior surgeon of the Flying Hospital, the army's first mobile surgical unit. Before he was thirty,

## The Doctor's Mob

In February 1788, a grave was robbed at Trinity, and an advertisement offered a one-hundred-dollar reward to anyone who could find out who stole the body. Debates in the paper over the next month show that grave robbing was a big problem. Medical students needed cadavers and were willing to fight for the right to dig them up.

Just over a month after the advertisement was placed, children playing outside of Columbia University allegedly saw a medical student waving a cadaver's arm out the window, and when word got around, a crowd broke into the college and hospital, determined to confiscate any bodies and perhaps even attack the students and their teachers. The mayor allowed the crowd to take the "specimens" away to be buried, likely at St. Paul's, and hustled several doctors to the jail, where the mob couldn't attack them. Among the doctors was Dr. Charles McKnight (page 97).

The next day, the mob grew larger and roamed the city, breaking into doctors' homes to find more "specimens" and attack doctors. Militias were called in, led by Revolutionary War veterans such as John Jay, Baron Von Steuben, and, likely, Hamilton, to fight the mob. It was, by some metrics, the first riot in the newly formed nation.

Details are hard to discern from firsthand accounts, as none of them are from people who were actually *involved* in the rioting. But contemporary commentaries give an interesting glimpse into how the founders viewed mobs, militias, and the shaky trust many people had that the new government would protect them.

McKnight was named physician-general, and in 1782, he was chief physician of the army.

When the war ended, he became a lecturer at Columbia, where John W. Francis wrote that "the profundity of his research, and the acuteness of his genius, gained for him the approbation of even the most fastidious."[147]

One surgery he performed toward the end of his life became a part of medical history: a woman had gone into labor without delivering a baby, and the extrauterine fetus was still inside her body over a year later. Dr. McKnight was able to remove the fetus, and the woman recovered.[148]

He died in 1791 from an old war injury.

Best viewed through the fence is a framed marker with an inscription that states it was restored by the daughters of RICHARD EDWARDS MOUNT (1786–1872) and MARIA BRANSON MOUNT (1792–1873, C7). One episode in Richard's life speaks well of him: in 1822, David Chase, an apprentice in Mount's brush making shop, died of yellow fever. John Lang of the *New York Gazette* alleged that he'd contracted it while committing a robbery in "the infected district." Mount fired off a vicious letter demanding an apology of Lang.[149] It's a nice contrast to the usually disparaging references to apprentices in the press.

There are several interments in the plot, including that of Maria's father, CAPTAIN WARE BRANSON (1753–1821), who sailed such vessels as the freighter *Sea Nymph*.[150] He must have been a Loyalist; in August 1776, George Washington named him among a handful of people who had been apprehended and were under guard at New Rochelle.[151] The first interment was likely that of THOMAS PETTITE (1744–1745).

The stone frame was added in 1885; the original stone has only a few legible words, though the haunting face can still be glimpsed above. The original epitaph, lost by 1897, featured one of the most dubious rhymes in the graveyard. It was for Captain Bronson's grandparents THOMAS WEAR (1680–1747) and JEAN WEAR (1680–1747):

> *They fled from scienes* [sic] *of mortal guilt*
> *Without Par Taking* [sic] *of the same*
> *They left their bodies Sleeping here*
> *Till Christ do come the Second time.*[152]

Well behind the Scott-McKnight section is an oblong stone marked with a plaque (H1) for a man who signed the Declaration of Independence.

In 1732, one Robert Elliston (died 1756) showed up at the churchyard and dug himself a vault. He does not appear to have had permission to do this, but vestry minutes show he agreed to pay "such reasonable sum as they shall think fit, it being but five feet wide." It's fun to imagine the vestrymen calling Elliston out in the middle of his digging and Elliston saying, "Oh, come on! It's just a little one!" Elliston seems to have been a merchant; his wife, Mary Elliston (died 1775), was selling wines and Indian goods after his death for "ready money."* Both are presumed to have been interred in the vault.

Late nineteenth-century vault records state that the location of this vault was unknown, but other records suggest that in 1839, the old Elliston vault was given to the Van Horne family to replace their old one, which was to be destroyed by the construction of the new church.

The Van Horne vault is located on the north side of the church, west of the McKnight graves, in a rather unusual spot for a vault, as nearly all of the old vaults are on the south side. The Van Hornes are recorded to have used it for only two interments, but there were seven coffins there in 1868.

* *NYM*, November 13, 1758.

## Francis Lewis

*No man should read novels until he has turned fifty.*
*—Francis Lewis, who read voraciously*

Francis Lewis (1713–1802, H1) was a New York merchant; advertisements for his shop in the 1740s list items such as linens, handkerchiefs, diapers, and snuff.[153]

During the Seven Years' War in 1756, General Montcalm captured Lewis, who was supplying uniforms to a fort in Oswego, and turned him over to a group of Natives. Lewis was certain he was going to be executed. But according to a family legend, he then realized that their language had words similar to the Gaelic and Cymraeg words he'd grown up with, and he managed to communicate with them. He was spared and sent to France; then he returned home after the Seven Years' War when he was granted five thousand acres of land by the Crown.[154]

There were many legends at the time that a Welsh prince had colonized the Americas in 1170 and rumors that there were still Welsh-speaking tribes on the continent to confirm it. Thomas Jefferson discussed the idea with his hired explorers Lewis and Clark.[155] Modern scholars are doubtful about the details of both the legend and Francis Lewis's story, as no surviving Native language much resembles Welsh. But Lewis's family always claimed to have heard it from Lewis himself, and explanations about exactly how he managed to survive captivity demanded *some* thrilling tale.

Of course, Lewis's life story hardly needed embellishing. Given the land grant, one might have expected Lewis to remain loyal to the British, but after retiring as a merchant, he became deeply involved in Revolutionary politics, eventually being elected to the Continental Congress, where he was one of the signers of the Declaration of Independence. He is the only signatory known to be buried in Manhattan.

Library records show he enjoyed the popular novelists of the day, such as Smollet and Fielding, and books about spies.[156] In 1791, he was one of a few Trinity residents who checked out *The Negro: Equalled by Few Europeans*, Lavalée's radical novel, though his record on slavery isn't spotless. He is known to have freed an enslaved man named King "in consideration of the fidelity, integrity, and sobriety ever manifested…in the course of a long service." This may be the man listed as "King, a Free Negro," who was buried at St. Paul's in 1803 (page 257).

> The location of the Lewis marker seems to be based on an old, vague rumor recorded in his file in the Trinity Archives, that he was interred in the Baker vault, under the church near N8. The Baker vault bears a date of 1813, too late for Lewis, and no one knew *why* he would be interred there. But dates on vaults can be seemingly arbitrary, and there were two unidentified coffins inside it in 1868. So, it's not impossible that Lewis was interred there.

A solitary grave beyond Lewis's, seen while proceeding on the sidewalk, is for merchant tailor WILLIAM BURRAS (CIRCA 1764–1798, J1). It has an epitaph taken from the hymn "When Blooming Youth Is Snatched Away," by Anne Steele:

*The voice of this alarming scene*
*May every heart obey*
*Nor be the heavenly warning vain*
*But let us watch and pray*

Behind this is a marker for Burras's mother, ESTER BURRAS (1724–1790, K2). It features a crisp epitaph, minus a few missing words on the first line; it's a common verse, beginning, "My flesh shall slumber in the ground." It also appears nearby on Captain Dickey's grave (I2).

It is unknown whose interment is marked by the stone to the left of Ester's (K1), but it is likely her husband, LAWRENCE BURRAS's (1720–1797), a periwig maker who is said to be buried in here in several nineteenth-century sources. Washington and his staff dined at the Burras home on Bowling Green after the Battle of Long Island.[157]

Section 1A contains one row on its west end where the inscriptions face the opposite direction of other stones. The best preserved, by far, is that of grocer CHARLES STEWART (CIRCA 1785–1819, L2). Obituaries show he was the son of Charles Stewart, also a grocer, who died in 1805, and Catharine Stewart, who died in 1812.[158] His parents are in the burial registry and are likely interred nearby, perhaps beneath the unidentified white stones to the left.

Walking as the path curves and heads east, with Section 1 to the right, past the faded box grave of wine dealer PHILIP KISSICK (CIRCA 1722–1790, I5), there's a small marker for tavern keeper SAMUEL LILLICK (CIRCA 1750–1791) and his daughter ANN LILLICK (1790–1791, F4). The grave, having its back to the western path, is hard to view, and the epitaph is usually covered by grass, but it reads:

*Ponder Then attend awhile*
*I died first and then my child*
*And as you read the state of me*
*Think on the fleeting hours for thee*

In 1871, a reporter transcribed the epitaph and noted, "It is seldom that the dead, as in this instance, speak of events that happen *after* their burial."

This practice of first-person epitaphs would eventually fall out of favor. An 1830 article wrote, "The penchant many have of making the dead speak to the spectator in language of quaint exhortion cannot have its foundation in good taste—for the departed are not there; all that would speak is far removed from the ashes of the grave, and therefore, direct addresses from the inhumed to the living partake of the revolting, if not the ludicrous."[159]

## Charlotte Temple: The Grave That Never Was

> *A dangerous illness and obstinate delirium ensued, during which he raved incessantly for Charlotte....He recovered, but to the end of his life was subject to severe fits of melancholy, and while he remained at New York frequently retired to the church yard, where he would weep over the grave, and regret the untimely fate of the lovely Charlotte Temple.*
>
> —*Charlotte Temple*

Along the sidewalk is a flat slab with a recessed space that looks as though there was a plaque there once and an unusually crisp epitaph reading "Charlotte Temple" (D6). It is the grave of a fictional character.

*Charlotte Temple*, Susanna Rowson's 1791 novel, tells of a teenage girl who is seduced and abandoned by a British officer. The officer repents when he learns that Charlotte has died in childbirth, begs her father to kill him, and then rushes off and kills a friend in a drunken swordfight before descending into madness.

Though not exactly a delightful romp, it was, by some accounts, the first best-selling novel in the United States. Most people knew the story was fiction, and no specific streets were mentioned in the book, but it became common for New Yorkers to show visitors places where Charlotte lived, just as it became common in later centuries to point out the restaurant from *Seinfeld.* The grave became one of the attractions of these "Temple tours" and was often held up as proof that Charlotte was real.

By the end of the nineteenth century, the marker was as well-known as the graves of Hamilton and Lawrence. Some pointed out that the lettering style was far more modern than one would see on an eighteenth-century grave, but true believers told a tale that the stone and plaque were added in 1800 by Charlotte's daughter and that the lettering was modern because it was added after the original plaque was stolen.[160]

The Charlotte Temple grave in the late nineteenth century and the same spot today. The cherub-topped grave for Henry Brasher Jr. is now missing, the Searle marker is badly deteriorated, and one behind it is lost. Strangely, the marker for Samuel Brown (1755–1756, D7) to the right of Charlotte was transcribed in 1897 but not visible when the earlier photograph was taken around 1876.

As early as 1890, a researcher noted that during the 1840s, when the third church was under construction, there were sheds, stones, and scaffolding all over the grounds, and gravestones were often displaced. He speculated that during this period, a worker had added the name to a stone, which matches the stones used in construction, as a prank. This is still the prevailing theory—it's notable that no mention of a Charlotte Temple grave has been found from before the 1840s.[161] If the inscription was a prank, it was a prank that fooled people for decades and continues to be talked about nearly two centuries on, which makes it an awfully successful prank.

But why would that worker have carved a place for a plaque? *Could* it have originally been the gravestone of someone else? Surely such a space couldn't have been unused in such a crowded burial ground.

In 2008, archivist Gwynedd Cannan had the stone lifted to see if a vault was underneath, but there was only packed earth.[162] The mystery lives on.

The fully illegible light-colored grave to the left of Charlotte's (D5) is for merchant JAMES SEARLE (CIRCA 1691–1745), who was known as "a gentleman of unspotted Reputation, [with] a happy Disposition, and an extensive charity."[163] The marker to the left (D4) is that of DAVID BRASEIR (CIRCA 1733–1758).

Old images of the Temple grave show a cherub-topped marker between Temple's and Searle's that is no longer present; it appears to have been for HENRY BRASHER JR. (1787).[164] The full text read, "Here lies intered the remains of Henry Brasher Jr. son of Henry and Genetta Brasher of this City who departed this life 19th September 1787 aged 9 months 15 days." Henry Brasher Sr., a Revolutionary War drummer, was probably a relative of the nearby David Braseir; their family appears to have been connected to Searle's by marriage. Henry Sr. worked as a realtor; Genetta left him a month before Henry Jr. died (he'd been indicted for abusing her earlier that year), and the next month, Henry Sr. died, too. Papers noted his death only in advertisements seeking the return of a twelve-year-old girl named Sill whom he had enslaved.[165]

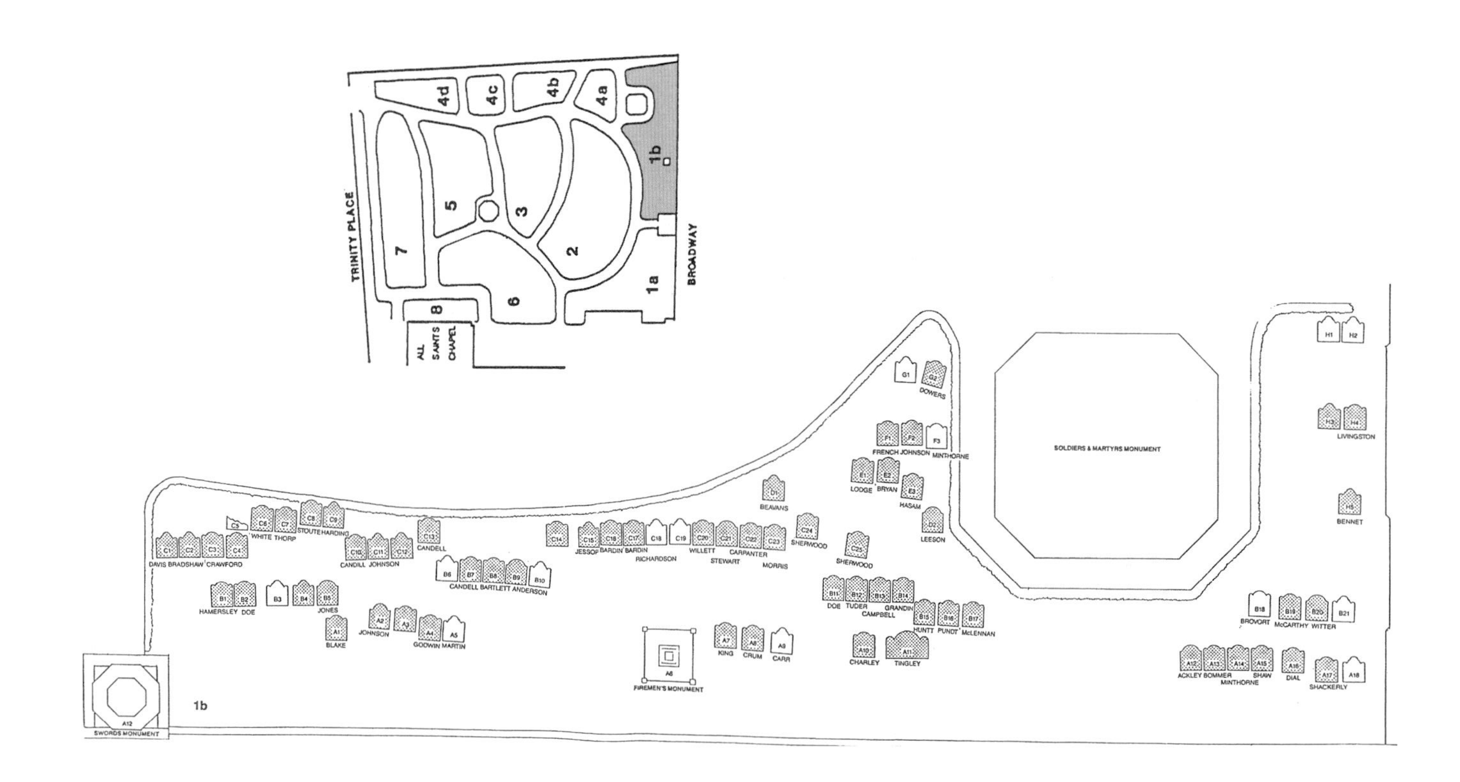

TRINITY PLACE
BROADWAY
ALL SAINTS CHAPEL
1a
1b
2
3
4a
4b
4c
4d
5
6
7
8
SWORDS MONUMENT
1b
DAVIS BRADSHAW CRAWFORD
WHITE THORP
STOUTE HARDING
CANDILL JOHNSON
CANDELL
HAMERSLEY DOE
JONES
BLAKE
JOHNSON
GODWIN MARTIN
CANDELL BARTLETT ANDERSON
JESSOP BARDIN BARDIN
RICHARDSON
WILLETT
STEWART
CARPANTER
MORRIS
SHERWOOD
SHERWOOD
BEAVANS
FIREMEN'S MONUMENT
KING
CRUM
CARR
DOE TUDER
CAMPBELL
GRANDIN
HUNTT PUNDT McLENNAN
CHARLEY
TINGLEY
LODGE BRYAN
HASAM
LEESON
FRENCH JOHNSON MINTHORNE
DOWERS
SOLDIERS & MARTYRS MONUMENT
LIVINGSTON
BENNET
BROVORT McCARTHY WITTER
ACKLEY BOMMER
MINTHORNE
SHAW
DIAL
SHACKERLY

# SECTION N1B

Section N1B begins at the fountain that sits outside of the fence (A12), designed in 1911 by Thomas Nash. It was commissioned by Henry Swords as a memorial to Ann Maria Cotheal Swords, his mother, who was buried at the Uptown Trinity Cemetery in 1897. It was one of two monuments in the north churchyard designed by Nash for people interred uptown, the other being the Astor Cross (page 145).

The section is distinguished by the number of interesting carvings on its stones, many of which are visible from the sidewalk on Broadway.

A little behind the fountain is a short stone, mostly buried, with a matronly soul effigy for William Crawford (died 1744, C3). "Wm Cr," as the marker styles him, was the son of Hugh Crawford, a vintner and tavern keeper. In 1749, the city celebrated the end of the War of Austrian Succession, a bloody conflict with several related battles that were fought in the colonies. It was noted that "the evening was concluded with Mirth, most of the houses being illuminated, especially Mr. Hugh Crawford's and Mr. Cock's Sexton

On the Blake stone, the word "also" looks to modern eyes like "alfo." It uses the long "s" that resembled a lowercase "f" (see page 29).

of Trinity Church who seemed to out-vie each other in their Demonstration of Joy."[166] Hugh's wife, Effie, carried on keeping his tavern after his death later that year.[167] It's likely that Hugh and Effie were interred at Trinity, though records don't survive.

Another interesting piece of art is located closer to the fence on the grave of Margret Blake (circa 1727–1752, A1), on which two winged death's heads almost appear to be giving each other a high five.

## The Fireman's Monument

In the middle of the section, fenced off near the street, is a firemen's monument (A6), added in 1865, the year that the various volunteer firefighting units in the city were finally organized into professional companies. It was originally built by the Empire Steam Fire Engine Company 42, which later asked that it be moved to Trinity. It features the names of six company members who had been killed, three in Civil War battles and three in the line of firefighting duty.

To the right of the firemen's monument is a broken but legible marker for John Crum (1722–1759) and his daughter Rachel Crum (1759, A8). The four-line epitaph doesn't break the lines on the rhyming words:

*Hark from the Tomb A Dolefull Sound*
*My Ears Attend The Cry Ye Living*
*Men Come View The Ground Where*
*You Must Must Shortly Lie*

The lines come from "Hark from the Tomb," a hymn by Isaac Watts, whose hymns were popular in epitaphs.

The now-illegible grave to the right of Crum's was for Elizabeth Carr (circa 1681–1709, A9), the wife of Robert. Though the inscription is now long lost, it was transcribed in 1871 as a fairly common verse:

*When on the Earth I did remain*
*Was filled with sorrow grief and pain*

*Adieu to friends and sins likewise*
*My journey is beyond the skies.*[168]

Most other versions of this epitaph use "foes" in place of "sins," which is somewhat suggestive. Did the person who picked the epitaph remember it imperfectly after seeing it elsewhere, or did they feel like pointing out some sin they associated with Carr?

Behind Carr's is a small monument with an elegant cursive script for DEBORAH SHERWOOD (1789–1796, C24). It's very hard to read today but is still a legible version of a fairly common epitaph:

*Tho in Deaths cold arms I make my bed*
*I only sleep until the great Assize*
*When the last Trumpet shall awake the dead*
*Then I with those that sleep in Christ shall rise.*

The "Great Assize" was a term for Judgement Day that was common at the time.

Behind Sherwood's is a marker for ELIZABETH BEAVENS (1749–1750) and her father, THOMAS BEAVENS (CIRCA 1712–1754, D1), topped by a soul effigy that features not only wings but also a feathered body beneath a serious-looking face. Beavans appears to have been a privateer whose ship *The Clinton* captured French vessels.[169]

Farther north is a marker with four soul effigies for the infant TINGLEY BROTHERS (A11). Family records show that their parents, Samuel and Agnes, were married in the 1730s; a son who lived to adulthood became a noted silversmith.

Just behind the Tingley marker is a stone with an almost comical, drowsy face. It marks the grave of SUSAN HUNTT ROUSBY (CIRCA 1715–1743, B15), whose father, Obadiah Huntt, has a tombstone inside of the church (page 171).

Nearby is a skull-topped marker for ELIZABETH MCLENNAN (CIRCA 1667–1733) and ANN MCLENNAN (1706–1730, B17). The stone once said that Ann was the only daughter of John McLennan (and presumably her mother, Elizabeth). John lived near the "Royal Bowling Green" and, like so many of

Rousby Huntt, Pundt, and McLennan.

his era, appeared in newspapers mostly in relation to slavery. A year after Elizabeth died, he advertised the sale of a twenty-year-old "mild and quiet" woman, who, besides "all sortes of household work…has another good Property she neither drinks rum nor smoke Tobacco, nor no strong liquor." The fact that he'd mention this at all is an interesting insight into the culture of slavery in New York at the time.[170]

## JAMES LEESON'S CRYPTOGRAM

It is not known when, exactly, anyone noticed that there was a secret code on the gravestone of JAMES LEESON (CIRCA 1756–1794, D2). Above his name are Masonic symbols. In the arch above these, though, are a series of strange markings that held a hidden message.

Early nineteenth-century articles on Trinity seldom mention Leeson, but the cryptogram became famous in the 1880s. Articles on the riddle circulated every so often thereafter, always including a solution. The "code" was made by laying letters across a series of marked tic-tac-toe boards, a code also used at St. Paul's on a grave for Captain Lacey (page 203).

The code translates to "remember death."

Though it's clear that Leeson was a Freemason—and it's a fair guess that he enjoyed puzzles—little more is known about him. One advertisement notes he kept a boardinghouse on Water Street, and his will indicates he

*Left*: The Leeson grave.

*Below*: The key to the cryptogam. *Trinity Archives.*

was a butcher.[171] One report states that his funeral was "attended by a great number of the masonic brethren….His loss will not only be lamented by his family, but by all who were acquainted or had any dealings with him; he has, ever since his residence in this country, supported the character of an honest man."[172] Of course, this is typical funeral report jargon and doesn't really tell us much about the man.

Below the main inscription, one may glimpse four faded lines of text that are completely illegible today. Old photographs show that this portion was underground for a time. A Pennsylvania article from 1859 seemed not to notice the cryptogram but did transcribe the four lines:

*While Life remained a Brother had a Friend*
*Till fleeting Moments fixt his Journey end.*
*Read this, and copy all those Acts of Love*
*Till all assemble in the Lodge above.*[173]

The verse, apparently original, seems almost as inscrutable as the puzzle. The word *read* was sometimes used to mean "solve," so "read this" may refer to the cryptogram above, but it's also possible that these lesser-known lines contain *another* hidden riddle still waiting to be deciphered.

A nineteenth-century postcard misidentified the grave as being at St. John's Burying Ground and still causes confusion. His obituaries state that he was interred at Trinity.

## The Martyr's Monument

The imposing gothic *Martyr's Monument* in the northeast corner of the churchyard was added in 1854, a tribute to the prisoners of war who died in the Livingston Sugar House on Crown Street (now Liberty Street). During the war, hundreds of prisoners were housed in the makeshift prison, and disease and starvation ruled the day. Every morning, dead bodies were carted away, and legend has it that they were unceremoniously buried in this section of Trinity Churchyard.

But these burials have never been confirmed, and the addition of the monument was an entirely political move.

For twenty years, aldermen had been passing resolutions to extend Albany Street or Pine Street through the north end of the churchyard, and the church had fought the plan again and again. Stories of the sugar house victims being buried where the street would go were the church's strongest argument, though it wasn't unheard of for someone to claim that an unmarked notable, such as John Lamb, was buried in that section, too.

Critics pointed out that Trinity had never expressed an interest in a monument to the martyrs *before* such a move might slow the attempts to build a road there and that the church hadn't objected to bodies being moved out of other nearby cemeteries, as had been happening constantly in the neighborhood for the past thirty years. The church itself had moved bodies from an old Lutheran cemetery when Grace Church was built over it, just south of Trinity. And of course, tossing old bones in to the "bone

## Trinity in the Revolution

Being a part of the Church of England, the clergy of Trinity Church remained loyal to the Crown as the Revolution dawned. When Washington's army came to the city in April 1776, things became awkward. Bishop Inglis wrote that the clergy were frequently threatened with violence. When Washington attended the church, Inglis fielded a request from one of his generals that prayers for the king be omitted from services. Inglis refused and "drew from him an awkward apology...which, I believe, was not authorized by Washington."

"One Sunday," Inglis wrote months later, "a company of about one hundred armed rebels marched into the Church with drums beating and fifes playing, and their guns loaded and bayonets fixed as if going to battle. The congregation was thrown into the utmost terror, and several women fainted, expecting a massacre was intended. I took no notice of them but went on with the service....The rebels stood thus in the aisle for near fifteen minutes, till, being asked into pews by the sexton, they complied." Inglis expected them to attack when he prayed for the king, but the prayer went on without incident. "I was afterwards assured that something hostile and violent was intended," he wrote. "But He who stills the raging of the sea, and madness of the people, overruled their purpose."

When independence was declared that July, Inglis closed the churches, feeling unable to continue to keep them open safely. In September, Washington's army fled as the British took over the city, and some plundered Inglis's home on their way out of town. One anecdote relates that Christopher Colles, an early advocate of the Erie Canal who was interred in an unmarked grave at either St. Paul's or St. John's (sources differ), was chased by British soldiers and hid in the then-neglected Trinity Churchyard, where the bayonets failed to find him among the tall grass and headstones.

Less than a week after the British army arrived, a fire destroyed a quarter of the city, including Trinity Church. Though the fire is generally believed now to have been started by burning shingles blowing off roofs, Inglis, like many at the time, believed that it was the work of rebel arsonists. He wrote, "The present revolution is one of the most causeless, unprovoked, and unnatural that ever disgraced a country."

Following the war, when Loyalists were expelled, Inglis took his congregation to form a new Trinity Church in Nova Scotia.* American members of the Church of England formed a new branch of the Protestant Episcopal Church, and the church was rebuilt, with Samuel Provoost, who had supported independence, installed as rector.

* Inglis to Reverend Hind, October 31, 1776.

hole" or charnel house to make room for new burials had been common in the old days.

One vocal critic even said that when Trinity had constructed a building just north of the churchyard, it had casually ignored the many bodies it disinterred in the process. "Large quantities of the remains of the dead were disturbed," he wrote. "Their ashes were scattered, and their bones were removed. I witnessed these proceedings, in passing the ground, almost daily, and I saw no exhibition of any peculiar delicacy or sensibility in the extensive exhumation."[174]

It was also noted that there no real evidence that the north end or any other part of the churchyard had really been used for prisoner burials. As a Loyalist church, Trinity might not have buried "rebels" during the war.

But the church insisted there had been thousands of burials of prisoners not just from the sugar house but also from the prison ships. General C.W. Sanford said that he "knew an old woman who daily got fuel from the board of the old coffins which were dug up" to make room for the prisoners' bodies and even claimed, despite being born in 1796, that he'd seen several bodies taken up himself.[175] Attorney Peter Cutler said, "That many such were buried there during the war is proved by tradition, and a tradition so generally believed in by the people would of itself be sufficient to establish any historical fact."

It was not a great argument, to say the least.

The debate was still raging when the monument was built, and everyone knew that it was being built less because of any evidence of burials on the spot than as an effort to intimidate the common council. One source at the time said that when the monument was first being built, it had a plaque with an inscription taken from Shakespeare's grave:

*Good frend for Jesvs sake forbear*
*To digg ye dvst encloased heare :*
*Bless be ye man yt spares thes stones,*
*And cvrst be he yt moves my bones.*[176]

The inscription was apparently removed before the monument was finished. Critics called the monument a "mockery," but the effort to extend the street was defeated.[177]

To the right of the Martyr's Monument is an elaborate marker for Anthony Ackley (circa 1725–1782, A12), a cooper, with stars around its head and the "Hark from the tomb a doleful sound" Isaac Watts verse that can also be seen on the nearby marker of John Crum (page 108). In his will, Ackley left his longest gun to his son John, the shortest to his son Anthony, and "a third gun, if there is one," (or money to buy one if not) to a son named Daniel.[178]

In the second row, near the fence, is a partly legible marker for Mary Witter (circa 1720–1746, B12), which is probably mostly buried. It must have been very tall when it was built; an 1871 article transcribed the epitaph and noted "there is an eccentricity" about it.

*Christian expectance of consummate blessing.*
*Here interred is ye body of Mary, late wife of Thomas Witters, who closed this mortle* [sic] *life the 17th day of April, in the year of our salvation 1746, in her 26 year, moreover with Herself is that of her beloved infant, whose decease was in 1742, and thus before His Parents That which Above are Their Invaluable Souls, That which beneath are their corruptible bodies for the Happy re-union and Joyful Rising again Eternally together.*[179]

Behind Mary's marker is that of Rachel Bennet (1776–1808, H5), on which only one line is currently above ground. The full epitaph, which is fairly common, reads:

*Her mind was tranquil and serene*
*No terrors in her looks were seen*
*Her savior's smiles dispelled the gloom*
*And smoothed her passage to the tomb.*

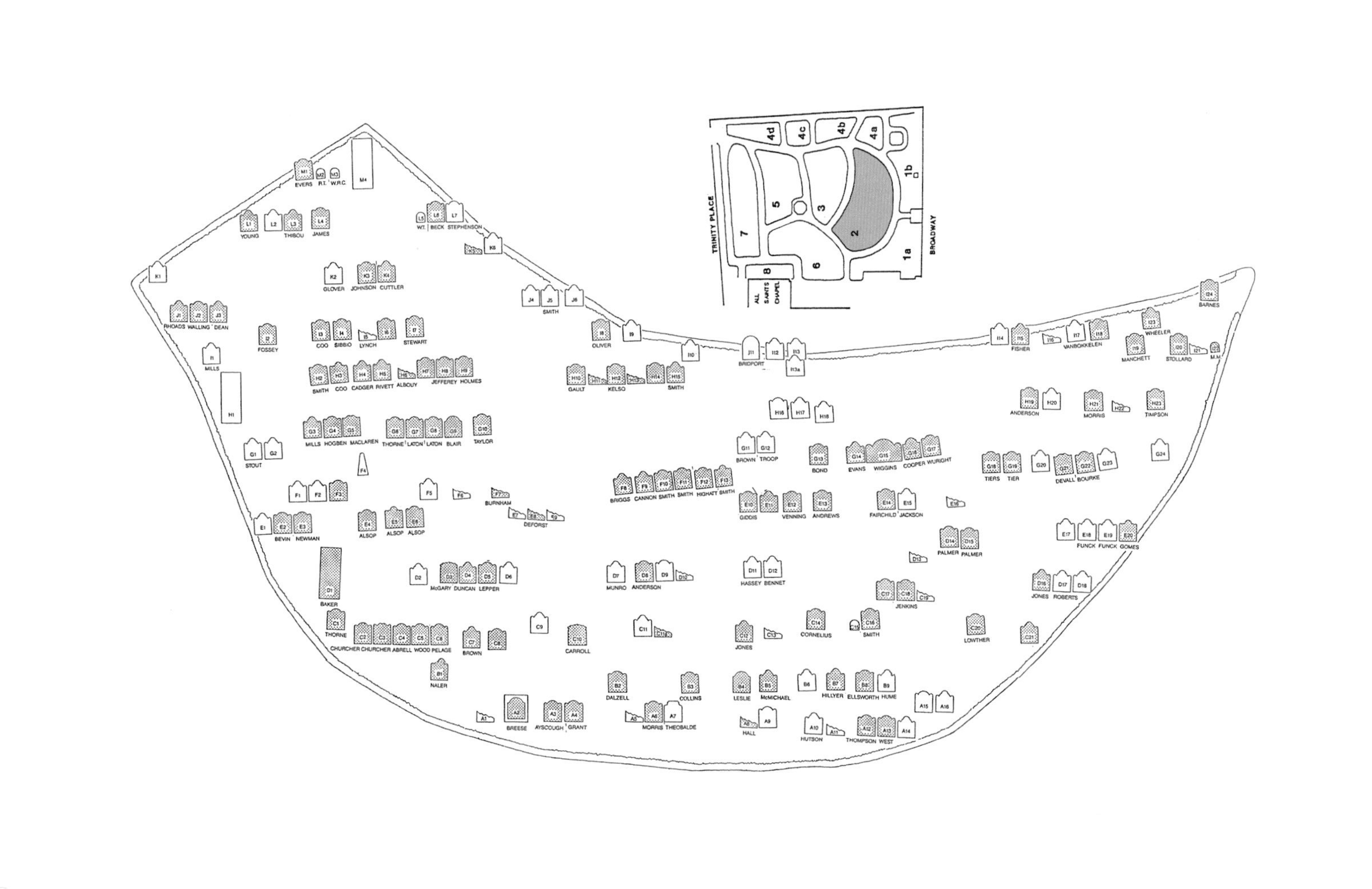
TRINITY PLACE
BROADWAY
ALL SAINTS CHAPEL
EVERS R.T. W.R.C.
YOUNG THIBOU JAMES
W.T. BECK STEPHENSON
GLOVER JOHNSON CUTTLER
SMITH
RHOADS WALLING DEAN
FOSSEY
MILLS
COO SIBBIO LYNCH STEWART
OLIVER
BRIDPORT
FISHER VANBOKKELEN
WHEELER
BARNES
MANCHETT STOLLARD M.M.
SMITH COO CADGER RIVETT ALBOUY JEFFEREY HOLMES
GAULT KELSO SMITH
ANDERSON MORRIS TIMPSON
MILLS HOGBEN MACLAREN THORNE LATON LATON BLAIR TAYLOR
STOUT
BROWN TROOP BOND EVANS WIGGINS COOPER WURIGHT
TIERS TIER DEVALL BOURKE
BURNHAM
DEFORST
BRIGGS CANNON SMITH SMITH HIGHATT SMITH
GIDDIS VENNING ANDREWS FAIRCHILD JACKSON
BEVIN NEWMAN
ALSOP ALSOP ALSOP
FUNCK FUNCK GOMES
PALMER PALMER
McGARY DUNCAN LEPPER
MUNRO ANDERSON
HASSEY BENNET
BAKER
JENKINS
JONES ROBERTS
THORNE
CHURCHER CHURCHER ABRELL WOOD PELAGE
BROWN
CARROLL
JONES CORNELIUS SMITH
LOWTHER
NALER
DALZELL COLLINS
LESLIE McMICHAEL HILLYER ELLSWORTH HUME
BREESE AYSCOUGH GRANT
MORRIS THEOBALDE
HALL
HUTSON THOMPSON WEST

# SECTION N2

Section N2 contains the oldest identified gravestones in the cemetery. There are few markers of well-known or well-documented people in this section, but their gravestones alone make them fascinating—and the section has a large number of poetic epitaphs that appear to be original, in some cases even written by the person they commemorate.

## The Churchers

At the southeast corner of the section is the marker of Richard Churcher (circa 1676–1681, C3), who died sixteen years before Trinity Church was even founded.

*W.C.*
*HER LYES THE BOD*
*OFRICHARDCHVRCH*
*ERTHESONOFWILLIA*
*MCHVRCHERWHO*
*DEID THE 5OF AOS*
*1681 OFAGE 5 YEARS*
*AND 5 MONTHS*

The Churcher section.

The "W.C." presumably refers to Richard's father, William. The back of the marker features a flying hourglass and a skull and crossbones, references to Richard's fleeting life. The last line is currently below the ground line.

With its unspaced letters, odd spelling and mid-word line breaks, the stone looks almost prehistoric next to the more ornate grave on the left for ANNE CHURCHER (1673–1691, C2), who is assumed to have been Richard's sister. Framed by floral ornamentation and a death's head, it mentions that she died on May 14, 1691, and then adds: "BURYED MAY THE 16 1691."

Including both the death *and* burial dates is unusual; perhaps whoever decided on the epitaph felt moved to point out that Anne was buried on a momentous day in the history of the city: May 16, 1691, was the end of Leisler's Rebellion.

The Catholic King James II had been deposed in 1688 and replaced by the Protestant William III and Mary II, making England and the colonies officially Protestant. But some Protestant colonists feared that the colonial governors who had been installed by James would continue to impose Catholic rule. A militia in New York took over Fort James, dismissed acting governor Nicholson, and installed militia captain James Leisler as acting governor until William and Mary could duly appoint someone to the post.

In 1691, William named Colonel Henry Sloughter as the new governor. Bad weather delayed his trip, though, and when another ship carrying Major Richard Ingoldesby arrived first, without official papers but demanding control, Leisler refused to give up the fort. When Sloughter arrived weeks later, he arrested Leisler for treason.

Most of those involved in Leisler's "rebellion" were pardoned, but enemies of Leisler persuaded Sloughter to order his execution. (One tale holds that they got him drunk and had him sign a death warrant.) Leisler was publicly hanged and buried in his own garden, near the current site of the Franklin statue near the Brooklyn Bridge entrance, on May 16, 1691, the day Anne Churcher was buried a short walk away. From their choice to specify both the death *and* burial date, we can imagine that the Churchers saw this as an important event, though it's impossible to know which side they took.

The political tides soon changed; Lord Bellomont (page 255) worked to have Leisler's land and title restored to his family, and in 1698, Leisler's body was moved to the Dutch church on Garden Street (now Exchange Place). That church burned in 1837, and remnants salvaged from Leisler's grave are rumored be somewhere in the collections of the New York Historical Society.

The broken stone at the end of the row is for a woman whose headstone (C6) was said, in 1897, to have been for "THE WIFE OF WILLIAM PELAGE died Oct 20 1692." But this transcription doesn't quite match what little remains legible, notably a word ending in "-stian" (presumably part of "Christian"), and others just gave the last name as "Pel." It was apparently badly broken long before anyone took proper notice of it.

In the row just behind the Churchers' markers is a particularly fine stone featuring a chalice and an epitaph in script as elegant as the text on the Richard Churcher grave is primitive. It is for JAMES MCGARY (CIRCA 1792–1798, D3). Young James was the son of Thomas McGary, a painter, and died in a fire started by a candle left in the backhouse of a home his father had just built.[180]

Near McGary is an almost charmingly crude stone for Elizabeth Lepper (1746, D5) with a verse from an Isaac Watts hymn:

*Infinite joy or endless woe attend our every breath*
*And yet how unconcerned we go upon the brink of death*

Behind them is a triangular marker (f4) whose subject remains unidentified.

Just in front of the Churchers' row is a marker for Sarah Naler (1720–1766, B1) with a self-written epitaph:

*Let No*
*One Mourn the Reason*
*Why Her Soul Ascended*
*To God On High There*
*With Angels & Arch*
*Angels for to Dwell*
*Hallelujah Hallelujah*
*To God On High :*
*Made By Her Self*
*6 Days Before her Death*

John Flavel Mines noted that it was "engraved by a sculptor who evidently had no rhythm in his soul....Poor soul! Her little vanity causes a smile after all the years have passed."[181] Sarah was the wife of Michael Naler, a mariner.[182]

## Sidney Breese

A bit to the right of Sarah Naler's marker is a faded marker in a stone frame for another person who wrote their own epitaph, Sidney Breese (1709–1767, A2). It reads (with the last line usually invisible under the grass):

*Sidney Breese June 9 1767*
*Made by himself*
*Ha Sidney Sidney*
*Lyest thou here*
*I here lye*

*Til time has flown*
*To its Extremity*

Sidney's family history calls him "one of the wittiest, most eccentric, as well as one the of the handsomest men of his time."[183] Born in Shrewsbury, England, Sidney Breese came to New York as a boy and spent years as purser for the British navy. As a young man, he fought a duel with an officer and lived with a bullet in his abdomen for the rest of his life as a result.

In his civilian life, he opened a shop, where he sold a little bit of everything, though looking glasses were particularly common in his advertisements. This shop was so well known that its advertisements didn't even provide an address, and it's said that Breese was so honest that people would claim to be "as honest as Sidney Breese."

Breese ordered wine from England and had his own bottles made, each stamped with his name. Some of them are still extant. One night, he threw a dinner party for all of his creditors, and each found a check for the full amount they were owed under their plates. British officers loved his parties, though this made him unpopular when British rule fell out of favor; it's even said that he refused to let his son sing because his own singing had made him popular with the wrong crowd.[184] This son, Samuel, became a colonel in the Continental army. S.F. Breese Morse, inventor of the telegraph, was a great-grandson.

Sidney died of complications from gout in 1767. His wife, Elizabeth Pinkethman Breese, became an importer and merchant herself after his death; it's possible that she was buried near him when she died in 1779, perhaps in the empty space beside his stone. The "made by himself" is sometimes taken to mean that he not only wrote his own epitaph but also carved his own tombstone.

The next extant stone is for DR. RICHARD AYSCOUGH (1723–1760, A3), who was involved in the first known public demonstrations of surgery on cadavers in 1752.[185] Records also show that after the Battle of Lake George during the French and Indian War in 1755, he was paid for treating "John the Indian," who presumably would have been one of the Mohawk allies of the troops.[186]

His grave may be part of a Breese family plot; a family history says that Elizabeth Pinkethman Breese's stepfather was a doctor named Richard Ascough (probably this Richard) and further states that he was a direct descendant of Anne Askew, a poet who was tortured as a Protestant heretic in an attempt to get her to implicate Catherine Parr, the last wife of Henry VIII, as one who shared her then-radical views that laypeople should be allowed to read the Bible. She was burned at the stake in 1546.[187]

The trend of personally written epitaphs may continue with the marker nearby for MARY DALZELL (1736–1764, B2), a well-carved stone that reads:

> *Adiew* [sic] *my dearest babes and tender husband dear*
> *the time of my departure is now drawing near*
> *and when I'm laid low in the silent grave*
> *where the Monarch is equal with the slave*
> *weep not my friends I hope there be at rest*
> *to be with Jesus Christ it is the best*

Dalzell (*left*) and Stephen Theobalde (*right*).

Since the epitaph is written in the first person, appears to be original, and refers to death as something oncoming, not something that has already happened, it's possible that Mary did write this herself. But speaking in the voice of the dead in epitaphs was common (page 103), and it doesn't say it was "made by herself." The extremely progressive (for 1764) sentiment that equality is preferable to social hierarchies may or may not be Mary's own.

We do know that Mary was the wife of James Dalzell, who, the year before her death, opened a grocery warehouse at Burling Slip. There, he promised "as a young beginner [I] will make it [my] study to merit the Favour of the Public, by keeping every Thing of the best Kind, and selling at the smallest Profit."[188]

To the right are a few small markers, including a particularly eerie, faded cherub face on an otherwise illegible marker. Trinity records say it's the headstone of STEPHEN THEOBALDE, OR THEOBALDS (DIED 1780, A7). Stephen's faded stone is all that is known of him, but the 1897 transcription notes a now-missing or illegible stone for JOHN AND CAROLONE THEOBALDE in section N1; they may be his parents. John was a sea captain.

In the middle of the section is a marker for ANN SMITH (CIRCA 1735–1753, F13). The difficult-to-read epitaph rhymes, but the line breaks are uneven:

> *Such Early worth*
> *I must I will deplore the meek the*
> *Lovey Anna is no more peacibly* [sic]
> *Herein Innocence doth rest*
> *Her mortal Body but her soul*
> *How blest with God Above in*
> *Endless Tryumph She securely*
> *Sits from every Evil free*

This epitaph appears to be original; it is also written in the first person but in the voice of a mourner, not Ann herself.

The large, illegible, arched white monument behind Ann's marker is for ROBERT BRIDPORT (CIRCA 1784–1810, J11). It once contained the motto "fideli certa merces," or "reward to the faithful is certain." Robert was likely the brother of George Bridport, an artist and architect.[189]

Along the eastern portion of the section, among the most striking sights is the bold skull on the grave of NICHOLAS ELLSWORTH (1729–1731, B8). Several rows back is a well-cut inscription on the headstone of JOHN TIERS (1778–1793, G18):

*In early life the message came,*
*That rob'd me of my breath:*
*And all mankind must soon or late,*
*Yield to the dart of death*
*Let not your sighs be spent for me*
*But for yourselves take care;*
*To meet your judge at the last day*
*Be sure that you prepare.*

The poem, written in John's posthumous voice, appears to be unique, though the sentiments expressed are all common for epitaphs of the era.

## LOST MARKERS IN N2

There was a grave here for CAPTAIN RICHARD JEFFREY (DIED 1766), a privateer who commanded the *Greyhound* (page 24) and was the namesake of Jeffrey's Hook, located near the George Washington Bridge. Its epitaph, still legible in 1897, was so long that it almost *must* have been one of the unidentified box graves (H1, M4):

*Caption Richard Jeffrey Who in His Life Practiced Every Virtue And Was An Enemy To All Vice. He Was A Friend to the Poor And to the Afflicted A comforter A Tender Husband A Fond Father A Compassionate Master Compleated* [sic] *The Shineing* [sic] *Character of A Good Christian he Dyed as he Had lived in the humble assurance of God's Favour through Jesus Christ and in perfect charity with all men.*[190]

The epitaph was mocked in the *Evening Post* in 1875 as "the record of one who must have been the most perfect man of his day....In this eloquent array of perfections the trifling matter of dots is omitted."[191] The reference to him being a "master" might have referred to his being a ship captain but more likely referred to his slave ownership. The 1897 transcription also notes a now-lost marker for Richard's sons, one of whom died in 1740.

An 1855 *New York Times* article described a marker near Sidney Breese that featured "a cluster of grapes, an hour-glass, a skeleton lying on a tomb, the cross-bones, and Death himself, with an arrow in hand," with the epitaph, "Death cuts down all, both great and small."[192] Nothing like that is present today.

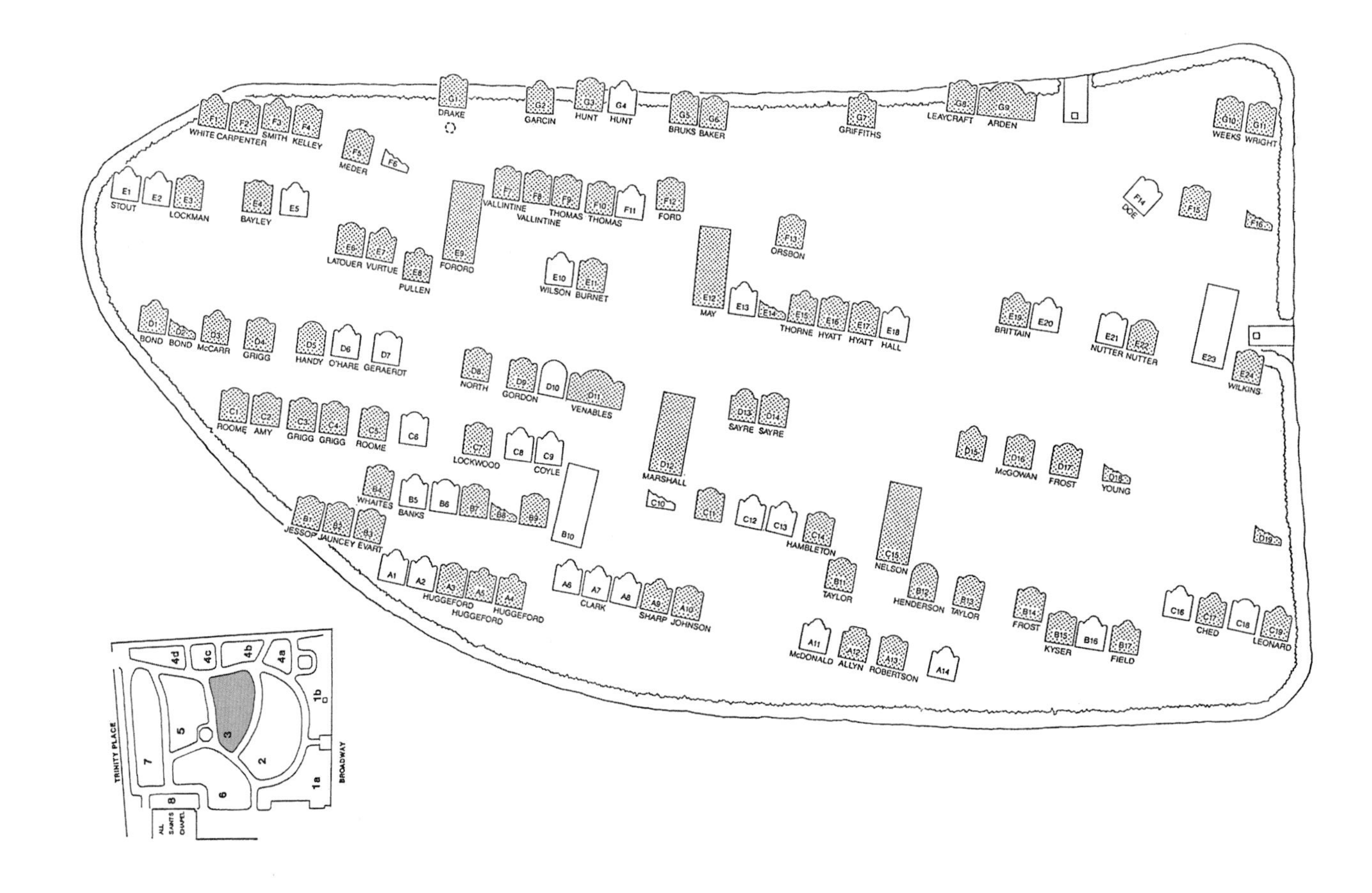

WHITE
CARPENTER
SMITH
KELLEY
DRAKE
GARCIN
HUNT
HUNT
BRUKS
BAKER
GRIFFITHS
LEAYCRAFT
ARDEN
WEEKS
WRIGHT
MEDER
STOUT
LOCKMAN
BAYLEY
VALLINTINE
VALLINTINE
THOMAS
THOMAS
FORD
DOE
LATOUER
VURTUE
PULLEN
FORORD
WILSON
BURNET
ORSBON
MAY
THORNE
HYATT
HYATT
HALL
BRITTAIN
NUTTER
NUTTER
WILKINS
BOND
BOND
McCARR
GRIGG
HANDY
O'HARE
GERAERDT
NORTH
GORDON
VENABLES
ROOME
AMY
GRIGG
GRIGG
ROOME
LOCKWOOD
COYLE
SAYRE
SAYRE
McGOWAN
FROST
YOUNG
MARSHALL
WHAITES
BANKS
JESSOP
JAUNCEY
EVART
HAMBLETON
NELSON
HUGGEFORD
HUGGEFORD
HUGGEFORD
CLARK
SHARP
JOHNSON
TAYLOR
HENDERSON
TAYLOR
FROST
KYSER
FIELD
CHED
LEONARD
McDONALD
ALLYN
ROBERTSON
TRINITY PLACE
ALL SAINTS CHAPEL
BROADWAY

# SECTION N3

The extant epitaphs in section N3 tend to be common epitaphs of the era, though a few are original and fascinating.

Beginning in the left (southern) "tip," one legible marker is for ANN BOND (1772–1796, D1):

*Vain world farewell to you*
*Heaven is my native air:*
*I bid my friends A short Adieu*
*Impatient to be there:*

This is from an Isaac Watts hymn, "The Heavens Invite Mine Eyes," which was particularly popular for epitaphs.

Two stones to the right is that of MARY ANN MCCARR (CIRCA 1794–1816, D3), whose last name is not visible on the stone, with an epitaph seen at more than one grave in the area:

*My parents dear, who mourn and weep*
*Behold the grave wherein I sleep:*
*Prepare for death, for you must die*
*And be entomb'd as well as I.*

Few will truly be entombed as well as Mary Ann, given that in-ground burials in Manhattan are extremely rare today.

Behind her and to the right is a stone for Anthony Latouer (1785–1793, E6) with a common epitaph:

*Reader reflect as you pass by,*
*As you are now so once was I*
*As I am now you soon will be*
*Prepare for death and follow me.*

There is an old joke about this sort of verse. As early as the 1850s, people were responding to the last lines with, "To follow you I'll not consent / until I know which way you went."[193]

At F3 is a marker for John Smith (1765–1766), notable for how many typos it contains:

*How loved, How valued*
*Once availd The Note*
*By whom Related, All By Whom Begot*
*A Heap of Dust Alone Remains of Thee*
*Tis All Thow Art And*
*All the Proud Shall Be*

These lines are a not-exactly-correct quote from Alexander Pope's 1717 "Elegy to the Memory of an Unfortunate Lady," ("how loved, how honour'd once, avails thee not, to whom related, or by whom forgot") which would become very popular as an epitaph, appearing on several graves at St. Paul's (page 239). This is a very early example of its use. Though later versions improve on the many typos here, many continued to use "how valued" on tombstones, though the actual line in the poem is "how honour'd," suggesting that that people were learning the quote from gravestones, not from the original source. Pope's poem appears on many graves at St. Paul's.

Behind an unidentified box tomb at D11 is a double-arched marker for hairdresser Charles Venables (circa 1764–1797), who arrived from London in the early 1790s and took out advertisements promising the ladies of New York "at least those who will favour him their commands, that he will dress them in the most modern style...on such terms as will give general satisfaction." Orders could be left for him at St. Paul's.[194] His stone has an inscription so neatly cut and well-spaced that it seems almost out of place. A now-hidden line says that it was erected by his wife, Martha, though the epitaph is written in Charles's voice:

*Fare well my Dear and Loving Wife*
*My children and my Friends*
*I hope in HEAVEN to see you all*
*When all things have their ends*

*And tho I die all in my prime*
*And in my Youthful Days*
*I hope the LORD will raise me up*
*To live with him all ways.*

The first four lines are taken from a poem attributed to Protestant martyr Robert Smith, who wrote several letters and poems before he was burned at the stake in 1555. They were published in John Foxe's hugely popular *Book of Matryrs* in 1563. The second four lines appear on a few tombstones in Britain.

## Captain Henry Ford

*Talbot, Brand, and Shehan arrived from the Indian council at the Miamis. They report to the governor that as soon as the Indians received the final message of the commissioners, they dispatched a large party, commissioned to seize us, with orders to cut off our noses, ears, &c., and to keep us prisoners until a peace could be obtained. These men arrived at Caldwell's the next morning after we sailed: I, therefore, congratulate your nose and ears as well as my own.*[195]

—*Captain Ford, 1793*

Behind Charles Venables's stone is a marker for Captain Henry Ford (died 1793, F12), described as "late commander of His Brittanic Majesty's Ship *Dunmore* on Lake Erie." Passing references to Ford suggest a life of narrow escapes and dangerous battles, though little is really known of him. One man who encountered him recalled, "[I] had a solid conversation with… Capt Ford…on slavery, war, swearing, and debauchery," but didn't really give a hint of Ford's position on these issues.[196]

Most references to him relate to a period when the *Dunmore* was used by commissioners negotiating the Treaty of Canandaigua, which established peace and friendship between the United States and the Six Nations of the Iroquois Confederacy. A 1793 letter from Secretary of State Pickering to President Washington said, "It may be proper for me to say that I think Captain Ford a man of honour. He is a very sensible man.…Captain Ford has come to the States for the recovery of his Health."[197] Ford died a few weeks after the letter was written.

The treaty was eventually signed a year later, offering the Six Nations $4,500 a year in goods and land rights. The government still pays the $4,500 in the form of bolts of cloth (at the Cayuga Nation's request), but the land rights agreements were soon ignored.[198]

To the right is a flat stone for Barbados-born tailor Edward Marshall (circa 1667–1704, D12). The last digits of the year of his death were illegible by 1897, but Walt Whitman had written about the stone in his 1852 novel *Jack Engle* and marveled that the man had died in 1704. Marshall's will was proved before Lord Cornbury (page 171).

Nearby is a stone for Catherine Thorne (circa 1740–1752, E15) that is almost entirely underground today. An 1871 transcription shows that it was already half-buried at the time, and by the time of the 1897 transcription, only a few lines below the soul effigy were visible, which is still the case. But a photograph in Trinity's archives shows the entire gravestone, unearthed during a restoration:

> *Here lyeth the Body of*
> *Catherine Thorne Daughter of Richard*
> *Thorne deceased who Departed*
> *This Life the 29th of June 1752*
> *Anno AEtatis 12 . Three days Fever*
> *Snatch'd her Breath and Bow'd her to*
> *triumphant Death. Tho' scarce twelve*

*Years had crowned her head. Behold in dust*
*Her peaceful Bed where every one must*
*Shortly lye For all that live live but to die*
*Her Soul we hope, will rest with God*
*And dwell within his blest Abode*
*Where human pains forever cease*
*Where flow* [illegible] *peace*
*Where every Seraph Gladly sings*
*To God, Eternal King of Kings*

The long poem appears to be original.

## Adam Allyn, Comedian

[From theatrical advertisements] *we gain a peep at our long-buried ancestors.... We see the beaux of 1761, with their powdered wigs, long stiff-skirted coats and waistcoats, with flaps reaching nearly to the knees of their inexpressibles...crowding and ogling the actresses on the stage. And we see the actor or actress going from house to house, presenting benefit bills, and soliciting patronage.*[199]

—*William Dunlap*

In the 1760s, three-dimensional faces were still relatively unusual on gravestones, so the solemn, closed-eyed face for Adam Allyn (died 1768, A12) is striking, particularly on a grave for a man whose epitaph gives his profession as "comedian." His coworkers gave him a rather suggestive epitaph:

*Sacred To the Memory Of Adam Allyn Comedian*
*Who Departed This Life February 15, 1768*
*This Stone Was Erected By the American Company*
*As a Testimony Of their Unfeigned Regard*
*He Posesed* [sic] *Many good Qualitys* [sic]
*But as he was a man He Had the Frailties*
*Common to mans Nature*

Adam Allyn, comedian, who had "the frailties common to man's nature."

Exactly what "frailties" they were alluding to are left to the imagination, though the fact that his friends seemed compelled to carve them into stone implies that they were significant and probably not just a reference to his mortality. Records may give some hints: an Adam Allyn was listed as being bankrupt in England in 1752. In 1759, a Philadelphia theater announced Allyn would appear in George Farquhar's bawdy farce *The Stage Coach* "in which will be introduced The History of Mr. Allyn and the Three Lawyers." This suggests that there had been some incident involving Allyn and the law that all of Philadelphia knew about, though the text of the play offers no real clues as to what it might be.

The American Company of Comedians formed in 1752 (page 203) and was active for over forty years. Some consider them the fathers of the American stage, as there had never been a professional dramatic company in the colonies before.[200]

Beginning in 1759, Allyn appears in most of their newspaper announcements. He appeared in many serious plays (he was the Friar in *Romeo and Juliet* and the grave digger in *Hamlet*), but was known for broad comedy roles, such as Fribble in David Garrick's *A Miss in Her Teens*.[201] He was the first in the country to appear in Garrick's *Lethe* as Lord Chalkstone, a proudly drunken old oaf who rants on every subject and "would not abstain from French wines and French cookery to save the souls and bodies of the whole college of physicians."

Some advertisements indicate that tickets for the shows could be purchased at Allyn's lodgings "at Mr. Hubbard's on Nassau Street." Beyond this minor bit, cast lists in newspapers form nearly all we know of Allyn; no one is known to have commented on his performances or personality.

Papers on February 15, 1768, announced that Allyn would appear in two shows that night, including in a small role in *The Recruiting Officer*. But that would be the day of his death, which we can only assume was unexpected.

Around the bend is a marker for JEFFRY LEONARD (CIRCA 1740–1807) and his wife, MARY STEDDEFORT LEONARD (1743–1816, C19), with a prose epitaph:

> *Honor thy Father with thy whole heart*
> *and forget not the sorrows of thy Mother*

*Remember that thou was begotten*
*and how canst thou recompenst them*
*the things they have done for thee*

The verse comes from an essay, "Dutifulness to Parents Is the Foundation of Religion," by British philanthropist Jonas Hanway, though he was paraphrasing from The Book of Sirach, a Jewish text that was part of the Anglican Apocrypha. Hanway was known for his opposition to tea drinking and is often credited with being the first man in London to carry an umbrella, which, in the 1750s, were "a luxury hitherto only confined to the ladies."[202]

Along the northern edge of the section, next to a box grave (E23) whose subject's identity is lost to time, stands a marker to VALENTIN WILKINS (1792–1793) and ISAAC WILKINS (CIRCA 1789–1794, E24), featuring a particularly interesting epitaph:

*We were born to die*
*Tis but expanding thought*
*And life is nothing*

Though hardly a mirthful sentiment, this line is from English playwright Richard Steele's 1703 comedy *The Lying Lover*. In the play, Young Bookwit, a champion liar, brags of his sexual conquests so much that a friend becomes jealous and challenges him to a duel. Bookwit wounds him, apparently fatally, and is hauled off to jail. Unaware that his friend is only faking being dead to teach him a lesson, Bookwit says the line from the epitaph while expecting to be hanged during a long, pious "reformation" scene that is generally blamed for the play becoming Steele's biggest flop.

The play is not known to have been performed in New York, but the lines appeared in several dictionaries of quotations. Out of context, it reflects a common idea from the time: that life was nothing, and only the afterlife was important. This attitude was often used to keep people from complaining about lives of drudgery and servitude that were, in the words of philosopher Thomas Hobbes, "nasty, brutish and short."

# Lost Markers in N3

Many old articles spoke of the gravestone of Captain Isaac Berryman (circa 1773–1808), which read:

> *Boreas' blasts and Neptune's waves*
> *Have tossed him to and fro*
> *But by the sacred will of God*
> *He's anchored here below*

This verse, mixing Greek and Roman mythology with Christian themes, was common on sailors' graves (see page 203).

The slate marker (D15) beside the Uzal Ward–carved ledger grave for Captain John Nelson (circa 1712–1762, C15) is completely illegible but is a good candidate for Berryman's lost marker. Multiple nineteenth-century sources state that it was close to Nelson's marker, and *Valentine's Manual* even points to this spot on a map.[203]

The epitaph gave an accurate idea of Berryman's stormy career. On one voyage from the Bay of Hondorus to New York, his ship the *Horatio* sprung a leak amid storm winds that "carried away the foreyard and sprung the foremast." He was somehow able to get the ship to Norfolk.[204] The next year, he was attacked and robbed by three men near the now-lost Collect Pond.[205]

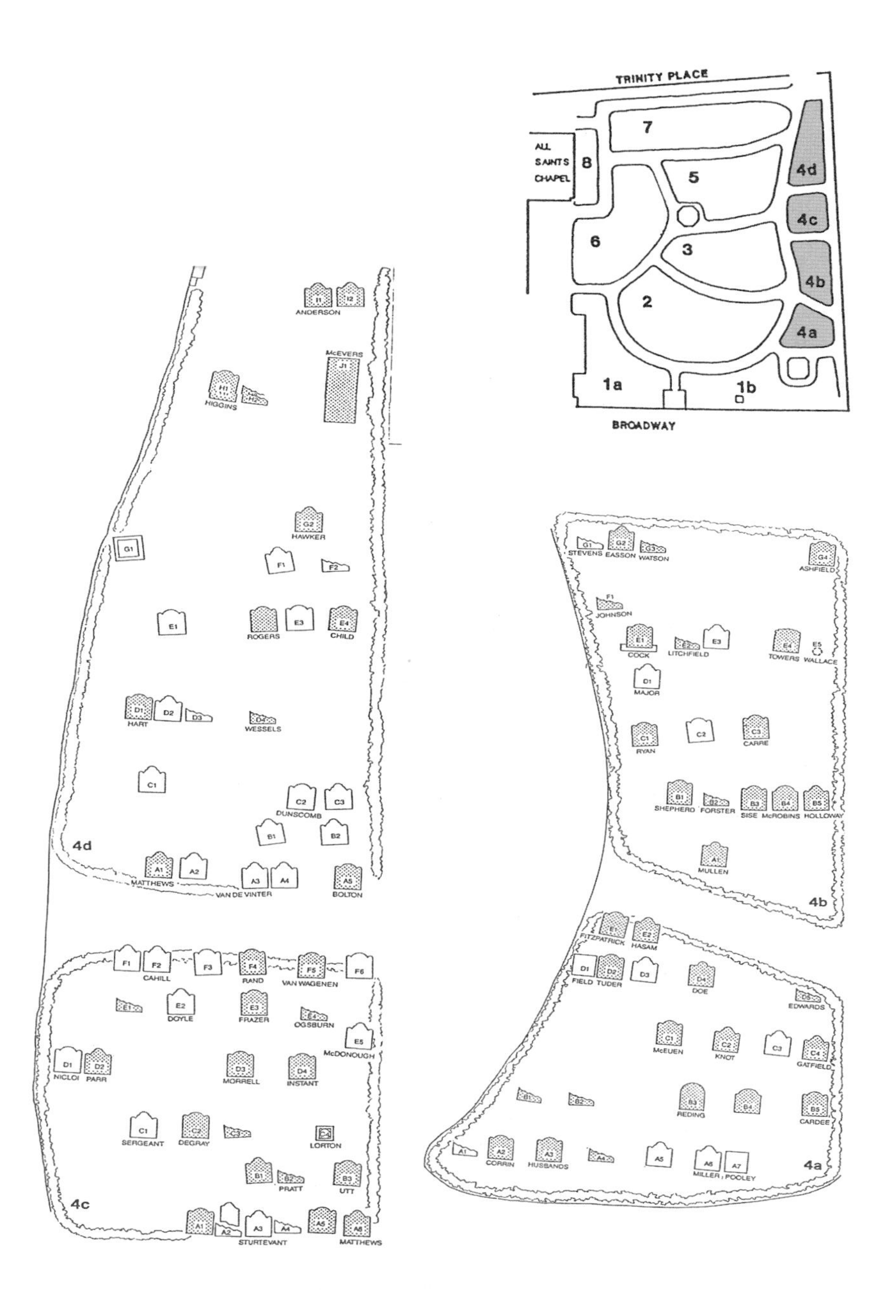

TRINITY PLACE
ALL SAINTS CHAPEL
8
7
5
6
3
2
1a
1b
4d
4c
4b
4a
BROADWAY
ANDERSON
McEVERS
HIGGINS
HAWKER
ROGERS
CHILD
HART
WESSELS
DUNSCOMB
4d
MATTHEWS
VAN DE VINTER
BOLTON
CAHILL
RAND
VAN WAGENEN
DOYLE
FRAZER
OGSBURN
McDONOUGH
NICLOI
PARR
MORRELL
INSTANT
SERGEANT
DEGRAY
LORTON
PRATT
UTT
4c
STURTEVANT
MATTHEWS
STEVENS
EASSON
WATSON
ASHFIELD
JOHNSON
COCK
LITCHFIELD
TOWERS
WALLACE
MAJOR
RYAN
CARRE
SHEPHERD
FORSTER
SISE
McROBINS
HOLLOWAY
MULLEN
4b
FITZPATRICK
HASAM
FIELD
TUDER
DOE
EDWARDS
McEUEN
KNOT
GATFIELD
REDING
CARDEE
CORRIN
HUSBANDS
MILLER
POOLEY
4a

# SECTION N4

Walking along the southern path that runs alongside the subsections of N4, one can see a few striking markers—note the calligraphy in the carving for CAPTAIN THOMAS TUDER (1737–1770, D2). Tuder was only twenty when he became captain of the brig *Mary*.[206] On a voyage from Bermuda with his crew (and his wife) in 1762, the brig began to leak. At 5:30 a.m., it was determined that the leak could not be stopped, and the entire party took to a lifeboat, where they watched the ship "take a Heel and go down." With very few provisions, they were adrift in the lifeboat for twenty-six hours before they were rescued by the schooner *Paragon*.[207]

In the middle of 4B is a mostly buried stone with a floral border and soul effigy for LEWIS CARRE (CIRCA 1659–1744 4B-C3), one of the earliest-born people in the cemetery; he would have been older than Richard Churcher (page 117). Lewis (or Louis) was a Huguenot (page 141) who came to New York in 1688 with his wife, Pregeante (who later went by Bridget). He became a prominent merchant with a home in the Stadt Huys block, near what is now Pearl and Broad Streets. A major archaeological investigation of the block in the 1980s indicated that people in Carre's home enjoyed expensive cuts of meat more than anyone else on the block.[208] There's a good chance that Bridget was buried near him when she died in 1750.[209]

Assuming it was carved around the year of Carre's death, the ornate soul effigy was far ahead of its time. Most of the stone is now buried. Preservationist Miriam Silverman believed it was likely carved by Ebenezer Price, a pioneer in the field of soul effigies.

*Above*: The mostly buried Carre marker.

*Left*: The unique Rogers soul effigy.

Just in front of Carre's marker is that of MARY SISE (CIRCA 1682–1762, 4B-B3), with a death's head by Uzal Ward.

In 4C, the top portion of the marker for JAMES RYAN (CIRCA 1748–1796, C1) is legible; beneath it was once the inscription:

*The hour of death draws nigh*
*'tis time to drop the Mask*
*fall at the feet of Christ and cry*
*He gives to all that ask.*

This comes from a hymn by Joseph Hart, a Calvinist minister.

Section 4D contains a marker for ISAIAH ROGERS (1756–1795, E2), featuring a cherub whose face, turned to an unusual three-quarter portrait, seems to be formed from the same calligraphic swirls as its wings. It resembles no other cherub, death's head or soul effigy in the cemetery. Rogers himself lived a quiet life, appearing in very few records. (He is not the same Isaiah Rogers who designed the Astor Hotel.)

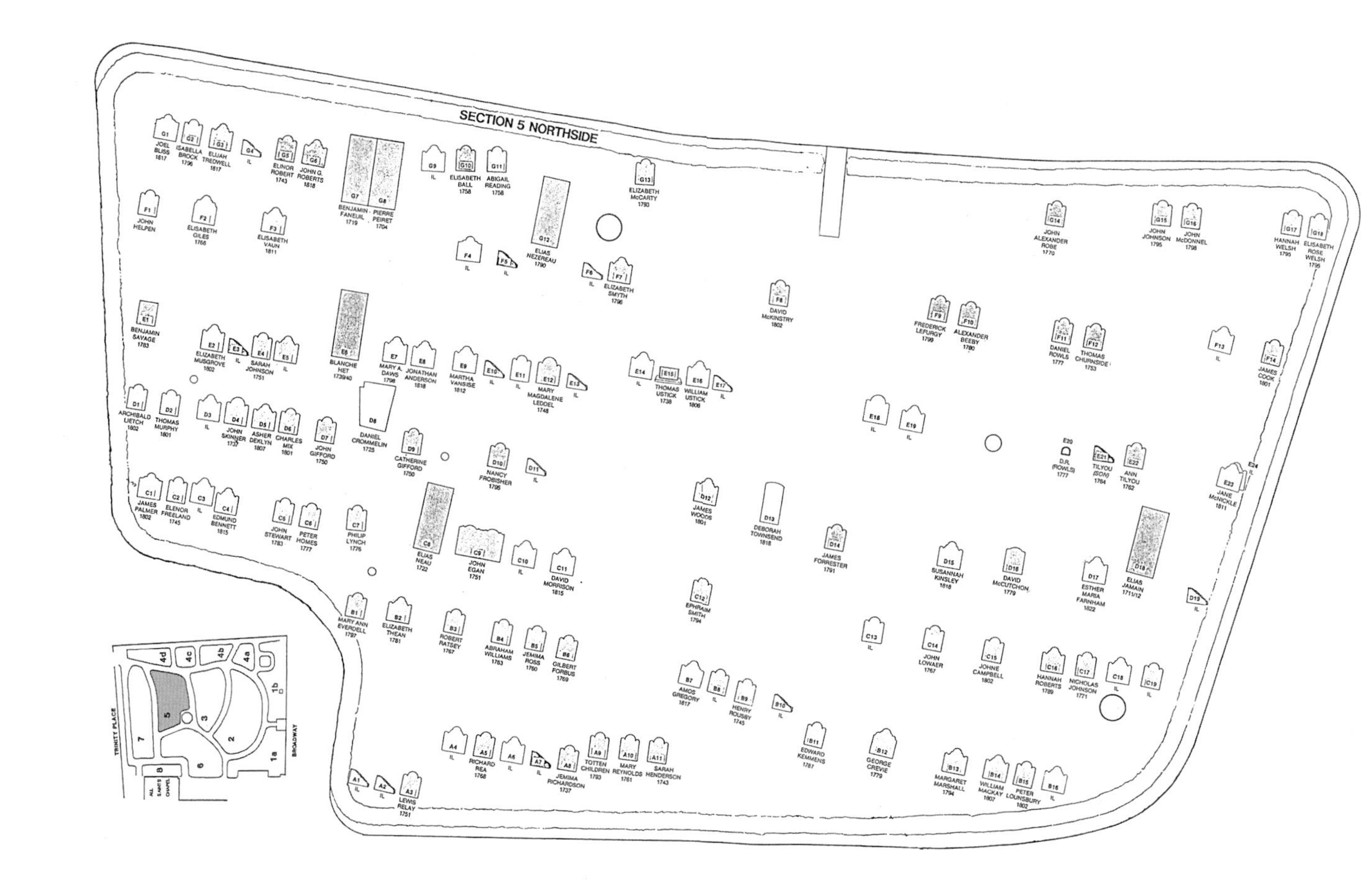

SECTION 5 NORTHSIDE
G1 JOEL BLISS 1817
G2 ISABELLA BROCK 1796
G3 ELIJAH TREDWELL 1817
G4 IL
G5 ELINOR ROBERT 1743
G6 JOHN G. ROBERTS 1818
G7 BENJAMIN FANEUIL 1719
G8 PIERRE PEIRET 1704
G9 IL
G10 ELISABETH BALL 1758
G11 ABIGAIL READING 1758
G12 ELIAS NEZEREAU 1790
G13 ELIZABETH McCARTY 1793
G14 JOHN ALEXANDER ROBE 1770
G15 JOHN JOHNSON 1795
G16 JOHN McDONNEL 1798
G17 HANNAH WELSH 1795
G18 ELISABETH ROSE WELSH 1795
F1 JOHN HELPEN
F2 ELISABETH GILES 1766
F3 ELISABETH VAUN 1811
F4 IL
F5 IL
F6 IL
F7 ELIZABETH SMYTH 1796
F8 DAVID McKINSTRY 1802
F9 FREDERICK LEFURGY 1799
F10 ALEXANDER BEEBY 1780
F11 DANIEL ROWLS 1777
F12 THOMAS CHURNSIDE 1753
F13 IL
F14 JAMES COOK 1801
E1 BENJAMIN SAVAGE 1783
E2 ELIZABETH MUSGROVE 1802
E3 IL
E4 SARAH JOHNSON 1751
E5 IL
E6 BLANCHE HET 1739/40
E7 MARY A. DAWS 1798
E8 JONATHAN ANDERSON 1818
E9 MARTHA VANSISE 1812
E10 IL
E11 IL
E12 MARY MAGDALENE LEDDEL 1748
E13 IL
E14 IL
E15 THOMAS USTICK 1738
E16 WILLIAM USTICK 1806
E17 IL
E18 IL
E19 IL
E20 D.R. (ROWLS) 1777
E21 TILYOU (SON) 1764
E22 ANN TILYOU 1762
E23 JANE McNICKLE 1811
E24 IL
D1 ARCHIBALD LIETCH 1802
D2 THOMAS MURPHY 1801
D3 IL
D4 JOHN SKINNER 1737
D5 ASHER DEKLYN 1807
D6 CHARLES MIX 1801
D7 JOHN GIFFORD 1750
D8 DANIEL CROMMELIN 1725
D9 CATHERINE GIFFORD 1750
D10 NANCY FROBISHER 1795
D11 IL
D12 JAMES WOODS 1801
D13 DEBORAH TOWNSEND 1818
D14 JAMES FORRESTER 1791
D15 SUSANNAH KINSLEY 1818
D16 DAVID McCUTCHON 1779
D17 ESTHER MARIA FARNHAM 1822
D18 ELIAS JAMAIN 1711/12
D19 IL
C1 JAMES PALMER 1802
C2 ELENOR FREELAND 1745
C3 IL
C4 EDMUND BENNETT 1815
C5 JOHN STEWART 1783
C6 PETER HOMES 1777
C7 PHILIP LYNCH 1776
C8 ELIAS NEAU 1722
C9 JOHN EGAN 1751
C10 IL
C11 DAVID MORRISON 1815
C12 EPHRAIM SMITH 1794
C13 IL
C14 JOHN LOWAER 1767
C15 JOHNE CAMPBELL 1802
C16 HANNAH ROBERTS 1789
C17 NICHOLAS JOHNSON 1771
C18 IL
C19 IL
B1 MARY ANN EVERDELL 1797
B2 ELIZABETH THEAN 1781
B3 ROBERT RATSEY 1767
B4 ABRAHAM WILLIAMS 1763
B5 JEMIMA ROSS 1760
B6 GILBERT FORBUS 1769
B7 AMOS GREGORY 1817
B8 IL
B9 HENRY ROUSBY 1745
B10 IL
B11 EDWARD KEMMENS 1787
B12 GEORGE CREVIE 1779
B13 MARGARET MARSHALL 1794
B14 WILLIAM MACKAY 1807
B15 PETER LOUNSBURY 1802
B16 IL
A1 IL
A2 IL
A3 LEWIS RELAY 1751
A4 IL
A5 RICHARD REA 1768
A6 IL
A7 IL
A8 JEMIMA RICHARDSON 1737
A9 TOTTEN CHILDREN 1793
A10 MARY REYNOLDS 1761
A11 SARAH HENDERSON 1743
TRINITY PLACE
BROADWAY
ALL SAINTS CHAPEL
1a
1b
2
3
4a
4b
4c
4d
5
6
7
8

# SECTION N5

In 1589, the Edict of Nantes granted Huguenots (Protestants) freedom to live in Catholic France. In 1685, King Louis XIV revoked the edict and required Huguenots to convert to Catholicism. Thousands of refugee Huguenots settled in New York; 5N contains a number of individuals from the first and second generations of French refugees.

Standing near the Astor Cross (page 145) and looking into the section, one can still read the gray slab for perhaps the best-known Huguenot of his era: a sailor, songwriter, enslaved person, prisoner, rebel, and celebrity who founded New York's first school for enslaved people.

## Elias Neau

*I am not loved because I fight corruption, they mockingly call me "The New Reformer." I can tell them that the money and the mud of the streets are the same in my heart.*

—*Elias Neau*[210]

ELIAS NEAU (1662–1722, C8) fled from religious persecution in France when he was just a teenager.[211] He worked as a sailor until 1692, when a ship he was commanding in the Caribbean was captured by privateers working for King Louis XIV. Brought to France, he refused to convert to Catholicism and was sentenced to life as a galley slave. He was put onto a ship after a thirty-seven-day march, during which he was chained to other men and suffered from dysentery.

After years of rowing as an enslaved man, he was imprisoned in the Chateau d'If, the prison island that would later appear in Dumas's *Count of Monte Cristo*. He shared his dungeon, "where darkness reigned at high noon," with chained men whose bodies were reduced to skin and bones, their long beards infested with vermin.

He was occasionally allowed to write letters, and stories of his suffering and piety made him famous. "Would you not confess," he wrote, "that one could call this life a living death? But…the sun of grace darts its beams into our hearts. If I should tell you that this sort of life is more sweet and agreeable than all the most eminent temporal prosperities, what would you say?"

In 1697, King William III persuaded the French to free Neau on the grounds that he was a British subject. Neau returned to his family in New York, where the joined the Church of England in 1704.

Once he was established in the young city, Neau opened a school to teach religion to enslaved people. Some neighbors told him that the enslaved didn't have souls to save. "Upon telling their Masters they wish to be baptised [*sic*]," he wrote, "[many of my students] are either threatened to be sold to Virginia or else be sent into the country if they come any more to school. Good God! What sort of religion have these people?…For my part, I can't help saying that they have none at all."[212]

Initially teaching only catechism and creed, Neau found success in adding the singing of psalms to his classes and noted, "I observe with pleasure that they strive [to] sing the best.…This draws an abundance of people to see and hear them."[213] Records show that among those he taught were people enslaved by Lord Cornbury (page 171) and Trinity Church rector William Vesey.[214] (Neau often complained in letters that Vesey disliked him.)[215]

Even having been an enslaved man himself, Neau was not opposed to slavery in and of itself and, in fact, wrote that "the Christian religions inspires in their slaves love and obedience to their masters and mistresses."[216] Given the culture of the day, the success of his school depended on him saying things like that. After an attempted uprising of enslaved people in 1712, Neau found himself a pariah. "Mr. Neau durst hardly appear abroad for some days," one early historian wrote. "[For] his school was blamed as the main occasion of this barbarous plot."[217] He eventually persuaded people that his teaching had actually kept his students from participating in the revolt.

The goals of Neau's school were strictly spiritual, not focused on betterment in this lifetime. But at least one modern historian has posited that his efforts likely "resulted in increased self-confidence, as well as in a growing desire to be truly free. The prayers, the teaching, the encouragement to sneak out at night to attend the school, and the ability to read and write that Neau afforded them could have created a 'subversive force' that Neau did not realize he was encouraging."[218]

SUSANNA NEAU (1660–1720), his wife, likely helped him in his imprisonment by getting his letters to people such as preacher Cotton Mather, who used Neau's sufferings to bring attention to his plight (and to inspire fear of Catholics). Their inscription was restored by descendants in 1846.[219]

Behind Neau's marker and to the right is a particularly fine headstone with a floral border and drooping, elongated wings on its soul effigy. It is for another Huguenot, MARY MAGDALENE LEDDEL (CIRCA 1682–1748, E12). Within the border is a prose epitaph: "Beloved wife of Joseph Leddel who's [*sic*] duty was Her delight she exchanged A Life of labour and sorrow (as we hope) for Eternall Joy and Rest."

Below the floral border is an additional bit of verse:

*The Sweet Remembrance of the Just*
*Shall flourish when he sleeps in dust*

The closing lines are from a 1696 translation of Psalm 112, which was standard in Anglican churches. Though odd to see the "he" pronoun on a gravestone for a woman, they may not have wished to alter the wording of scripture, even if it was a rather recent—and not at all literal—translation (though the Isaiah Rogers stone changes it to "they," page 139). It could also be taken as a clue that Joseph Leddel may have been buried nearby upon his death in 1753.

Little is known of Mary, except that a friend of her husband left her a choice of "one of my finest tea kettles" in his will.[220] Joseph Leddel and his son, Joseph Jr., were both noted engravers, and one of them may have

*Left*: A Leddel tankard showing scenes from the life of the biblical Joseph and a soul effigy bearing similarities to the one on Mary's gravestone. *Yale University*.

*Below*: Ledell soul effigy.

carved this stone. Some of their extant pieces include pewter engravings of a style one writer called "virtually unknown on colonial American silver" and feature soul effigies resembling the one here.[221] Their work is also full of gruesome anti-Jacobite imagery, such as a silver beaker engraved with execution scenes, hellfire, and couplets attacking the "pretender, devil and pope," reflecting Joseph's background as the son of Huguenot refugees. (page 141).

## OTHER HUGUENOTS IN N5

A little behind Mary's marker is a gray ledger stone for Huguenot ELIAS NEZEREAU (CIRCA 1622–1709, G12), who fled from France on the same ship as the REVEREND PIERRE PEIRET (CIRCA 1644–1704, G8), whose own ledger is located nearby. Peiret began preaching in France in 1677 (though he was suspended for a year when his daughter was born only six months after his marriage to Marguerite Latour).[222] His church was closed after the Edict of Nantes was revoked.

Adjacent to Peiret's marker on the left is a matching slab for Huguenot merchant BENJAMIN FANEUIL (1668–1719, G7). Benjamin's brother Anthony was a merchant in Boston and left his fortune to one of Benjamin's sons on the strange condition that the young man never take a wife. When he *did* marry, the huge inheritance went to one of Benjamin's other sons, Peter, who founded the famous Faneuil Hall in Boston.[223]

### THE ASTOR CROSS

Nestled between Sections 4 and 5 is the massive Astor Cross, a Thomas Nash–designed monument for Caroline Astor, usually known simply as "Mrs. Astor," the queen of New York's high society. The upper elite of New York in the Gilded Age are sometimes said to have been called "The 400" because that was how many people fit in Mrs. Astor's ballroom. This is probably just a legend, but there's some truth in it: to be invited to Mrs. Astor's ball was a coveted status symbol. She was buried in the Uptown Trinity Cemetery when she passed away in 1908; the cross was added here in her memory here six years later.

Benjamin himself occupies a footnote in history: he is the first known person to have freed an enslaved person in New York. In 1708, he freed a man named Nero. The only other recorded manumission over the next decade in the city came in 1712, when a man named Fortune was freed by ELIAS JAMAIN (1668–1712), who has a ledger similar to Benjamin's at D18 with a French inscription and an example of "double-dating" with the death date "1711/12" (see page 150).

In the center of the section is a marker for JAMES WOODS (CIRCA 1758–1801, D12) with an epitaph that appears on a few New York–area graves, but stands out among those of the French Huguenots surrounding him:

*Unseen to mankinds view;*
*An exile of old Erin true,*
*His principle was just and good*
*And for his country freedom stood*

Woods is said to have fled to New York after the disastrous Irish Rebellion of 1798.[224] Inspired by the French and American Revolutions, the Society of United Irishmen fought for an end to British rule and freedom for Catholics. Some in New York saw the rebellion as a parallel to the American Revolution; one journalist asked, "If taxation and representation in 1775 were held to be inseparable…why ought they not be…for three millions of Catholics in Ireland who have not had (Great God of Liberty) a single vote?"[225] But Federalists, who dominated the American government at the time, feared that any turmoil abroad could lead to war on American soil and avoided supporting the society.[226]

Despite help from the French, the rebels were decimated, and Irish immigration to the United States surged. (Though being Catholic had been a serious crime quite recently, the assistance of the French in the Revolution, and the changing views of the Age of Enlightenment had helped attitudes evolve remarkably quickly.)

Toward the back corner is a marker with three cannons in the tympanum for DANIEL ROWLS (CIRCA 1723–1777, F11), a carpenter whose epitaph says he "Belong'd to the company of artificers sent to this place by the honorable board of Ordnance under the direction of Major Dixon, Chief Engineer of America."

The Board of Ordnance was a British body that regulated artillery; Major Matthew Dixon was a particularly minor figure whose time in New York is largely forgotten. How Rowls came to die in his service seems to be unknown; perhaps Dixon paid for the stone.

Two stones in the northwest corner mark the graves of HANNAH WELSH (CIRCA 1755–1795, G17) and her adopted daughter, ELIZABETH ROSE WELSH (1786–1795, G18). The poem on Hannah's stone is broken off, but it read:

*While night in solemn triumph reigns*
*Ascend, my soul, the heavenly plains*
*Thy flight to those gay regions take*
*Angels and God are still awake*
*The smiling stars will light thy way*
*To the gladsome realms of day*
*While drowsy men, with idle themes*
*Fantastic joys, and airy dreams*

This is an excerpt from a poem that appears in Elizabeth Singer Rowe's *Friendship in Death*, a book of imaginary letters from the dead to the living. It was one of the most popular books of the eighteenth century.

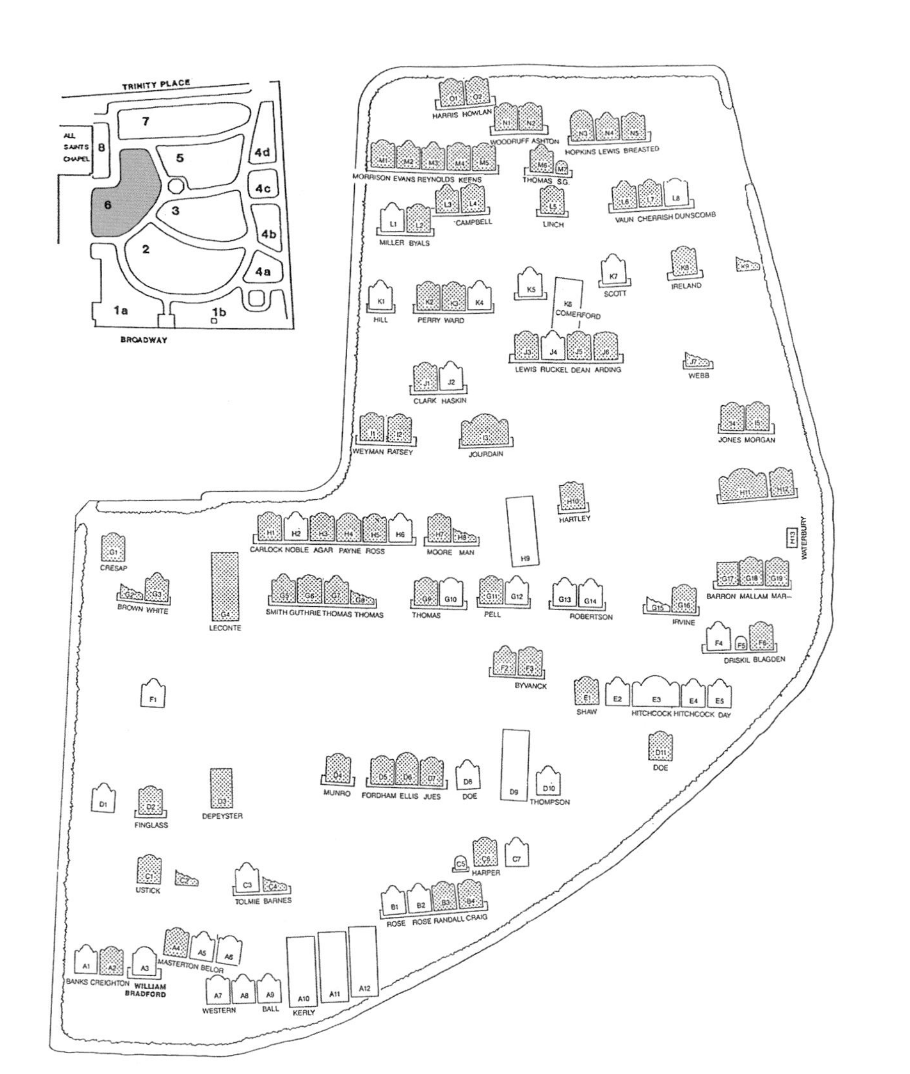

TRINITY PLACE
ALL SAINTS CHAPEL
8
7
5
6
3
2
1a
1b
4a
4b
4c
4d
BROADWAY
HARRIS HOWLAN
WOODRUFF ASHTON
HOPKINS LEWIS BREASTED
MORRISON EVANS REYNOLDS KEENS
THOMAS S.G.
CAMPBELL
LINCH
VAUN CHERRISH DUNSCOMB
MILLER BYALS
HILL
PERRY WARD
COMERFORD
SCOTT
IRELAND
LEWIS RUCKEL DEAN ARDING
WEBB
CLARK HASKIN
WEYMAN RATSEY
JOURDAIN
JONES MORGAN
HARTLEY
CARLOCK NOBLE AGAR PAYNE ROSS
MOORE MAN
WATERBURY
CRESAP
BROWN WHITE
LECONTE
SMITH GUTHRIE THOMAS THOMAS
THOMAS
PELL
ROBERTSON
IRVINE
BARRON MALLAM MAR–
DRISKIL BLAGDEN
BYVANCK
SHAW
HITCHCOCK HITCHCOCK DAY
DOE
MUNRO
FORDHAM ELLIS JUES
DOE
THOMPSON
FINGLASS
DEPEYSTER
USTICK
TOLMIE BARNES
HARPER
ROSE ROSE RANDALL CRAIG
MASTERTON BELOR
BANKS CREIGHTON
WILLIAM BRADFORD
WESTERN
BALL
KERLY

# SECTION N6

Section N6 has a number of stones that were reset in concrete footings in 1965. Most seem not to have been moved much from their original locations.

A walk around N6 begins with the gravestone of GIDEON HARPER (CIRCA 1700–1750, C6), which features a backward N in his name and gives his date of death as "March the 13 1749–50."

Given the backward letter, one might wonder if the person who carved the stone wasn't sure on *which* March 13 Harper died. However, the date is a relic of an era just before England finally switched from the Julian to Gregorian calendar in 1752. Until then, the official beginning of the year in England was March 25 (nine months before Christmas). Anticipating that England would soon catch up with much of Christendom and begin years on January 1, by 1750, some people (including almanacs and newspapers like the *New York Post*) had started simply changing the year in January, and others modified the way dates were written from January 1 to March 25, showing the Julian year (1749 in this case) followed by the Gregorian (1750). (See also: the Gautier bowl, page 75).

The double-dated Gideon Harper headstone.

Nearby is the marker of JOHN RANDALL (CIRCA 1776–1803) and his daughter JANE RANDALL (1800–1803, B3), who died about six weeks after he did (the cause of their deaths is not known, but it was a bad year for yellow fever). John was a hairdresser; his wife, Sarah, carried on the business after his death.[227] Sarah may have been the author of the apparently original poem on the stone:

*Thus to the tomb her dearer half consigned*
*And at his side a tender pledge resign'd*
*How lonely is the parent widow's fate*
*At once to mourn her offspring and her mate*
*Thy virtues John although nameless here*
*Shall long be told by Sarah's silent tear*

The two illegible stones to the left are those of CAPTAIN JOSEPH ROSE and his wife, BARBARA ROSE (CIRCA 1744–1806, B1-2). Captain Rose's 1773 house at 273 Water Street still stands, though it's no longer on the banks of the East River, as it would have been prior to landfills. Rose, who was in the business of importing mahogany, was able to keep the schooner *Industry* docked right behind the house. A bit of the culture of the day can be seen in the advertisements Rose took out, seeking the vandals who'd broken onto the ship in 1777; he was keeping live goats and decorative iron crows on the ship.[228]

In the 1860s, the Rose house was bought by Kit Burns of the Dead Rabbits Gang. He called it Sportsmans Hall, though it was perhaps better known as The Rat Pit. Burns used it to host dog fights, boxing matches and dances. Between rounds, Burns's son-in-law, Jack the Rat, would bite the heads off rodents for quarters. A reporter who visited the house reported that one spectator said, "I know all Watts hymns [but] I'd like to be an angel and bite Gabriel's ear off."[229]

Now once again known as The Captain Joseph Rose House, the building houses luxury apartments.

To the left of the markers for the Randalls and Roses are a white marble ledger and a white box tomb, both unidentified, and a table-style marker for MARY BARNES KERLY (CIRCA 1737–1807, A10) and her husband,

ARCHIBALD KERLY (CIRCA 1751–1811). Their wedding was listed as being held at Trinity in 1781, officiated by Reverend Inglis, but the church had not been rebuilt from the fire yet, so it was likely held at the Dutch church. Archie was a delegate to the state constitutional convention in 1801, as well as a contributor to the Free-School Society of New York, which established schools for poor children who didn't belong to any religious society.[230]

Just behind Mary and Archibald's table grave is the beautifully carved but partially broken monument to JAMES BARNES (CIRCA 1719–1747, C4), Mary's brother, which features an elaborate floral pattern surrounding a heart. He captained the sloop *Midnight*, which his father, Thomas, a privateer, had also captained in his younger days.

The worn marker to the left is for James and Mary's sister, PHEBE BARNES TOLMIE (CIRCA 1732–1795, C3), though biographical data says that she died in England after the death of her husband, Captain Normand Tolmie.[231] Captain Tolmie fought on the British side during the Revolution. Besides a handwritten receipt for the purchase of a woman named Pegg, Tolmie appears in a couple of records: in one affidavit, he swore to the Continental Congress that another officer had said that those who opposed the Stamp Act ought to be hanged and "might kiss his arse." He was brought to court himself for accusing Francis Lewis (page 100) of fraud and remained a zealous supporter of the Crown after the war. Normand and Phebe's wills suggest a difference of opinion; his refers to 1765 as "the sixth year of the reign of our sovereign," and hers calls 1791 "15 of our independence."

The Kerly section.

Remains of the exquisite Barnes marker.

Captain Tolmie died in 1788 in New York and was likely buried near Phebe. It's possible that Captain Thomas Barnes or other family members are buried here as well, perhaps under the unidentified box graves or headstones nearby.

## WILLIAM BRADFORD

> *If I print one thing to-day, and the contrary party bring me another to-morrow, to contradict it, I cannot say that I shall not print it. Printing is the manufacture of the nation, and therefore ought rather to be encouraged than suppressed.*
>
> —*William Bradford, 1689*

To the left of the Barnes-Kerny-Tolmie family plots is a tall, crisp gravestone for WILLIAM BRADFORD (1663–1752, A3), who was New York's first professional printer.

Born to a family of London printers, Bradford joined William Penn's colony of the Religious Society of Friends (Quakers) in Pennsylvania, where he first published an almanac in 1685, with a note to readers stating, "After great Charge and Trouble, I have brought the great Art and Mystery of *Printing* into this part of *America*, believing it may be of service to you in several respects."

He immediately ran into trouble with censorship, libel, and other issues related to what would one day be known as "freedom of the press." He was once ordered to blot out the "Lord" in mentions of "Lord Penn" in his almanac, and another time, he was ordered to print only things that met with the approval of the Society of Friends, who would become such a thorn in his side that he would eventually call them "my most inveterate enemies." He may have only joined them in order to marry ELIZABETH SOWLE BRADFORD (CIRCA 1663–1731), whose Quaker father he had apprenticed under.[232]

Elizabeth, too, seems to have braced against the Society's rules; she was a poet, even though early Quakers were suspicious of poetry. Her one published verse, a preface to a book by a Baptist poet, opens with a defense of poetry itself:

*One or two lines to thee I'll here Commend*
*This honest POEM to defend*

*From Calumny, because at this day*
*All Poetry there's many do gain-say*
*And very much condemn, as if the same*
*Did worthily deserve reproach and blame*
*If any Book in verse they chance to spy,*
*Away Prophane, they presently do cry*
*But tho this kind of Writing some dispraise*
*Sith Men so captious are in these our days*
*Yet I dare say, how e'er the scruple rose,*
*Verse hath express'd as secret things as Prose.*[233]

In the early 1690s, William printed several titles for George Keith, a Quaker dissenter, and was hauled into court, where he argued that he wasn't responsible for the material that his shop printed and that, even if he *was*, there wasn't even proof that he'd done the printing at all (the case against him fell apart when a juryman dropped the evidence and broke it). Fed up, Bradford moved to New York. Taking the job of royal printer, he had a monopoly on printing in the city for decades and was the only printer in town when young Benjamin Franklin arrived (Bradford sent him to Philadelphia to work for his son). He was well into his sixties when he launched his first newspaper, the *New York Gazette*.

The Bradfords' original sandstone tombstone was damaged during the construction of the third church and was replaced by a marble replica to commemorate William's two hundredth birthday.[234] Due to a policy of maintaining original inscriptions, the new version still gave William's birth date as 1660, though by then it was known to be a typo. Such a mistake could be seen as appropriate, as Bradford's work, unburdened by competition, was famously error-prone and of poor quality. The weekly *Gazette* was filled mostly with months-old foreign news and featured a woodcut in the

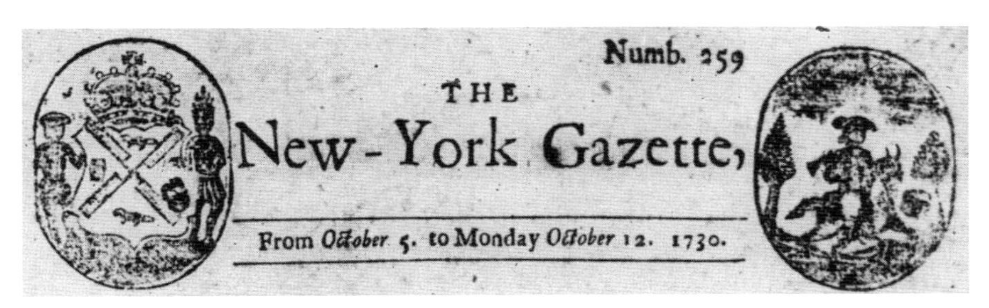


Masthead from Bradford's newspaper.

masthead that an early historian described as "a postman on an animal somewhat resembling a horse."[235]

A verse in the middle of the epitaph, apparently original, alludes to the advanced age William reached:

> *Reader reflect how soon you'll quit this Stage.*
> *You'll find but few atain* [sic] *to such an Age.*

## Cresap and Logan

In the corner of the section is a small marker—a nineteenth-century reproduction—for Michael Cresap (1742–1775, G1), a military captain who was briefly among the most famous Revolutionary figures in the country's collective imagination but ended up best remembered for an atrocity he didn't commit.

There was a time when being able to recite "Logan's Lament" was a standard part of education. Logan the Orator was a Cayuga leader, the son of Chief Shikellamy, who supervised the Six Nations and worked with the Iroquois Nation and the colonial government.

In 1774, Virginia settlers near Yellow Creek lured several members of the Mingo Tribe, with whom Logan had been living, into a cabin and murdered them. Several of the victims were Logan's family members. A speech Logan made in response became famous:

> *I appeal to any white man to say, if he ever entered Logan's cabin hungry, and he gave him not meat.…During the course of the last long and bloody war, Logan remained in his cabin, an advocate for peace.…Col. Cresap, the last spring, in cold blood, and unprovoked, murdered all the relations of Logan, not sparing even my women and children. There runs not a drop of my blood in the veins of any living creature. Who is there to mourn for Logan? Not one.*

Thomas Jefferson later recalled that the speech "became the theme of every conversation" for a time; he himself reprinted it in a 1782 book.[236]

Cresap, a frontiersman, was involved in a battle between several groups that were fighting for control of the Ohio Valley in the 1770s. After the Yellow Creek murders, newspapers mistakenly portrayed him as an "infamous" killer and even seemed to sympathize with Logan when he took revenge with retaliatory raids. For a time, Cresap was thought of as a villain who had badly damaged relations with Natives.[237]

But Logan, Jefferson, and the press had been misinformed—Cresap had nothing to do with the murders at Yellow Creek.

As the Revolutionary War broke out in earnest in 1775, Cresap formed a rifle company and used their journey to join Washington's army as a public tour, giving sharp-shooting performances along the route. Stories spread of their tricks, such as shooting shingles out of each other's hands.[238] They would perform dressed as Natives, and Cresap became, in one historian's words, "the Revolution's noble savage."[239] At a time when the battles of the Revolution had just begun and when people feared that Natives would join with the British, Cresap became a hero. The "tour" was an inspiration to many.

His rifle company ended their tour by joining with the Continental army, but Cresap, sick with what tradition says was a broken heart over being blamed for the murders but was actually a fever, went to New York City to recover. He died in October 1775 and was given a military funeral, one of only a few that would be given at Trinity Church to Revolutionaries until after the war. The funeral was covered in the press nationwide.

Sorting fact from fiction in the tale of Logan and Cresap would prove an obsession to some in the coming decades, and it's hard to know what Cresap really thought of the Yellow Creek Massacre and whether the "tour" was done to benefit his own reputation or to support his country. Nearly everything written about Cresap was intended to portray him as some sort of symbol. But Cresap's fame as a soldier would be eclipsed by the lasting fame of Logan's speech. Over a century later, John Flavel Mines noted, "Many a schoolboy of my day declaimed the noble speech of Logan…without the least idea that Logan's foe slept quietly in Trinity churchyard.…Alone and apart from all their kindred are the graves of Cresap and Logan. It may be a mere coincidence, but the student of history may think otherwise."[240]

Cresap is not exactly apart from his kindred; though no one seems to have noticed it at the time of her death, he was the grandfather of Eleonora Martin Keene (page 78).

Proceeding back around on the path, it is nearly impossible to miss the marker for MARGARET BARRON (1767–1772, G17), which features two soul effigies looking down on what appears to be a realistic portrayal of Margaret herself, a necklace around her neck and long hair flowing behind her back. Little is known of her, and enough people had the same name as her father to make researching him and his family tricky.

Though the identity of the artisans who carved the stones at Trinity is rarely known, there's a good chance that some older ones were carved by ROBERT HARTLEY (CIRCA 1735–1772, H10), who has a grave a little behind and to the right of Margaret Barron's, beside an unidentified white box grave. His marker notes that he was a "stone cutter." Around the early 1770s, Hartley came to New York from Kingston upon Hull and said in his newspaper advertisements that he made "marble monuments, tombs, grave stones, head-stones &c…in the neatest and best manner."[241] His time in New York before his death was short, however, so he had few opportunities to carve the monuments here.

The haunting Barron monument.

# LOST MARKERS IN N6

One marker said to be near Bradford's in 1855 was a "noble monument" for THOMAS CAHUSAC (CIRCA 1772–1817). The memorial was the work of his fellow medical students at New York State University.

Another in N6, still present in 1897 but lost by the 1980s, featured two skulls in an unusual profile view, topped by only the initials "T.S." and "H.L.," followed by more initials under "T.S." and the date 1731 on each side. It attracted a good deal of comment in its day; John Flavel Mines wrote, "As a bid to provoke curiosity, the inscriptions are a success." In 1885, the gardener told a reporter he'd never been able to find anything out about it.[242] We do know that in two months in 1731, over five hundred New Yorkers—

The now-lost "initial" marker sketched in 1876, with the extant Jones marker (H11) visible behind it. *Harper's Weekly.*

between 5 and 10 percent of the population at the time—died of smallpox. Odds are good that this was a case of a family decimated by the disease.

An 1876 illustration of the marker clearly shows the extant John Jones marker (H11) in the background, which would place it between H10 and H11.

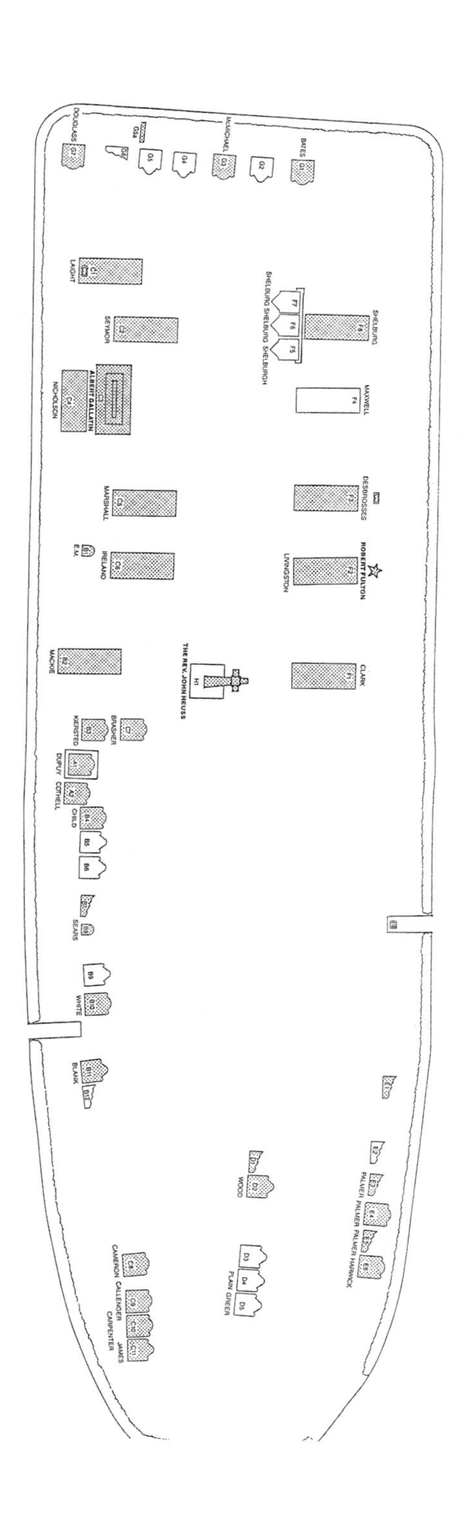
DOUGLASS
BATES
McMICHAEL
LAIGHT
SEYMOR
ALBERT GALLATIN
NICHOLSON
SHELBURG
SHELBURG SHELBURG SHELBURGH
MAXWELL
MARSHALL
DESBROSSES
E.M.
IRELAND
ROBERT FULTON
LIVINGSTON
MACKIE
THE REV. JOHN HEUSS
CLARK
KIERSTED
BRASHER
DUPUY
COTHELL
CHILD
SEARS
WHITE
BLANK
WOOD
PALMER PALMER PALMER HARWICK
PLAIN GREER
CAMERON CALLENGER
CARPENTER
JAMES

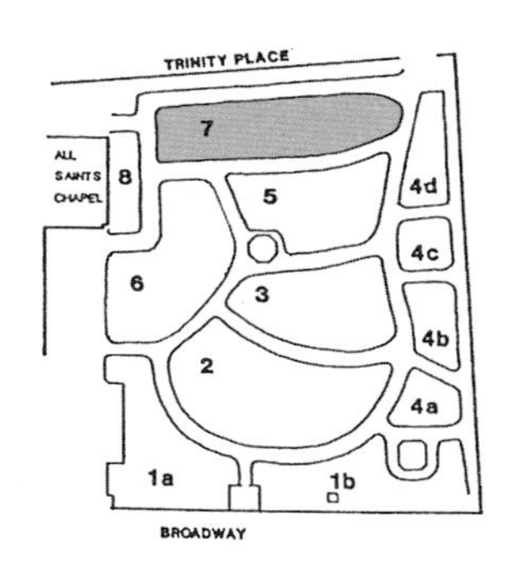
TRINITY PLACE
ALL SAINTS CHAPEL
8
7
5
4d
4c
6
3
4b
2
4a
1a
1b
BROADWAY

# SECTION N7

At the time in-ground burials stopped, Section N7 seems to have been remarkably empty. Old images of the churchyard show only a few scattered headstones here, despite all the stories of the churchyard being overcrowded.

In the 1960s, when the Manning Wing was added to the south portion of the church, contents from nine of the old vaults were moved over to new concrete vaults built in this section.[243] Rather than using subterranean stairs to a doorway, the entrances to the new vaults are located atop the vaults, covered by 1,300-pound slabs of bluestone a few feet underground. In most cases, the crumbling remains and plates found in the old vaults were consolidated into one or two new burial cases, though lead coffins were moved intact.

## Albert Gallatin

*I am to be presented to the King this evening. It is a parade that I wish was over.*

*—Hannah Nicholson Gallatin to Dolley Madison, Paris, 1816*[244]

The Gallatin monument (C3) eclipses the vault of COMMODORE JAMES NICHOLSON (1736–1804, C4), who built his original vault in 1790—both the monument and vault were moved from the south churchyard in the 1960s. A British navy veteran, Nicholson joined the Continental navy when the Revolution broke out, and as the most senior officer to join, he became commodore-in-chief. He commanded the barge that sailed President-elect Washington into New York to take the oath of office.

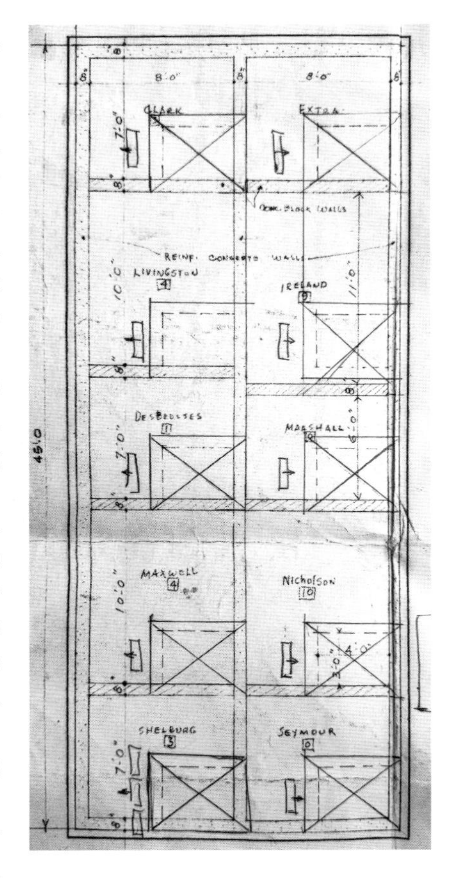


After the war, Nicholson became a fierce rival of Alexander Hamilton (page 40), whom he accused of making large investments in British funds. Eventually, Hamilton challenged him to a duel. Nicholson countered that the proposed duel must be fought sooner than Hamilton requested, before his family found out and intervened. The two resolved the matter through a series of very polite letters.[245]

Nicholson's son-in-law would fight Hamilton in an entirely different way. As secretary of the treasury under Presidents Jefferson and Madison, Swiss-born ALBERT GALLATIN (1761–1849) was tasked with trying to undo Hamilton's financial system. He was unable to find the errors in it that Jefferson hoped to find and maintained much of it, though he shifted the focus of the office to cutting down the national debt.

Later in life, Gallatin fought against slavery; George Templeton Strong (page 73) saw him speak at a rally against annexing Texas in 1844 and noted that he "spoke with more force and more physical strength than one would have anticipated from his appearance, for he's very old and looks infirm."[246]

Before Albert took office, he and his wife, HANNAH NICHOLSON GALLATIN (1766–1849), went back and forth between New York and the Pennsylvania frontier, where he had business ventures. Hannah, a true city woman, always counted the days until they could return to New York. An early biography of her husband notes that as a young woman, Hannah and

*Opposite*: Diagram of the new vaults in section 7N. *Trinity Archives.*

*Left*: Albert Gallatin, by Mathew Brady. *Library of Congress.*

her sisters wrote letters full of notes about New York society, with "allusions anything but friendly to Alexander Hamilton."[247] For a time, she was courted by Thomas Paine.

Albert is also known as the "father of American ethnology." He had become fascinated with Native languages and published *A Table of Indian Languages of the United States* in 1826, which contained one of the first tribal language maps.

## THE FEW SISTERS

Albert and Hannah Gallatin died three months apart after fifty-five years of marriage. Albert died overseas; his body was transported back to New York on a steamship named for Robert Fulton, who is interred in a vault nearby (page 165). Theirs were among the coffin plates found in 1885 when the vault was opened for the remains of FRANCES FEW CHRYSTIE (1789–1885), a granddaughter of Commodore Nicholson. Her diary from an 1808 Washington, D.C. trip survives; when she dined with President Jefferson in 1808, she noted, "The president was only to be distinguished by the shabbiness of his dress."

Her sister, Mary Few (1790–1872), exchanged hundreds of letters with Mary Telfair, a Savannah, Georgia woman who described Mary as her "Siamese twin." Over decades of correspondence, Mary Few would only meet her friend in person in New York and never visited her in Savannah, as she was reluctant to travel to the South. (Mary and Frances's father, William Few, was one of Georgia's first senators but moved to New York in 1799 because of his antislavery views.) The letters Telfair wrote chronicle an extraordinary long-term friendship. It's rumored that the two were romantically linked, and while the letters don't explicitly confirm the rumor, they also don't do much to discredit it. Neither Few nor Telfair ever married, and one letter notes that Frances Few was tired of hearing Telfair talk of how little she thought of "the ruder sex." Few's replies to the many letters are not known to survive, which, like Burr's lost letters, allows modern historians room to speculate.

Many of the letters were collected in the book *Mary Telfair to Mary Few* in 2007.

## Lord George Drummond

The Ireland vault (C6) contains the remains of George Essex Montifex Drummond (1856–1887), Viscount of Forth. His was a story that newspapers loved: Young Drummond had shocked his English family by marrying Eliza Harrison, a servant in his grandmother's house. The story goes that when George was told what would be expected of him as a British lord, he eloped with Eliza and fled. Making the tale all the more scandalous, Eliza was reportedly not divorced from her first husband at the time. In some versions, she had been Drummond's governess.

The couple moved to New York, where George worked a number of odd jobs. He worked as an elevated train ticket chopper, as a Long Island fisherman, and as a clerk in a clothing firm, besides a stint in the press room of the *New York World*.[248] One friend recalled that he "was universally liked…the first to step in and lend a hand. He would tell a lie to shield a companion if the truth would have caused trouble." Many times, the family reportedly offered him a life of ease in his ancestral home if he left Eliza, but he always refused.[249]

When George died of tuberculosis in 1887, his lawyer John B. Ireland (1822–1913) arranged for his body to be interred in the Ireland family vault.[250] George and Eliza's daughter later tried to claim an inheritance, but she could never prove that her parents' marriage was legal. In the early twentieth century, she was widely reported to be working in a Brooklyn ice cream parlor and as a "hello girl" for a telephone company.

The old vault had originally been built for John Ireland in 1787. The first recorded interment here was that of Horatio Ireland Lawrence (1805–1884) nearly a century after it was built, but an 1868, a vault inspection had found three decayed coffins, which shows how little data there is on specific vault interments. Drummond's lead coffin was moved intact.

## The Livingston Manor Vault: Robert Fulton and (Perhaps) Angelica Schuyler Church

*By "my amiable" you know that I mean your Husband, for I love him very much and if you were as generous as the Old Romans you would lend him to me for a little while.*

*—Angelica Schuyler Church to Eliza Schuyler Hamilton, 1794*

The Walter and Robert Cambridge Livingston vault (F2) is a particular puzzle in a graveyard full of them. The Livingstons were an immensely powerful merchant family in 1700s, but most of them (such as Robert R. Livingston, who helped draft the Declaration of Independence, and the vault's namesake, Robert Cambridge Livingston) were buried in the family crypts in or near Livingston Manor, over one hundred miles upstate.[251]

A miniature portrait by Samuel Shelley, possibly of Angelica Schuyler Church, whose remains are possibly in the Livingston Manor vault.

Records on the vault are rather unclear. Fourteen bodies were removed from it to other cemeteries in the 1840s and 1850s, which should have left only a few in the vault, according to the best guesses as to who was in it. But when the vault was inspected in 1868, there were twelve coffins inside. When the vault was moved in the 1960s, only one coffin was found; the piecemeal remains from the others had been consolidated into the single box long before. Also found, though, was a locket containing a lock of hair and coffin plates for Cornelia Schuyler Livingston (circa 1746–1822) and Cornelia Juhel Le Ray de Chaumont (1803–1823) (whose mother had been born Cornelia Livingston).

A third plate had the name "James Crawford" and probably referred to James Crauford (circa 1744–1811). A former member of parliament, Crauford was spoken of as a "gallant, but lazy" young man who gambled away a fortune before being given a post as governor of Bermuda.[252] His wife, Alice Swift Livingston Crauford (1751–1816), who had been the widow of Robert Cambridge Livingston, is in the burial registry and was likely in the vault as well. The two are mentioned in George Washington's diary as dinner guests.

Though the stone bears the names of Robert C. Livingston and Walter Livingston (1740–1797), Robert's obituary states that his body was interred in the family vault at Livingston Manor, and contemporary records give no specific burial place for Walter.[253] However, a coffin plate shows that his wife, Cornelia, was interred here, and it's reasonable assume he was as well. Their daughter, Harriet, married inventor Robert Fulton, who was interred in the vault (though his personal memorial is located in section S1-D, see page 46).

Rumors have long held that Angelica Schuyler Church (1756–1814) was interred in the Livingston Manor vault (her grandmother was a Livingston). A sister of Eliza Schuyler Hamilton (page 40), Angelica was a socialite who knew everyone in Revolutionary society and enchanted them all. Much of her correspondence with Jefferson, Washington, Lafayette, and others still survives.

Angelica eloped with John Church in 1777. After the war, the couple moved to Europe, though they returned to attend Washington's inauguration and moved back to New York in 1799. On the morning of her brother-in-law's fatal duel, she wrote to a friend of "that wretch Burr," with whom her husband had fought a bloodless duel himself a few years before. (John is buried in London.)

Articles about Angelica from the late nineteenth century stated that she was interred in this vault, but they never provided a source.[254] Her coffin plate was not among those found, and records state only that she was buried *somewhere* at Trinity. Records for the vault in the archives usually mention her but also always point out that her interment here is not confirmed.

The headstones lining the south end of the section were moved here along with the vaults. Among these is the headstone for JOHN BATES (1730–1770), who kept a shop that sold wools and furs; his wife, Rachel, took over the shop after his death.[255]

During the debates about expanding a street through the church (page 112), it was charged that Trinity had discarded countless bones during the construction of the present church. The sexton denied it, saying, "A very few skulls were unearthed, as is always the case when any excavation is made in a churchyard, but they were carefully coffined and placed in the Bates vault."[256] There is no record of Bates having a vault. Perhaps he meant the John Clarkson vault, which did contain a coffin full of skulls around the time of the construction (see page 71).

In the middle of the section is the enclosed and restored marker for JOHN DUPUY (1679–1744, A1), a Huguenot who left France in 1682. The British Crown sent him to Jamaica to be a fort surgeon at Port Royal around 1711, and he came to New York three years later. His will carefully laid out which of his enslaved laborers, Rose, Jack, Phillis, and Caesar, went to which family member.

None were bequeathed to his son, JOHN DUPUY JR. (1717–1745), who instead was given a "great garden" and all of John Sr.'s medical supplies; John Jr. was a physician as well. Upon John Jr.'s death the next year, an obituary described him as a "man midwife," indicating that he was one of few doctors who handled births (a job generally left to nonprofessionals in those days). In noting this role, the obituary said, "It may be truly said here, as David did of Goliath's sword, 'There is none like him.'"[257]

DuPuy Jr. once had a headstone here carved by Nathaniel Emmes, bearing a coat of arms surrounded by Latin text that was far more elaborate than other headstones in the section, but it was later moved inside the church.

Behind Dupuy's is a marker for MARY BRASHER (CIRCA 1769–1794, C7), the wife of James, who is memorialized with a poem that begins with four original lines before ending with a particularly maudlin couplet that appears on other graves in the region as well:

*Mary thy Love to James were known*
*The want of thee he does bemoan*
*But while he grieves the loss of thee*
*Thy happiness he trusts to see*
*And when the Lord sees fit to end my time*
*With thy beloved dust I'll mingle mine.*

This was the sort of sentiment that inspired cringes from the next generation. And mixing the apparently original lines four lines with the fairly common final two creates an amusing muddle; it makes it appear that the poem was written by a third party, *not* James, who planned to mingle their dust with Mary's.

In any case, little is known of Mary besides the poem, and it is not known whether James's "dust" (or anyone else's) was ever interred here, as the epitaph promised.

# BURIALS IN THE CHURCH

There are several burial vaults located underneath the church, primarily underneath the Manning Wing, but a few are located under the main structure. John Flavel Mines recalled sneaking into them as a boy in the mid-nineteenth century: "Huge was my delight," he wrote, "when, with two or three companions, we could escape the eye of old David Lyon, the sexton, and hide down into the crypt beneath the chancel. There we saw yawning mouths of vaults, revealing to our exploring gaze bits of ancient coffins and forgotten mortality, and we poked about these subterranean corridors with dusty jackets and whispered words, finding its atmosphere of mould and mystery a strange delight."

Some vaults, such as the Bleecker vault, can be accessed under the church. Others have been inaccessible for ages. During construction around 2019, the ground beneath some pews gave way, exposing the McVickar family vault below, including six caskets, the most recent of which would have been that of PROFESSOR THOMAS EGLESTON (1832–1900), a geologist who married AUGUSTA MCVICKAR EGLESTON (DIED 1895). Records suggest, but are not conclusive, that merchant JOHN MCVICKAR (CIRCA 1761–1812) was interred here; he was remembered as being so generous with credit and assistance that people would commonly ask, "Who has McVickar helped today?"[258]

Next to the McVickar vault would be the vault of JOHN SANDERS (1713–1791), a cooper, which may contain the remains of his son-in-law, Hercules Mulligan (see page 84). It may not have been opened since the 1881 interment of Catherine Ann Livingston Velasquez (circa 1799–1881), a daughter of Ann Sanders Livingston. Catherine was married to Mariano Velasquez, who was private secretary to King Charles IV of Spain before coming to New York, where he made his living teaching Spanish.

Maps also show a block of six vaults just west of McVickar and Sanders, two of which were unknown as of 1868. One, last used in the 1830s, contained fourteen coffins at the time.

Another was listed only as "vault in the south corner which can only be partly opened; all coffins decayed."[259] This southern vault was "discovered" during 1964 construction; plates found at the time suggest it was the vault of merchant John Shaw (circa 1744–1817).

In the first church, the one built in the 1690s, a person could be buried under the chancel for five pounds, which was more than fifteen times the cost of a burial in the south churchyard. In 1864, a chart was drawn up showing twenty burials under the chancel, and that list didn't include a few that had been noted before.

After visiting the church in 1774, future president John Adams wished to note in his diary only that Benjamin Pratt (1710–1763), former chief justice of New York, was buried under the chancel.[260] Mutual friends told Adams legends of Pratt's astounding memory and ability as a lawyer. After Pratt's death, among his papers was a poem titled "Death," which was frequently published in years after. It ends with the lines:

> *Death buries all diseases in the grave*
> *And gives us freedom from each fool and knave*
> *To worlds unknown it kindly wafts us o'er—*
> *Come death, my guide, I'm raptured to explore.*

Funeral reports also state that James De Lancey (1703–1760), who served as colonial governor, was buried under the middle aisle of the first church.[261]

Neither De Lancy nor Pratt are included in the 1864 report.

## THE MAN WHO NAMED THE CHURCH

The north monument room contains an old tombstone from the churchyard, that of OBADIAH HUNTT (1676–1760), whose epitaph credits him with naming the church. Its original location may have been near the stone of his daughter, Susannah Hunt Rousby, in Section N1B (page 109). The inscription read:

> *Obadiah Huntt from Birmingham in Warwichshire with his wife Susannah from Credley in Heartford Sheir in Old ingland* [sic] *with sundry children and grandchildren who departed this Life Oct 22 1760 and was at ye founding of this church in ye year 1695 and named Trinity Church.*

It's interesting to note that Huntt would have been a teenager when he named the church. Huntt kept a tavern at 35 Pearl Street for nearly twenty years. After retiring, he traveled frequently; in his eighties, he was still taking trips to the Caribbean. These trips probably involved slave trading, as he is known to have enslaved people named Tobey, Wooster, and Warwick, the latter of whom was apparently named after Hunt's hometown.[262] In 1719, Obadiah and Susannah also took in a young orphan named Susana Maria Beyer, who was apprenticed to them for nine years to learn housework.[263]

The tombstone doesn't give a date for the death of SUSANNAH HUNTT, though a writer in 1904 noted with a chuckle that the epitaph made it look as though Obadiah, Susannah, and the "sundry children and grandchildren" had *all* died on October 22, 1760: "If the above statement be true there must have been fearful mortality in the Hunt family on the day specified."[264]

## CATHARINE O'BRIEN, LADY CORNBURY

Though any number of the people involved with and interred at Trinity Church have inspired urban legends, few approach Lord and Lady Cornbury in tales of their eccentricities.

CATHARINE O'BRIEN HYDE, LADY CORNBURY (1673–1706), was laid to rest in the original church, under the steeple. According to one legend, her husband, Edward Hyde, third Earl of Cladendon, known as Lord Cornbury, attended the funeral wearing one of her dresses.

While many of the stories of Lord Corbury dressing in drag were not written until nearly two centuries after his death, some do date to his lifetime. In 1708, Elias Neau (page 142) wrote a letter about him, stating, "Lord Cornbury has…an unfortunate custom of dressing himself in women's clothes, and of exposing himself in that garb upon the ramparts to the view of the pubic; in that dress he draws a world of spectators…especially for exposing himself in such a manner [at] all the great Holidays, and even an hour or two after going to the Communion." Neau also noted that Cornbury was addicted to "debauch and abominable swearing."

Lord Cornbury was governor of New York and New Jersey at the time. Though some stories about him may have been smears from political rivals, almost nothing flattering about him was ever written.

Stories of his relationship with Lady Cornbury are mixed. In one account, "[Cornbury] had fallen in love with her ear, which was very beautiful. The ear ceased to please, and he treated her with neglect. Her pin-money was withheld, and she had no resource but begging and stealing.…As hers was the only carriage in the city, the rolling of the wheels was easily distinguished, and then the cry in the house was 'There comes my lady; hide this, hide that, take that away.'"[265]

Other accounts state that Lord Cornbury was at Catharine's deathbed day and night when she took ill and was prostrated by grief when she died. At her funeral, the preacher noted, "The great passion which afflicts and oppresses her honourable consort…are an unexceptionable testimony [to] how dearly he loved her."[266] Stories that say he was in her clothing on that particular occasion came long after.

The sermon preached at her funeral was mainly a religious speech about the nature of death, but noted, "[Lady Cornbury] professed…that she was most willing to leave the world, that she died in the faith of the Church of England.…She had strength and vigor which promised a much longer life, but the frequent returns to her Distemper put her in mind that her body was to return to the dust."

During construction at Trinity in 1839, her grave was discovered; it contained fragments of a coffin and a plate with her name from the lid. The relics were reburied; modern records refer to the "Cornbury vault" just south of the tower.[267] One man who saw the fragments removed from the "vaulted grave" remarked that the artwork on the huge plate was still in good shape, "emblazoned by the hands of an unskilled artist…placed in its dark, cold repository, to be now brought forth again to the light of day to undergo the scrutiny of a generation of men who were not thought of in those days."[268]

Sketch of the large Cornbury coffin plate.

Old newspaper reports note that Katharine Rigby Hyde (1672–1733), had been interred in the Cornbury vault as well. She was the widow of the governor of North Carolina and was once descried as "a woman of abundance of life."[269] She was a cousin of Lady Cornbury.

Hyde's daughter, Anne Hyde Clarke (circa 1693–1740), was also interred in the vault. Anne was the wife of George Clarke, the acting governor of New York, who named New Hyde Park, Long Island, using her maiden name. Anne's unusually detailed obituary sang her praises and noted, "As it was a Pleasure to Her in her Life, to feed the Hungry, so on the Day of her Funeral a Loaf of Bread was given to every Poor Person that would receive it."[270]

# KNOWN BURIALS, UNKNOWN GRAVES

Burial records are missing for the years before the 1776 fire. Even among later records, funeral reports and tombstones show that many people were buried here who weren't mentioned in the record.

Likewise, both the registry and funeral reports show that a great many notably people are interred here without tombstones or even a rumor of where, exactly, they might have been buried.

## Captain Tollemache

Lowther Pennington was a passenger on a ship to New York captained by John Tollemache (died 1777), and during the voyage, Captain Tollemache "endeavour'd to thwart or ridicule" everything Pennington did or said.[271] Tollemache was said to be particularly annoyed by Pennington humming a song after dinner, remarking that "he was never so tired of anything in London as he had been of that tune." He even joked that he was going to shoot Pennington dead over it and said that Pennington "deserved to have his throat cut…and I would like to cut it."

It turned out he wasn't joking.

On September 26, 1777, the ship arrived in New York. The next night, Pennington was dining at Hull's Tavern, right next to Trinity, when, according to Pennington's own account, Tollemache swept into the room, made a remark about the bad lighting, and attacked Pennington with a sword. Pennington acquired a sword of his own and killed him. In a report the following Monday, the *Gazette* noted, "Captain Tallemache's Corpse were [*sic*] decently interred in Trinity Church yard last Saturday Evening."[272]

There is a general sense in letters of the day that Pennington's version of events, which got him acquitted of murder, was probably not entirely accurate. Later rumors suggested that Pennington wasn't singing a popular song but an insulting song he'd written about Tollemache's wife. One man, General Fitzpatrick, wrote to his sister-in-law, "Everybody concludes [Pennington] to have been in the wrong, from his general character. I cannot help pitying Lady Bridget [Tollemache], though she is a detestable woman."[273]

## James Gordon

Near the Lawrence monument, a small sign was added in the twenty-first century substituting for the unmarked grave of James Gordon. Gordon was known in England as a jovial man. General Cornwallis would later say he knew him as "gay in gay London," while remarking, "Who could have guessed how much lay in the man?"

Gordon became a major and was taken prisoner after Cornwallis surrendered to George Washington at Yorktown. In the heady period that followed, while the two sides tried to negotiate the treaty to end the war, a British soldier was wantonly killed by a mob. The British responded by hanging an American officer in revenge, an execution possibly ordered by William Franklin (page 253), one of the sons of Benjamin Franklin. William, a Loyalist, may have intended the hanging to disrupt his father's ongoing peace talks.

It came close to doing so. Public pressure to retaliate was intense. Washington ordered that an officer under Gordon's command be chosen by lottery to be hanged, and the lot fell to Captain Charles Asgill.

Gordon reportedly told Asgill, "I wish to God they would take me in your place. I am an old worn-out trunk of a tree, and have neither wife nor mother to weep for me." He remained with the young officer through his confinement and wrote to Washington to express his "astonishment" at the affair and to demand in the name of the king that Asgill be discharged.[274] Meanwhile, Alexander Hamilton wrote to Harry Knox that the "wanton and unnecessary" execution would be "repugnant to the genius of the age we live in."[275]

King Louis XVI of France requested that Asgill's life be spared, and Congress decided that they could save face by saying that calling the execution off was a favor to France. Major Gordon, worn out by the affair, died the next year of dropsy.

## JAMES CHEETHAM

> *I stated in my first letter that you had proclaimed Mr. Jefferson in your paper a hypocrite, a liar, a scoundrel, an assassin, and usurper....I have shown, from your own paper, that you have called Mr. Jefferson* [all but one of these]. *I have not found the word* scoundrel*; but I think, and your readers will agree with me, that the word* scoundrel *is merged in the superior epithets of disgrace which you so copiously applied to the executive.*
> *—James Cheetham's letter to the* New York Post, *September 1802*[276]

It may be the "calumnies" JAMES CHEETHAM (1772–1810) published about Aaron Burr throughout 1804 that pushed Burr over the edge.

Cheetham was an English-born hatter who, after coming to New York, became the editor of the *American Citizen*, a mouthpiece for the Democratic-Republican Party—to which Cheetham believed Burr was a traitor. In his angry, provocative rants, he seems like an early prototype for the cable news loudmouths of later centuries.

When Burr ran for governor, Cheetham published a rumor that he'd courted the votes of Black men by inviting them to a ball at his house where they were provided with sexual favors. At other times, Cheetham claimed that "the names of upwards of *twenty women of ill fame* with whom [Burr] has been connected have been obtained."[277] He even ran a letter from a reader stating that Burr "permitted a prostitute to insult and embitter the dying moments of his injured wife."[278] (Cheetham presumably didn't know that while Burr's wife was on her deathbed, a servant in the house was pregnant with Burr's child [page 39]—if he had, he absolutely would have printed it.)

After Burr killed Hamilton, Cheetham attacked both men but said that Burr had cheated in the duel by wearing a silk coat "impenetrable to a ball," by practicing ahead of time, and by shooting to kill knowing that Hamilton wasn't planning to shoot back.

Cheetham went on to write a highly critical biography of Thomas Paine, a former friend against whom he'd turned bitter. He continued to run the paper until his death in 1810. "He was certainly a man of uncommon natural talents," wrote the *New York Post*. "And with all his faults was possessed of many great virtues."[279]

Trinity records show he was buried somewhere in the churchyard, but there's no record indicating that he ever had a marker.

Another known to be "decently interred" somewhere in the churchyard is DAVID JAMISON (1660–1739).[280] In his native Scotland, Jamison joined the Sweet Singers, a religious order that denounced churches, names of months and days, and all sports. They believed in burning all books except the Bible—and would even burn those if it was a translation they had issues with. Jamison was arrested for burning a Bible himself and was condemned to hang, but he was instead banished to New York, where he was sold as an indentured servant to pay for his transportation costs. Later, he was admitted to the bar and was among the judges in the Jacob Leisler trial (page 118). He was dismissed from his post by Lord Bellomont (page 255), but after years in private practice, he served as chief justice of New Jersey and attorney general of New York.

Apparently cooling from his early religious fervor, he became a vestryman at Trinity.

## SARAH GOMEZ (AND OTHER PEOPLE OF COLOR KNOWN TO BE BURIED AT TRINITY)

When Trinity was chartered in 1697, a rule was made that "after the expiration of four weeks from the date hereof [October 25, 1697] no Negroes [may] be buried within the bounds and Limits of the Church Yard." But the existence of the rule implies that such burials had taken place there before then, and it only applied to the south yard, not the older burial ground north of the church. When the city turned the management of that ground over to Trinity in 1703, rules stated that it was to be available to anyone.

Most known burials of Black individuals in eighteenth-century New York took place at the African American Burial Ground a few blocks north (see next volume), but data suggests that the rules at Trinity were not always enforced; if they had been, the parish may not have felt it was necessary to rule in 1790 that there should be no burials of Black individuals (or "any except communicants") at Trinity or St. Paul's henceforth. That rule lasted until 1801, when the vestry decided that the children of Black communicants could be buried in the graveyards under their jurisdiction.

There are eight known interments of people of color at Trinity, though there may have been many more. Though the weddings of Black couples performed in the church are easy to find in the marriage records, ethnicity was generally not noted in the burial registry. Among those known is SARAH GOMES (OR GOMEZ) (CIRCA 1715 OR 1734–1814), who was buried at Trinity on November 27, 1814. Right Reverend Onderdonk noted that she was a person of color in his notes from attending her funeral, but nothing else is known of her, except that the registry gives her age as ninety-nine.

The other known people of color interred at Trinity, with their burial dates, are:

AN UNIDENTIFIED BLACK CHILD (DIED 1801), died of "fits" at eight months old on February 25, 1801.

"ANTHONY" (CIRCA 1717–1801) died of "old age" at eighty-four on March 14, 1801.

"ENEAS, A NEGRO" (CIRCA 1744–1801) died of "fever" at fifty-seven on May 22, 1801.

"MR. WHITE'S BLACK WOMAN" (CIRCA 1721–1803), died at age eighty-one on January 2, 1803.

"LUCY" (CIRCA 1731–1809) died at age seventy-eight on August 20 or 23, 1809.

AN UNIDENTIFIED BLACK WOMAN (CIRCA 1734–1812) died at age seventy-eight on May 17, 1812.

JOSEPH PANCAUST (DIED 1818) died at three months old on November 23, 1818.

None are known to have headstones.

# PART II

# ST. PAUL'S

St. Paul's in 2023.

Introduction

# ST. PAUL'S

St. Paul's Chapel is one of the oldest buildings in Manhattan. George Washington had a pew here after the Revolution. It re-entered national consciousness when it narrowly survived the September 11, 2001 attacks on the nearby World Trade Center. The church became a haven for the workers who cleared the rubble after the 2001 attack. The Bell of Hope, forged in the same foundry that cast the Liberty Bell and Big Ben, was added near the west porch in 2002, a gift from London to be rung every year on September 11. But the church's reputation as a survivor goes back much further; the church and graveyard had narrowly survived the New York Fire of 1776, the Vesey Street Fire of 1799, the Park Theater Fires of 1820 and 1848, and the burning of Barnum's Museum in 1868.

Built over two years beginning in 1764, with a steeple added a few decades later, St. Paul's was thought to be in a rather remote location when it was built. Though reminisces that it was "out in the country" are an exaggeration, its short distance from Trinity did make a difference. In 1867, rector Morgan Dix noted that older people heard stories of cattle straying into the churchyard to "browse among the monuments" and repeated a popular legend that one day, a horse wandered into the church and down the aisle in the middle of services.[281]

Having been in existence for far less time than Trinity when in-ground burials were stopped in 1822, it has far fewer markers and includes only around thirty vaults, about one-third the number at Trinity. It has been the subject of far less study than Trinity Church.

Though it is not without the graves of Revolutionary soldiers or famous names itself, St. Paul's has a somewhat smaller and arguably stranger collection of residents. One of most prominent monuments in the churchyard is that of an actor whose biographer said he possessed no virtues at all (page 213). Elsewhere are the graves of gamblers, prize fighters, scoundrels, and knaves, all mingling with the graves of soldiers, statesmen, and artists.

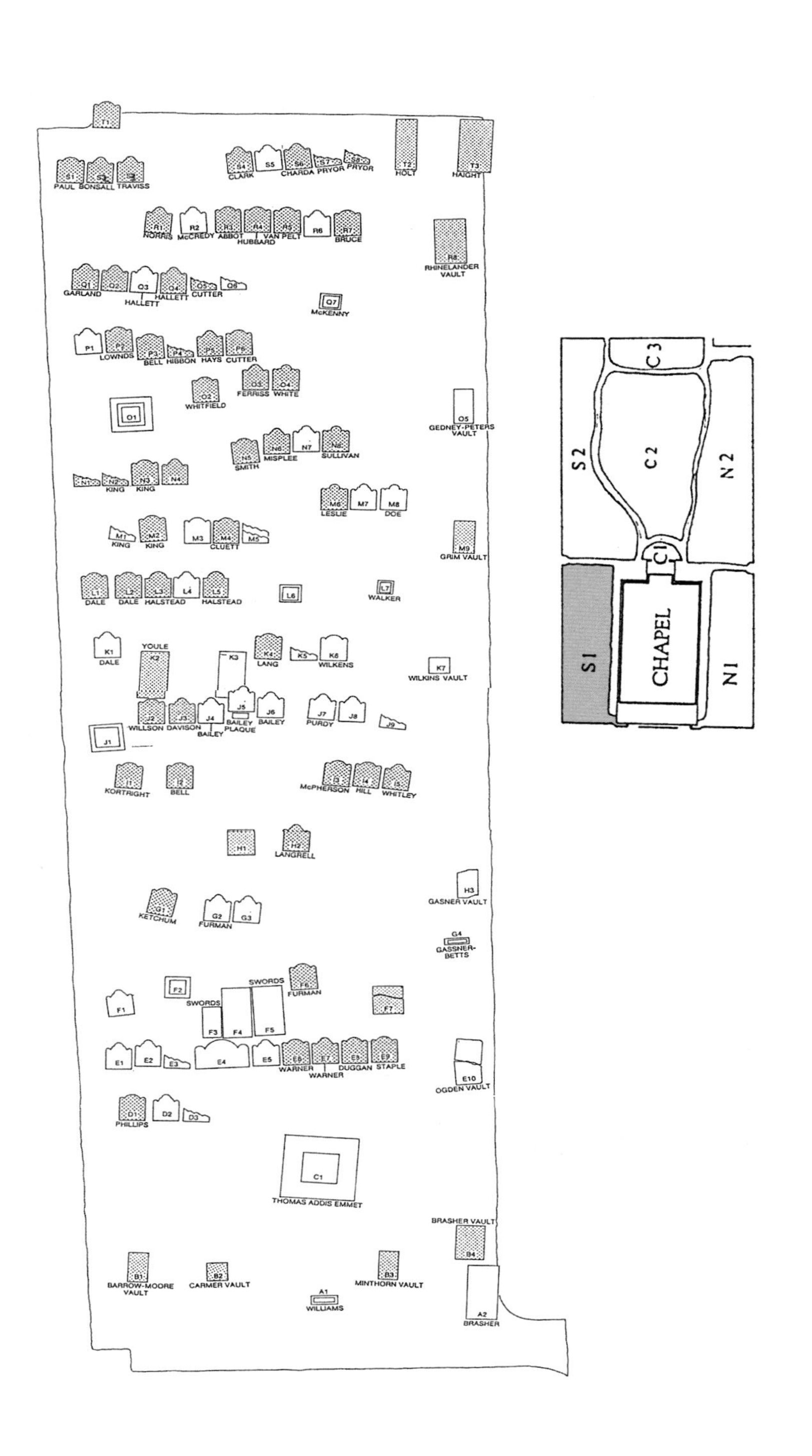

T1
S1 PAUL
BONSALL
TRAVISS
S4 CLARK
S5
S6 CHARDA
S7 PRYOR
S8 PRYOR
T2 HOLT
T3 HAIGHT
R1 NORRIS
R2 McCREDY
R3 ABBOT
R4 HUBBARD
R5 VAN PELT
R6
R7 BRUCE
R8 RHINELANDER VAULT
Q1 GARLAND
Q2
Q3 HALLETT
Q4 HALLETT
Q5 CUTTER
Q6
Q7 McKENNY
P1
P2 LOWNDS
P3 BELL
P4 HIBBON
P5 HAYS
P6 CUTTER
O1
O2 WHITFIELD
O3 FERRISS
O4 WHITE
O5 GEDNEY-PETERS VAULT
N1
N2 KING
N3 KING
N4
N5 SMITH
N6 MISPLEE
N7
N8 SULLIVAN
M1 KING
M2 KING
M3
M4 CLUETT
M5
M6 LESLIE
M7
M8 DOE
M9 GRIM VAULT
L1 DALE
L2 DALE
L3 HALSTEAD
L4
L5 HALSTEAD
L6
L7 WALKER
K1 DALE
K2 YOULE
K3
K4 LANG
K5
K6 WILKENS
K7 WILKINS VAULT
J1
J2 WILLSON
J3 DAVISON
J4 BAILEY
J5 BAILEY PLAQUE
J6 BAILEY
J7 PURDY
J8
J9
I1 KORTRIGHT
I2 BELL
I3 McPHERSON
I4 HILL
I5 WHITLEY
H1
H2 LANGRELL
H3 GASNER VAULT
G1 KETCHUM
G2 FURMAN
G3
G4 GASSNER-BETTS
F1
F2
F3 SWORDS
F4
F5 SWORDS
F6 FURMAN
F7
E1
E2
E3
E4
E5
E6 WARNER
E7 WARNER
E8 DUGGAN
E9 STAPLE
E10 OGDEN VAULT
D1 PHILLIPS
D2
D3
C1 THOMAS ADDIS EMMET
B1 BARROW-MOORE VAULT
B2 CARMER VAULT
B3 MINTHORN VAULT
B4 BRASHER VAULT
A1 WILLIAMS
A2 BRASHER
C3
S2
C2
N2
C1
S1
CHAPEL
N1

# SECTION S1

Looking through the fence from Broadway, in front of the larger cenotaph to Thomas Emet is the faded white stone for "beloved aunt" SARAH FURMAN WARNER WILLIAMS (1772–1848, A1).[282]

Sarah married Azarias Williams at Trinity Church in 1789. A newspaper ran a poem wishing them happiness, but after her father's death in 1825, Sarah moved back into the old family home on Bowery without Azarias, and the two apparently lived apart from then on.[283] The quilts and embroidery attributed to her are some of the finest and most creative examples of early American stitchery that have ever been found. Several are held by museums, including an Indian palampore–influenced coverlet now held by the Metropolitan Museum of Art.

The lengthy inscription from the poem "The Loved and Lost," attributed to Martha C. Canfield, was probably illegible fairly soon after it was carved, but it would have read:

*A thousand old familiar things*
*Within our childhood home*
*Speak of that absent cherished one*
*Who never more may come.*

*They wake with mingled bliss and pain*
*Fond memories of thee*
*But would we call thee back again*
*We mourn but thou art free.*

*For thou hast gained a brighter home*
*And death's cold stream is past*
*Thine are the joys at God's right hand*
*That shall for ever last.*

*A crown is on thy peaceful brow*
*Thine eye the King doth see*
*Thy home is with the seraphs now*
*We mourn but thou art free.*

Nearby is a broken grave for MARIA WARNER (1786–1792) and ELIZA WARNER (1790–1792, E7), who died two months apart, likely of yellow fever. The first two lines of the epitaph (the common "weep not for us") are vaguely visible. The last two were a variation on the common "prepare for death and follow me" epitaph:

*The debt is paid our grave you see*
*Prepare for Heaven's felicity*

Behind the Emet monument are two white ledger stones (E7). The marker on the right reads:

*Near this spot were deposited the remains of*
*Lieutenant THOMAS SWORDS*
*Late of his Brittannic Majesty's 55th Regt of Foote*
*who departed this life on the*
*16th of January 1780*
*in the 42nd year of his age*
*And underneath this tomb lies*
*all that was mortal of MARY SWORDS*
*relict of the said Liet. Thomas Swords*
*who on the 15th day of September 1798*
*fell a victim to the pestilence which then*
*desolated the city of New York.*

One of Sarah's quilts, held by the Henry Ford Museum until it was damaged in a 1970 fire. The church in the middle may be St. Paul's.

Thomas Swords (circa 1738–1780) was wounded in an attack on Ticonderoga in 1756 and later put in command of Fort George before he resigned from the army in 1766. When he later refused a post in the Continental army in 1776, he was arrested in Albany and, before his release to New York, contracted an illness that proved fatal.

Mary Swords (died 1798) petitioned the British government for financial relief, stating that besides her husband being "imprisoned and deprived of all his substance," her son was killed in battle.[284] "I don't believe there is one person come from the continent of America," she wrote, "that has been a greater sufferer than myself." She was granted a pension but spent the rest of her life fighting for more compensation and took an oath of allegiance to the United States in 1795.[285] The visitation of yellow fever in which she perished killed some two thousand people, roughly one in thirty people in New York at the time.

Beside them is a smaller slab for Eliza Davidson Swords (1795–1796, F3), a granddaughter, with a poem by Richard Bingham Davis:

*Vain was the fond parental prayer*
*Affections warmest tears were vain*
*And Fruitless was the tenderest care*
*Her gentle spirit to retain*
*For Heaven its precious gift resumes*
*Eliza leaves our weeping sight*
*Sweet flower. She fades but now she bloom*
*In gardens of celestial light.*

Davis was a New Yorker who wrote a number of elegiac poems. He once wrote a piece mocking one Mr. Martlett as a "buffoon" who had no luck with the ladies; it was later revealed that "Mr. Martlett" was an alias for himself. His work was published by Thomas and Mary Swords's sons, who

A large obelisk commemorates Thomas Addis Emmet, an Irish rebel who was jailed in England. He became attorney general of New York and was noted for his antislavery work. The monument was placed here in 1833 at the behest of his friend William Macneven (page 237). However, Emmet was never interred here; he was laid to rest in the Jones vault at St. Mark's (page 259) and later moved to Ireland.

grew up to be printers; the poem on the stone, "Epitaph for an Infant," may have been written specifically for Eliza.

Some ways behind Mary, usually marked with military paraphernalia but difficult to see from the path, is the marker of a man who made swords for George Washington. John Bailey (1736–1815, J5) was among the New Yorkers who fled to outlying areas as the British army approached. Washington mentioned him in a 1779 letter to Nathanael Green, suggesting that he enlist "Mr. Bayley" to make him a penknife—one with two blades—to replace an old favorite he had lost.[286]

By 1790, Bailey had written Washington to request a grant to mint coins, saying that he hoped the general remembered him, and, "I have actually struck at the rate of 56 coins a minute....I am acquainted with the whole mystery of coining."[287] Washington would have perhaps best remembered him for making him the stylish green-hilted battle sword he used in the final years of the war.

Among the stones visible through the fence on the south side of the churchyard, near the subway entrance, is that of Elizabeth Kortright (circa 1743–1789, I1).

> *The remains that lie beneath this Tomb*
> *Once had Rachel's face and Leah's fruitful womb*
> *Abigail's prudence and Sarah's faithful heart*
> *Martha's care and Mary's better part*
> *HER JUST CHARACTER*

Though the stray final line is unique, variations on the verse are seen in North America on stones dating to at least the 1690s. Elizabeth and her husband, Nicholas, were relatives of Elizabeth Kortright Monroe, whose marriage to future president James Monroe was performed at Trinity in 1786.

The sword Bailey made for Washington appears in several portraits, including the famous painting of Washington crossing the Delaware in 1776—though the sword likely wasn't created until 1778. *Metropolitan Museum of Art.*

Farther along the fence is a marker for Elatha Dale (circa 1741–1789, L1), with a popular bit of verse from Pope's "Elegy to an Unforunate Lady" (page 128). Though Elatha's marker also calls her "a sincere Christian," contemporary critics like John Wesley disapproved of Pope's poem, as the "Unfortunate Lady" it memorialized was thought to have died by suicide.

The small, illegible white marker in front of Elatha's is one for her husband, Captain Robert Dale (circa 1730–1804, K1), and it once read, "Death comfortably ends a well-spent life."[288]

A little way back at P3 is the marker for Robert Bell (1753–1778), whose epitaph is partially buried:

*Reader*
*Whoe'r thou are Whome choice hath led*
*To trace these faded Memorials of the dead*
*Learn since lifes airy vision soon is ore*
*To wait the great teacher Death & God adore.*

This is another Alexander Pope reference; though most of the epitaph appears to be unique, the last line is from Pope's "Essay on Man."

## The House Carpenter's Spirit

One of the broadside "ballads" sold along the fence on Fulton Street (page 192) may have been the poem written about Abijah Abbot (circa 1735–1768, R3), a young carpenter who died in the construction of a house. His stone is visible through the fence toward the back of S1, but only a few of its letters can now be made out. It once said that he "died accidentally."

Poet Peter St. John wrote an elegy for Abijah in his voice and that of Mary, Abijah's wife of six years, titled "A Dialogue Between Flesh and Spirit: Composed Upon the Decease of Mr. Abijah Abbot."

In the poem, the "Flesh" (Mary) laments,

*The time as well as manner of his Death*
*That awful hour when he resign'd his breath.*

In 1864, a reporter penned a Dickensian description of the scene around the church, when the sidewalks were swarming with peddlers who spilled right into the graveyard. Rumors had it that P.T. Barnum paid them to set up there, away from his nearby museum, and that the church made money by charging rent for spaces on the fence.

> *At the corner of Fulton Street was a dealer in old coins, tokens, medals, Confederate notes, foreign postage stamps, &c. Opposite him, on the curbstone, was a lemonade, cake, and fruit stand. Extending down the street a wholesale ballad-monger stretched his printed songs and ballads, ignominiously held in their places by a double line of cords, along the railing for at least 300 feet, entirely monopolizing the trade on that side of the churchyard....*
>
> *On Broadway there was first a shoeblack...next came a bouquet man...two newsboys succeeded him, who were "challing" each other while waiting for the third edition of the evening papers.*
>
> *Then there were three or four walking advertisements, one with a great oil-cloth overcoat on, painted in big letters, which set forth the virtues of some particular invention, and the others bearing staring placards like banners with strange devices above their shoulders; then came a dealer in the red gutta-percha balloons which little folks delight in; then the mosquito net man...then a boy with three Newfoundland puppies in a basket; then a naturalist with glass globes containing gold fish; then another naturalist with whistles, on which he imitated the singing of birds; then an iced-lemonade man, then a penny-a-glass ice cream woman.... Then an old woman with two baskets of pop corn, pink and white; then a candy stand, with love mottoes inscribed on the candies, then a thin-faced easterly wind-looking individual who dealt in barometers, then a disconsolate woman with green apples and stunted peaches....*
>
> *Directly on the corner of Vesey street was an old established newspaper stand....Then a candy and peanut stand, then a row of ballads, "Johnny's Gone to Sea," "Root Hog or Die," and others of a similar character....*
>
> *Then more ballads, then a lot of bright colored lithographs....Then a display of varnished maps of the seat of war, and colored charts descriptive of events in the Bible; then a medley of brooms, shoe brushes, small mirrors, combs, pins, knives, forks, &c. Then more ballads; then an old sailor with sponges and a collection of sea shells; then a dealer in ribbons and lace; then more ballads; and then, lastly, a clothing shop....*
>
> *If the policeman who is partial to driving decent colored people out of the cars will only make these peddlars move along...he will be doing his duty, and gratifyingly serving the public.**

* "The Congregation of Peddlers Around St Paul's Churchyard," *NYP*, July 27, 1864 (edited for clarity).

Lunchtime, circa 1909. The churchyard was a popular lunch spot for women who worked in nearby offices in the late nineteenth and early twentieth centuries. Men were not allowed. *Trinity Archives.*

Echoing many of the shorter epitaphs in the cemetery, the "Spirit" (Abijah) says his maker

> *Took but the Breath, which his own Spirit gave*
> *and hides the casket in The silent grave*
> *he saw 'twas best in this surprising way*
> *to take the spirit from this lump of clay.*

At the far northwest corner of S1 is a table-style marker for the family vault of real estate investor William Rhinelander (1790–1878, R8), whose family mansion in Greenwich Village was a landmark for years and whose children funded many charitable institutions. Among the interments is that of a daughter, Julia Rhinelander (1830–1890), whom one newspaper suggested was "the richest spinster in America." It was believed that she never married because she wanted to manage her finances herself: "[She] entirely refuses to listen to the endless offers of the male sex to take care of her money."[289]

Her sister, Serena Rhinelander (died 1914) was also known as being financially savvy, handling most of the affairs of the family's vast property empire herself. There was a small scandal when she died and her will left nothing to a nephew who had been largely disinherited and banished from New York for marrying a servant. He was apparently still not forgiven forty years later.[290]

## John Holt: The Radical Printer

> *As to* [Benjamin Franklin]*'s private Character, I have always greatly respected the Doctor. He was always hospitable kind and friendly; and as a natural philosopher I have the highest Opinion of him; but I have long thought his public Conduct mysterious and suspicious, and have been obliged to consider him as a dangerous person, primarily attentive to his own interest, and always acting in Subserviency to it.*
>
> —*John Holt, 1778*[291]

Near the western edge is a ledger stone for printer John Holt (1721–1784, T2). The epitaph reads, in part:

> *The tongue of slander can't say less*
> *Though Justice might say more*
> *In token of Sincere affection, his disconsolate widow*
> *Hath caused this monument to be erected*

The reference to "the tongue of slander" doesn't come from nowhere. Many of people said a lot of things about John Holt—and it wasn't *all* slander.

No one could say how Holt became mayor of Williamsburg, Virginia, in 1752. He had no real political experience and no great reputation, either. But once in office, he used his position for petty revenge—he and a shopkeeper had accused each other of selling alcohol to enslaved people, and Holt, as mayor, stopped anyone from putting out a fire in the shopkeeper's house.[292] Facing bankruptcy and possible jail time, he abandoned the office and fled Virginia for Connecticut, where he found work as a printer and newspaperman under James Parker, who was urged to take Holt under his wing at the *Connecticut Gazette* by Benjamin Franklin.[293]

While working for Parker, Holt accused one Charles Roberts, an indentured servant, of stealing lottery tickets and had his indenture extended from three years to forty, effectively rendering him an enslaved man. Roberts, who was of mixed ethnicity, was literate, played the fiddle, and dressed in wigs, escaped. Holt took out advertisements accusing him of being a "villain," a cheat and a con artist. Parker, Holt's boss, said all the same things of Holt and was likely among the many who believed that Holt had stolen the lottery tickets himself.[294]

But Holt's willingness to make enemies and pick fights paid dividends during the Revolution. In 1760, he took over the *New York Gazette*, which he stuffed with anti-English essays until it became the local voice of the Revolution. It's likely that Holt's paper did much to make formerly radical views mainstream.

Though former partners continued to speak of Holt as "a viper, indeed, a knave," John Adams and other members of the Continental Congress made sure to visit "Friend Holt, the Liberty Printer," after touring Trinity and St. Paul's in in 1774.[295] (Adams noted that "the building [St. Paul's] taken altogether does not strike me.")

On July 9, 1776, Holt printed copies of the Declaration of Independence to be sent to government officials. Soon after, he fled New York to escape the oncoming British army and ran newspapers in Poughkeepsie before returning to New York to resume his *Gazette*. Upon his death, his widow, Elizabeth, took over as publisher; she was buried in Philadelphia. The marker is said to have been based on the memorial cards Elizabeth printed; she may have written the epitaph herself.[296]

## Phillip Brum: The Lost Sailor's Marker

*Dear wife—I have now nothing else to do, therefore I cannot omit writing…I forgot to mention a remarkable circumstance of a cock onboard the Saratoga, who got up into the rigging on the commencement of the battle and began crowing, and continued to do so until the end of the battle.*

*—Philip Brum to Susan Brum, October 24, 1814*

Among the more recently lost stones is a plain marble marker for Philip Brum (circa 1776–1818), a transcript of which read:

*In Memory of Philip Brum who departed this life June 1, 1818, aged 42 years. He was sailing master of the United States ship Saratoga, at the memorable battle of Lake Champlain, September 11, 1814, AND DID HIS DUTY*

Philip Brum had studied for the ministry, but as one contemporary put it, "he early determined to gratify a passion common in the bosom of many young men to roam abroad upon the seas" and was in the navy during the War of 1812.[297]

Sailors in the New York Flotilla regularly let their families visit them. Shortly after an order stopped the practice, Master Commandant Jacob Lewis found that Sailing Master Brum was still letting his sick wife sleep in a ship's infirmary. Outraged, he roared that Brum was "neglectful of his duty" and reassigned him to the *Saratoga* on Lake Champlain, where conditions were so bad that some sailors resigned rather than serve there.

In the Battle of Lake Champlain, the USS *Saratoga* and the British *Confiance* fought to a standstill. The starboard guns of the *Saratoga*, those on the side facing the enemy, were nearly all out of commission, but so were the guns facing them from the other ship. Brum oversaw a maneuver to wind the ship around so that it's still-intact portside guns were facing the now helpless *Confiance*, which quickly surrendered.

British and American delegates were already negotiating a peace treaty. The burning of Washington a month before the battle put the British in a good position to demand the United States give up some territory, but after their Lake Champlain defeat, this leverage was gone. Partly because of Brum, the war ended with territorial control much the same as it had been at the beginning.

Brum (whose name is sometimes given as "Blum") was wounded by shrapnel in the battle and for a moment was thought to be dead, until he leaped to his feet, made an apron of his pocket handkerchief, and fought on. However, his obituaries four years later said he'd developed his fatal illness from the wound.[298] The line that he "did his duty" on the stone could be seen as his wife's rebuke of Commandant Lewis.

The stone was restored in 1862 and transcribed (except for the last line) in 1897, but it is now apparently gone. It was described as being near the Broadway entrance, where it was overshadowed by the Emmet monument. It may be one of the unidentified marble markers near the obelisk.

# Other Lost Markers in S1

In 1875, librarian Robert Kelby made notecard sketches and transcriptions of hundreds of graves at St. Paul's, some of which include a rough sketch of the stones' shapes and copies of their carvings. These can be very useful for lost graves, but he seldom gave even vague locations.[299]

Some of the larger monuments in this area (F2, J1, O1, and O6) are unidentified. It's tempting to attempt to match any known inscription that can't be matched to an extant stone to one of them. One epitaph at St. Paul's that was transcribed several times in the 1860s:

> *Rising Sun Chapter No 16 of the Royal Arch Masons and Rising Sun Encampment of Knights Templars have conjointly erected this stone in commemoration of their respect for the affection and virtues that once glowed in the heart and animated the soul of their dead Companion and Sir Knight, Thomas Freeborn. He died the 3d day of May, 1815, aged 43 years, 3 months, and 22 days.*
>
> *In the various excellencies that flowed from the relations of husband, parent, and friend he has not been surpassed, seldom equalled* [sic], *has left to the brotherhood, his example for their imitation*

Two of the larger unidentified monuments.

Kelby's 1875 sketch suggests it was a very tall, narrow monument with a tympanum featuring a skull and crossbones, a pyramid, and other masonic imagery. A masonic author transcribed the stone, which he noted was made of marble, in 1866 and boasted that "it will be as admirable and as admired a hundred years hence. Such is masonry!"[300] However, it was apparently fully illegible or completely gone by 1897.

Though the monument praised him as a family man, Thomas Freeborn (circa 1772–1815) was a member of so many fraternal organizations that one wonders if his wife and seven children saw much of him. When he died after a short illness, his popularity among members of Trinity Lodge was noted in obituaries.[301]

The 1897 transcriptions show a number of other epitaphs in this section that are no longer present. One for Fitz Randolph (1774–1798) read:

*I've gone unto a pleasant shore*
*Where pain & sorrow is no more*
*And left my friends for those above*
*And blessed with the almightys love*

A marker for Andrew Tombs (1798) and Annie Tombs (1801–1806), children of Andrew and Maria Tombs, noted that Annie was born at sea.

A grave for Sarah Cluck (1768–1804) read, "Time how short; Eternity how long."

One report spoke of a small marker for Dr. Phillip Turner (1740–1815) near the southeast corner. It is said to have mentioned his Revolutionary service; Turner he was made surgeon general of the eastern department. Even in 1875, Robert Kelby's sketch simply said "Doctr. Philip (Turner?)." The 1897 transcription, strangely, was able to make out a bit more, noting a couple of illegible lines before one that included the words "In the revolution."

An 1830 article mentioned a marker for merchant Lawrence Read Yates (circa 1735–1796) with an epitaph taken from Shakespeare's *Julius Caesar*:

*His life was gentle and the elements*
*So mixed in him that nature might stand up*
*And say to the world, This was a man*[302]

The marker was described as "a tablet near the southern wall." Robert Kelby's sketch in 1875 called it a "large flat stone raised on foundation" and noted that the epitaph below the name and dates was illegible. It was apparently no longer extant at all by 1897. Yates partnered with his brother to import rum and sugar from Jamaica.

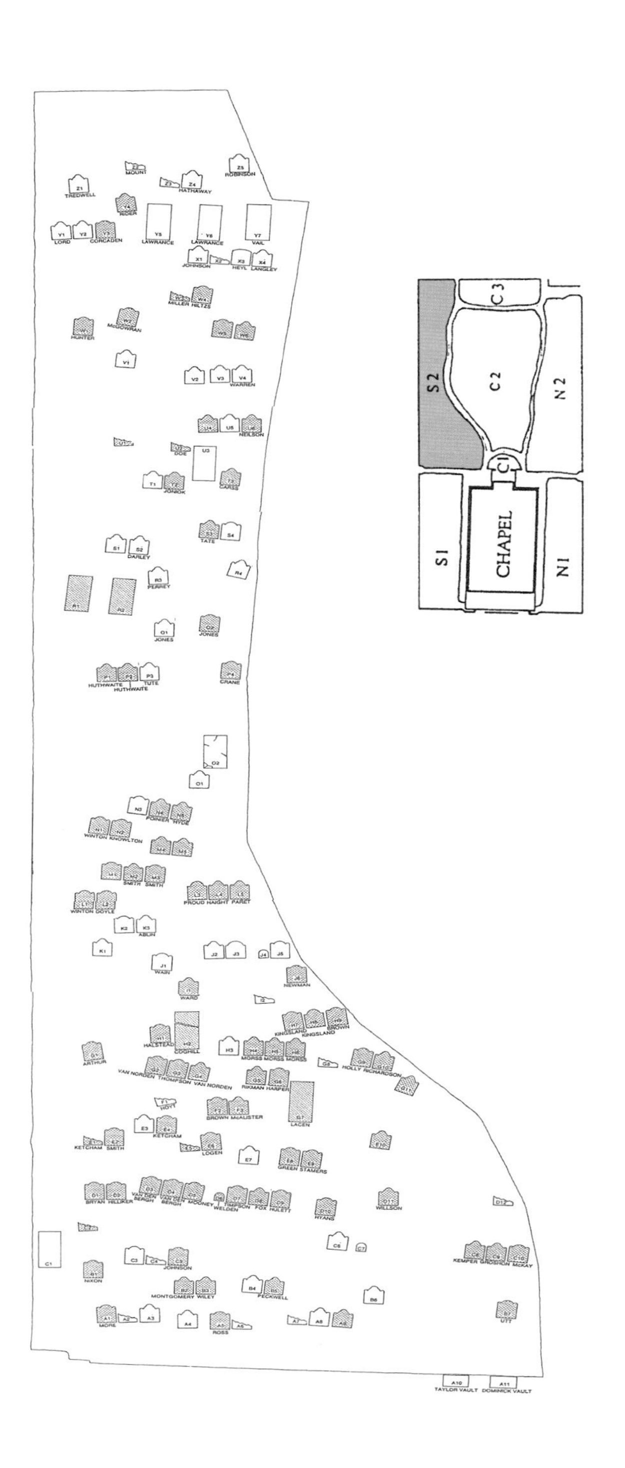
Z1 TREDWELL
Z2 MOUNT
Z3
Z4 HATHAWAY
Z5 ROBINSON
Y4 RIDER
Y1 LORD
Y2
Y3 CORCADEN
Y5 LAWRANCE
Y6 LAWRANCE
Y7 VAIL
X1 JOHNSON
X2
X3 HEYL
X4 LANGLEY
W3 MILLER
W4 HILTZS
W1 HUNTER
W2 McGOWRAN
W5
W6
V1
V2
V3
V4 WARREN
U4
U5
U6 NEILSON
U1
U2 DOE
U3
T1
T2 JONIOK
T3 CARSS
S3 TATE
S4
S1
S2 DARLEY
R4
R3 PERREY
R1
R2
O1 JONES
O2 JONES
P1 HUTHWAITE
P2 HUTHWAITE
P3 TUTE
P4 CRANE
O2
O1
N3
N4 POINIER
N5 HYDE
N1 WINTON
N2 KNOWLTON
M4
M5
M1
M2 SMITH
M3 SMITH
L3 PROUD
L4 HAIGHT
L5 PARET
L1 WINTON
L2 DOYLE
K2
K3 ABLIN
K1
J2
J3
J4
J5
J1 WAIN
J6 NEWMAN
I1 WARD
I2
H7 KINGSLAND
H8 KINGSLAND
H9 BROWN
H1 HALSTEAD
H2 COGHILL
H3
H4 MORSS
H5 MORSS
H6 MORSS
G1 ARTHUR
G2 VAN NORDEN
G3 THOMPSON
G4 VAN NORDEN
G5 RIKMAN
G6 HARPER
G7 LACEN
G8
G9 HOLLY
G10 RICHARDSON
G11
F1 HOYT
F2 BROWN
F3 McALISTER
E3
E4 KETCHAM
E1 KETCHAM
E2 SMITH
E5
E6 LOGEN
E7
E8 GREEN
E9 STAMERS
E10
D1 BRYAN
D2 HILLIKER
D3 VAN DEN BERGH
D4 VAN DEN BERGH
D5 MOONEY
D6 WELDEN
D7 TIMPSON
D8 FOX
D9 HULETT
D10 HYANS
D11 WILLSON
D12
C2
C1
C3
C4
C5 JOHNSON
C6
C7
C8 KEMPER
C9 GROSHON
C10 McKAY
B1 NIXON
B2 MONTGOMERY
B3 WILEY
B4
B5 PECKWELL
B6
B7 UTT
A1 MORE
A2
A3
A4
A5 ROSS
A6
A7
A8
A9
A10 TAYLOR VAULT
A11 DOMINICK VAULT
C3
S2
C2
N2
C1
CHAPEL
S1
N1

# SECTION S2

Among those markers visible inside the gates from the path between S1 and S2 are several graves with almost cartoonish soul effigies, among the few examples of artwork seen at St. Paul's. One is the marker for infant JAMES MOONEY (1781, D5), with an Isaac Watts verse:

*Why do we mourn departed freinds* [sic]
*And shake at Death's alarms*
*It is the Voice that Jesus sends*
*To Call us to his arms*

Along the north path, one of the first legible graves is that of JACOB KEMPER (CIRCA 1772–1792) and RACHEL KEMPER (1793, C8), with a verse of a Philip Doddridge hymn:

*O happy dead in peace that sleep*
*Tho o'er your mouldering dust we weep*
*A faithful saviour soon will come*
*That dust to ransom from the tomb*

Down the path toward Church Street, a few rows into the section, is a marker for CHARLOTTE FOX (CIRCA 1765–1810, D8). Both its distance from the fence and its faded inscription make the stone difficult to read, but it says:

*In early life she wisely sought her God*
*And the straight path of smiling virtue trod*
*Fond to oblige, too gentle to offend*
*Belov'd by all, to all the good a friend*
*The bad the censur'd by her life alone*
*Blind to their faults, severe upon her own*
*In others grief a tender part she bore*
*And with the needy shar'd her little store*

The couplets come from a poem that was published widely; one early version gives the title "On the Much Lamented Death of Mrs. Anne Wale, Widow of Mr. Johne Wale, Earls Colne Priory, Ye 9th Feb., 1770" and names the author as William Beauchamp. Other versions had other titles and included different lines, such as the couplet "Her front with virgin modesty she bound / and on her lips the law of truth was found."

Cartoonish soul effigies on the Bryan and Hilliker markers.

Continuing along, just as the road bends, there is a flat slab, slightly elevated, that includes elaborate calligraphy for Captain James Lacey (1755–1796, G7) and the same style of cryptogram—and the same cryptic message when decoded—that appears on James Leeson's grave at Trinity (page 110). Captain Lacey piloted the passenger sloops *Edward* and *Sally* between New York and Vermont. Much of his estate was willed to the Trinity Lodge of Freemasons.[303]

Below the name, only a few words of the inscription remain, but early transcripts give it as a variation on the once-common epitaph for seafarers, such as the lost Berryman grave at Trinity (page 135).

*Tho' Boreas' blasts and boisterous waves*
*Have tost me to and fro*
*In spite of both you plainly see*
*I harbor here below*
*Where safe at anchor though I ride*
*With many of our fleet*
*Yet once again I must set sail*
*My admiral Christ to meet*

## Mrs. Harper, the Comedian

Mrs. Malaprop, the language-mangling character in Sheridan's *The Rivals*, was arguably the very pinnacle (or, as she would say, "the very pineapple") of comedy roles on the eighteenth-century stage. And the *New York Gazette* said that there was no better Mrs. Malaprop than Frances Harper (circa 1754–1791, G6) of the American Company of Comedians. Her marker is adjacent to Lacey's.

Frances was one of the first women to make her living in comedy in New York, performing alongside her husband in The Old American Company of Comedians, which returned to the city after spending the war years in Jamaica. Theater itself was controversial and sometimes even banned in the early years after the Revolution, but The Old American became known for finding ways around the law.

Comedian Frances Harper's marker and Captain James Lacey's marker with its cryptogram.

Frances caused some controversy herself in 1787, when she starred in George Farquhar's 1706 play *The Recruiting Officer* as Sylvia, a character who declares, "I am heartily sick of my sex," and disguises herself as a male soldier. One militia captain who saw Frances perform said she did the military drills better than most of his men, but a pearl-clutching critic for the *Daily Advertiser* accused her of being both too sexy *and* too "masculine" in the role, causing indelicate excitement among the women who came to the show.

The play was not new; Adam Allyn (page 131) had played a small role in it as a member of the same company a generation before. But with the Constitution still being debated, people were also debating what sort of country the United States would be culturally. Some argued for a morally upright path without such impurities as plays like *The Recruiting Officer*. The *Advertiser* critic insisted that the play had been written "for an age and court distinguished for depravity, deism, and voluptuousness" and didn't belong in modern New York, "where delicacy and innocence of manners should prevail."[304]

But no one criticized Mrs. Harper's skill in the role.[305] The controversy died down, but for the rest of her career she was better known for her turns as comedic old ladies, such as Mrs. Malaprop. Like Adam Allyn, she also played dramatic roles, such Queen Gertrude in *Hamlet*, but received her best reviews for comedy.

Upon her death after a long illness in 1791, a memorial poem was published in the *Gazette*:

*A real friend attempts to speak thy praise*
*Tho' not in graceful, yet sincerest lays*
*Just were thy actions in this busy life,*
*Thro' all the scenes of daughter, friend, and wife*
*On this poor stage your merits all confess'd*
*Your virtue now applauded by the blest.*

## John Coghill Knapp: The Pettifogger

*I* [have] *no desire of greater Gain than to keep the WOLFE (if possible) from the Door, till, the great Point weather'd, I may return under a flowing Sheet to my NATIVE SPOT, with a CHARACTER to disperse the heavy Cloud, under which (by Misconduct shipwreck'd) I was cast on this distant Shore.*[306]

—*John Coghill Knapp*

A little beyond Frances Harper's marker is a ledger grave for John Coghill Knapp (circa 1729–1784, H2), who was known as a "pettifogger," or a sleazy lawyer.

In 1763, Knapp had been brought to trial in England as "a notorious sharp and cheat" and was sentenced to seven years of banishment. As he was led from court, people he'd defrauded cried, "Hang him! Hang him! Let him be well flogged before he goes!"[307]

Arriving in New York, Knapp began taking out lengthy advertisements in papers. He was barred from practicing law but offered "legal advice" for one dollar, as well as debt collecting services, written conveyances, and help for "seafaring men and other strangers who often met with difficulty not altogether relative to the law."[308] In all dealings, he vowed "utmost secrecy." Knapp's advertisements were very much the 1760s equivalent of commercials for smarmy lawyers on daytime television in later centuries; indeed, he may have invented the form. No other lawyer in town took out advertisements like his.

When papers exposed his history, Knapp simply made it a part of his advertising. In his ongoing series of advertisements, he openly referred to his shady past, developing a larger-than-life persona as a much-abused sinner trying to make things right by helping his "fellow creatures." He would ramble about how humble he was (while dropping references to his Oxford education). To back up his claims of being so abused, he accused John Morin Scott (page 95) of beating him up when he tried to collect a debt. Local lawyers seem to have considered him a thorn in their side. He called them "hypocrites, pretending with ease to see the mote in their brother's eye, [when they] cannot behold the beam in their own."

In an advertisement celebrating the repeal of the Stamp Act, he droned about his love of "dear liberty, the birth right and much boasted pageant of a Briton," even though John Watts (page 57) said Knapp was the only lawyer in town who supported the act.[309] Despite his many rants in praise of liberty, many of his advertisements offered to broker sales of "negroes of both sexes" for a two-shilling commission and noted that in such sales "this office hath been particularly successful."[310]

Knapp returned to England when his banishment was up, but in 1781, he was taking out advertisements announcing his return to New York and resumption of his old business.[311] Cornwallis having just surrendered, Knapp was now in a new country. He set up an office across from Trinity Churchyard (where the church itself was still in ruins) and wrote, "The courts of justice being so long shut, the Law lies as in a trance, consequently its fundamentals...are more likely to be trampled" and warned people that any dealings they made now or before "the present unhappy troubles" could be nullified under a new government if they didn't hire him to help.[312]

The Latin ledger for "Johannis" Coghill Knapp.

His ledger-style stone says that with the loss of this friend, the Republic has lost a useful man. It speaks of him as a man who came from the great families of England, worked for the poor, and merited respect for his good manners. Written entirely in Latin and calling him "Johannis" instead of John, the stone in an extension of his self-important persona. Though the authorship of epitaphs is almost always anonymous, it's safe to assume that Knapp dictated this one himself.

Directly behind Knapp is Captain William Ward (circa 1759–1796, I1), with an epitaph common on masonic graves of the era:

*Here, call'd from labor to repose*
*A weary mason resting lies*
*Till the last awful trumpet blows*
*And bids each human atom rise.*

Behind the markers of Frances Harper and Captain Lacey lie the markers for the Morss family, with a particularly maudlin epitaph for Mary Morss (died 1802, H5) that appears to be unique, though similar lines appear on other graves:

*Beneath this sod in mouldering dust now lies*
*The best of mothers and the best of wives*
*If domestic merit ever deserved a tear*
*What friend to virtue can refuse it here?*

Further along is a much-faded brown stone for Elsie Paret (circa 1804–1809, L5) that features a barely legible epitaph from an interesting source:

*This tender plant once flourishing & fair*
*Whose happy exit claims a parent's tear*
*Shall lovelier far to full perfection rise*
*Unfold its charm and flourish in the skies*

This was a poem by Frances Greensted, who wrote while working as a household servant and published a 1796 collection, *Fugitive Pieces*, for the benefit of her aged mother. It sold thousands of copies. Some critics said it was only because of Greensted's inspirational backstory, but one British critic said that she "may be fairly called one of the handmaids of the Muses," and at least one New Yorker loved her work enough to use as in an epitaph.[313]

Behind three box graves is an upright marble stone for Beverley Robinson. Several early articles identified this as the grave of the Beverley Robinson who played a major role in facilitating Benedict Arnold's treason, but that man died in 1792 in England. This is his son, Beverley Robinson Jr. (died 1816).

While his father was trying to remain neutral as the Revolution spread, the staunchly Loyalist Robinson Jr. went to New York to join the British army, in which he become a lieutenant colonel. Some of his recruits were discovered and exposed by Enoch Crosby, the agent who is said to have inspired James Fenimore Cooper's *The Spy*.

Following the war, the British government gave Robinson Jr. a lucrative office in New Brunswick, where he fathered ten children and wrote letters to his wife chastising her for laziness, scolding her for letting the doughnuts she made him get dry, and assuring her that even though she needed glasses now, he'd always remember how beautiful she used to be.[314]

Though he was banished from New York on penalty of death if he ever returned, Robinson Jr. came to visit his son and consult with doctors in 1816. As if natural causes were doling out the penalty, he died while he was in town.[315]

## Lost Markers in S2

The oldest marker in the churchyard was a brown stone for one Francis Dring (circa 1739–1767). It was still extant as of 1909, when a guidebook marked it as being near A1.[316] Robert Kelby's 1875 notecard sketch shows an upright stone with "Time how short, Eternity how long" along the arch of the tympanum and the common "My flesh shall slumber in the ground" verse below the name and dates. In a corner of his card, he wrote, "Chipped at mouth." Only the name and dates were transcribed in 1897, and it was lost or totally illegible by the 1980s.

A 1919 *New York Sun* sketch of the now-lost Dring marker, which was the oldest in the churchyard. Based on the sketch, it may have included the common epitaph "My flesh shall slumber in the ground / til the final trumpet sound."

Many of the box graves in the section are unidentified. One of them may have been for Sarah Mary Ann Moore (1788–1802), who had a lengthy inscription in this section per the 1897 transcriptions:

> *In memory of Miss Sarah Mary Ann Moore, daughter of Mr. Edward Moore of this city. Merchant. She died on the 16th of May 1802. Aged 13 Years & 7 months. She was beautiful amiable and for her years highly accomplished.*
>
> *Come unto me for such is the Kingdom of Heaven. St Matthew 19 C 14 V. I love them that love me and those that seek me shall find me. Proverbs 8 c 14 v.*

A newspaper obituary for Sarah—rare for someone so young—said that she died "of a decline" and agreed that she was "amiable," "accomplished," and "beautiful."[317] Kelby's 1875 sketch omits the scriptural quotes and gives no shape at all, which perhaps suggests that it was a box grave (the shape of the notecard).

There was also a grave here for Francis Scott (circa 1767–1811), whose epitaph read:

> *A native of England who, to save a child, was himself drowned in the east river Sept 8 1811. Aged 44 years; of Nedlam Yorkshire.*

Indeed, in September 1811, a pleasure boat near the Battery upset, throwing nine people overboard. All were saved except for Francis Scott.[318] As of 1875, Kelby couldn't decipher anything on the stone past "drowned in the" (his sketch suggests no particular shape, which again allows the possibility of it being a box grave), but the 1897 transcription was complete.

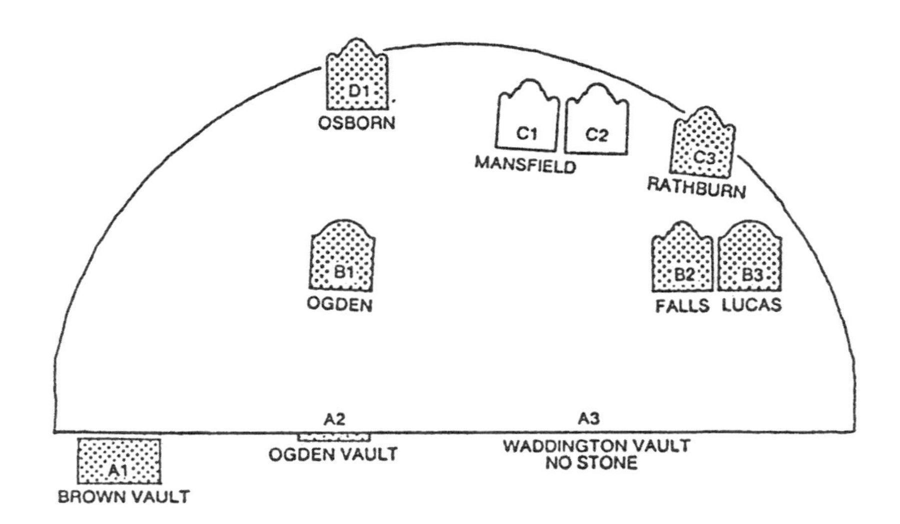
D1
OSBORN
C1
C2
MANSFIELD
C3
RATHBURN
B1
OGDEN
B2
B3
FALLS
LUCAS
A2
A3
A1
BROWN VAULT
OGDEN VAULT
WADDINGTON VAULT
NO STONE

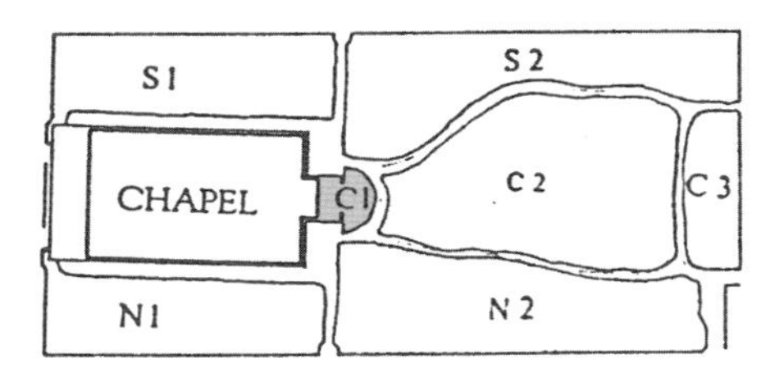
S1
S2
CHAPEL
C1
C2
C3
N1
N2

# SECTION C1

Underneath the porch are two brick vaults that are normally buried but were partially exposed during repairs in 2012.

One is the family vault of JOSHUA WADDINGTON (1755–1844), a founder of the Bank of New York. Beside it is the vault of THOMAS L. OGDEN (1773–1844), one of Hamilton's last legal partners. The families were connected; Ogden's niece GERTRUDE OGDEN WADDINGTON (DIED 1850) married Waddington and is in his vault.

Both vaults were built in 1814; the Ogden vault was reportedly permanently sealed after the 1942 interment of FANNY OGDEN (1848–1942), Thomas's granddaughter.

Fanny may have had vague memories from childhood of her great-great-aunt Eliza Schuyler Hamilton (page 40). Perhaps she even attended her burial at Trinity in 1854. Her aunt RUTH SCHUYLER OGDEN (1813–1901), who is also in the vault, would likely have had more memories of the last of the Revolutionary-era Schuylers. Ruth died six hours apart from her husband, broker THOMAS W. OGDEN (1810–1901).[319]

A small marker in C1 commemorates the Ogden vault. The most notable of the other headstones in the small section is that of MARY LUCAS (CIRCA 1729–1780, B3), the wife of cutler Sebastian Lucas, whose advertisements included offers for "steel trusses and steel collars for children," which were used to improve posture.[320] The stone features a double cherub beneath a beaming cloud that is very well preserved, especially relative to the space below, where nearly all of the inscription past "Here Be Lieth Inter'd the Body" has been missing for decades.

The double soul effigy for Mary Lucas.

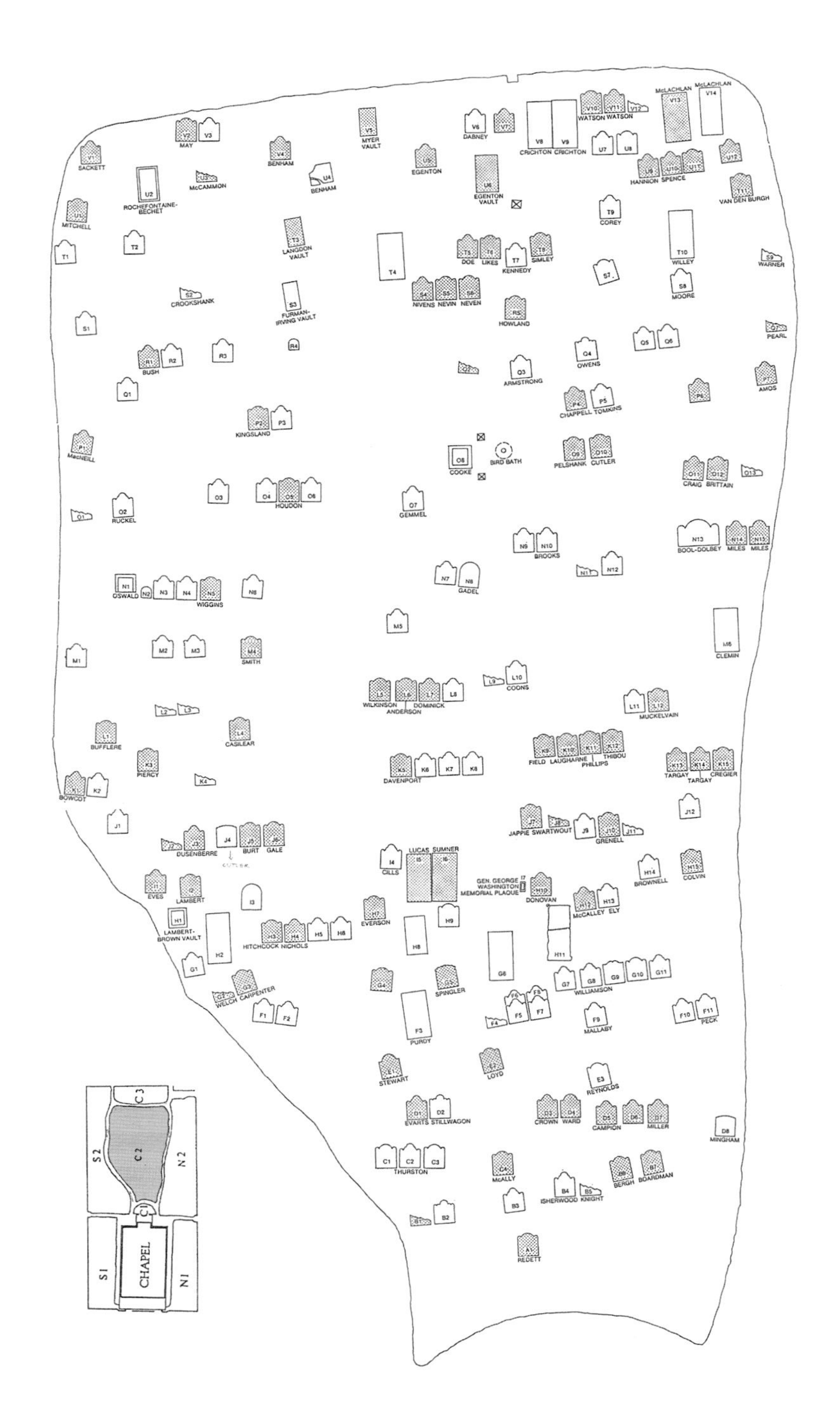

McLACHLAN
V13
McLACHLAN
V14
V10
V11
WATSON WATSON
V12
V8
V9
CRICHTON CRICHTON
V6
DABNEY
V7
V5
MYER
VAULT
V4
BENHAM
U4
BENHAM
V2
MAY
V3
V1
SACKETT
U2
ROCHEFONTAINE-
BECHET
U3
McCAMMON
U5
EGENTON
U6
EGENTON
VAULT
U7
U8
U9
HANNION
U10
SPENCE
U11
U12
T11
VAN DEN BURGH
U1
MITCHELL
T1
T2
T3
LANGDON
VAULT
T4
T5
DOE
T6
LIKES
T7
KENNEDY
T8
SIMLEY
T9
COREY
T10
WILLEY
S9
WARNER
S7
S8
MOORE
S4
NIVENS
S5
NEVIN
S6
NEVEN
R5
HOWLAND
S2
CROOKSHANK
S3
FURMAN-
IRVING VAULT
S1
R4
R1
BUSH
R2
R3
Q1
Q2
Q3
ARMSTRONG
Q4
OWENS
Q5
Q6
Q7
PEARL
P7
AMOS
P6
P4
CHAPPELL
P5
TOMKINS
P2
KINGSLAND
P3
P1
MacNEILL
O8
COOKE
BIRD BATH
O9
PELSHANK
O10
CUTLER
O11
CRAIG
O12
BRITTAIN
O13
O1
O2
RUCKEL
O3
O4
O5
HOUDON
O6
O7
GEMMEL
N9
N10
BROOKS
N11
N12
N13
BOOL-DOLBEY
N14
MILES
N15
MILES
N1
OSWALD
N2
N3
N4
N5
WIGGINS
N6
N7
N8
GADEL
M5
M6
CLEMIN
M1
M2
M3
M4
SMITH
L9
L10
COONS
L5
WILKINSON
L6
ANDERSON
L7
DOMINICK
L8
L11
L12
MUCKELVAIN
L2
L3
L1
BUFFLERE
L4
CASILEAR
K9
FIELD
K10
LAUGHARNE
K11
PHILLIPS
K12
THIBOU
K13
TARGAY
K14
TARGAY
K15
CREGIER
K3
PIERCY
K5
DAVENPORT
K6
K7
K8
K1
BOWCOT
K2
K4
J1
J12
J7
JAPPIE
J8
SWARTWOUT
J9
J10
GRENELL
J11
J2
J3
DUSENBERRE
J4
CUTLER
J5
BURT
J6
GALE
I4
CILLS
I5
LUCAS
I6
SUMNER
GEN. GEORGE
WASHINGTON
MEMORIAL PLAQUE
I7
H10
DONOVAN
H14
BROWNELL
H15
COLVIN
I1
EVES
I2
LAMBERT
I3
H12
McCALLEY
H13
ELY
H1
LAMBERT-
BROWN VAULT
H2
H3
HITCHCOCK
H4
NICHOLS
H5
H6
H7
EVERSON
H8
H9
H11
G8
G1
G2
WELCH
G3
CARPENTER
G4
G5
SPINGLER
G7
G8
WILLIAMSON
G9
G10
G11
F1
F2
F3
PURDY
F4
F5
F6
F7
F8
F9
MALLABY
F10
F11
PECK
E1
STEWART
E2
LOYD
E3
REYNOLDS
D1
EVARTS
D2
STILLWAGON
D3
CROWN
D4
WARD
D5
CAMPION
D6
D7
MILLER
D8
MINGHAM
C1
C2
C3
THURSTON
C4
McALLY
B4
ISHERWOOD
B5
KNIGHT
B6
BERGH
B7
BOARDMAN
B1
B2
B3
A1
REDETT
C3
S2
C2
N2
C1
S1
CHAPEL
N1

# SECTION C2

C2 is by far the largest section in the cemetery, making up the grounds directly in front of the porch (which would have been the entrance at one time, facing the Hudson River before the area was developed). With the fences on the edge of the path, many of the monuments in the middle are now difficult to see. The central space is dominated by a large marker, which stands not to a politician or war hero but to the British actor GEORGE FREDERICK COOKE (1756–1812, 08), who is interred here, minus his skull and one of his fingers.

## COOKE: THE HEADLESS ACTOR

*Ah ha! Ha! Ah ha! I astonished the yankee actors. I gave it them! I'll show these fellows what acting is!*

—*G.F. Cooke*

G.F. Cooke was an exasperating genius. There were legends of him refusing to go onstage unless he was paid a huge sum and then throwing the money right into the fire after the show. A proud subject of King George III, he reportedly refused to perform for President Madison, stating, "It is degradation enough to play before rebels; but I'll not go on for the amusement of…the contemptible king of the yankee doodles!"[321] He even claimed that

Section C2 of St. Paul's with the World Trade Center looming above.

as a British soldier in the Revolution (which he may or may not have actually been at all), he had very nearly killed George Washington.

He was brought to America by Park Theater manager Stephen Price (pages 72, 86, 214 and 232). While in the United States in 1811, Cooke traveled

*Left*: The Cooke monument.

*Right*: Cooke as Richard III by Thomas Sully. *Pennsylvania Academy of Fine Arts.*

with theater historian William Dunlap, who found him to be consumed with blazing talent but constantly battling his own demons. Several nights a week, Cooke would awe audiences with his portrayals of Richard III or Iago and then get "in his cups" and go on rampages or declaim rants that left Dunlap to remark, "What a strange animal." In the morning, Cooke would charm his way back into everyone's good graces and then repeat the cycle at night.[322] On one occasion, Cooke promised to stay inside, sober for the night, and the grateful Dunlap went to bed. His next day's diary entry begins, "The old wretch went out to his whores again as soon as I was gone." Later, he wrote that Cooke was "formed by nature for the attainment of every virtue without possessing one—I fear not one!"

But Cooke's skill as an actor was beyond doubt. Washington Irving, who experienced the agony of trying to keep Cooke sober, nonetheless called his Macbeth "sublime."

Cooke died of liver trouble in New York while stranded in the country by the War of 1812. Initially, he was interred in something known as "the stranger's vault," the meaning of which is now unclear (every historical reference to it is about Cooke). In 1821, through the efforts of actor Edmund Kean, the body was moved to its current spot, and the current monument was added, with a sculpted flame that pointed to the Park Theatre (then likely visible from the monument)[323] and featuring an original epitaph, possibly written by Kean himself:

*Three kingdoms claim his birth*
*Both hemispheres pronounce his worth.*

Of the couplet, one 1830 magazine wrote, "Expressing no opinion as to the merits of the man, or the much contested merits of the epitaph, [it] has the recommendation of being brief."[324]

But the story doesn't end here. The coffin was badly decayed, and when it was moved, Cooke's skeleton was exposed. Kean is said to have "gazed with profound emotion…and for hours lingered, mused, and quoted Shakespeare in the moonlit cemetery, making the night-breeze musical with his plaintive singing of 'Those Evening Bells.'"[325] He helped himself to one of Cooke's finger bones and took it home to England, where his horrified wife threw it away. (Dunlap later noted that Kean "exceeded [Cooke], if not in skill, certainly in depravity.")[326]

Not to be outdone, Dr. John W. Francis, who'd tended Cooke on his deathbed and supervised the removal, helped himself to Cooke's skull (it seems fitting that Francis would later be Edgar Allan Poe's doctor).

Years later, when the Park Theater needed a skull for a production of *Hamlet*, Dr. Francis loaned them Cooke's, allowing the actor to make a posthumous return to the stage to play Yorick.[327] (In most accounts, it was a night when Charles Kemble was playing the melancholy Dane in a benefit performance, which may place the date of Cooke's posthumous comeback on October 18, 1833).[328] Dunlap claimed that on his deathbed, Cooke said, "I have played every speaking part in *Hamlet*, from the prince to the grave digger; the next will be the skull."[329]

The tale became a theatrical legend. Though the story is difficult to truly verify, the *New York Mirror* told it as early as 1836, and Dr. Francis wrote about it himself. As stories of this sort go, it's remarkably well-sourced.

Dr. Francis's son eventually donated the skull to his own doctor, who donated it to Thomas Jefferson University in Philadelphia. One tooth was given to Edwin Booth; it was last said to be at the Museum of the City of New York, though the museum says it no longer has a record of it.

In the eastern portion of the section is a finely detailed brown stone with a soul effigy for Jane Spingler (circa 1732–1790, G5) that features an epitaph now difficult to read:

*Waked by the trumpet sound*
*I from the dead shall rise*
*And see the judge with glory crowned*
*And see the flaming skies*

*Arrayed in glorious grace*
*Shall saints forever shine*
*And every shape and every face*
*Be heavenly and thine*

The first four lines are from a hymn by Charles Wesley; the next are from another Wesley hymn, "And Must This Body Die," but they were rewritten, perhaps to be less gruesome. The original sixth line is "shall these vile bodies shine," and the rest of the hymn speaks of "mouldering," worms, decay and dust. Such topics were less in favor on tombstones by 1790.

## Samuel Purdy and the Great Race

The table-shaped marker beside Spingler (F3) shows the names of Sarah Purdy (1785–1813) and Samuel Purdy (1775–1836).

Purdy was the primary jockey of the horse American Eclipse, who was known as "the pride of the North" at a time when horse racing was far more popular in the South. In 1822, soon after slavery was formally delineated as a North-South issue and conflict between the regions intensified, a man named William Ransom Johnson challenged Eclipse's owner to a race against a Southern horse on a new track on Long Island for an enormous purse of $40,000. The owner accepted.

Johnson took every unfair advantage he could, scouting horses for months to find the one with the best chance against the aging Eclipse, fully determined to humiliate the North and "set straight the blind and foolish judgements of all those who dispute us." Excitement for the race was intense; newspaper reports suggested that not a man was left in Manhattan because they'd all gone to Long Island. Future president Andrew Jackson and former vice president Aaron Burr are said to have attended. Some Southerners were said to have bet hundreds of enslaved people and even their whole estates in what they saw as the final battle to establish Southern supremacy.[330]

The mere fact that Purdy was white made the race unusual to viewers from the South, where enslaved jockeys were far more common. He was nearing fifty, paunchy and stiff, and Eclipse's owner picked a different jockey for the big race. But Purdy arrived in his racing silks, just in case. He was pulled from the crowd to take over after the first heat and won the race by three lengths in the end. Congressman John Randolph had cheered hard for the Southern horse, Sir Henry, but gave a speech in praise of the victor, saying, "It required something more than human to compete successfully with Samuel Purdy."[331]

After his racing career, Purdy lived on Bowery Street and became an alderman; an obituary noted, "Although [he] was fond of the sports of the turf, he indulged in none of the vices attendant on that species of amusement; on the contrary he was a man of strict moral deportment, and in all the relations of life was beloved as a citizen and a father."[332] An inscription on the monument to him and Sarah, no longer visible, once said that it was "erected to their memories by their affectionate children."[333]

Near Purdy's marker is an arched white stone, badly faded, broken and currently patched together by metal braces (G5). Pictures from a century ago show that it was once mostly sunken into the ground. It's the grave of Lydia Stringham (circa 1783–1813), and early transcriptions give the inscription as:

> *Stranger tread lightly on this sod*
> *It covers the earthly remains of one who*
> *Was not only a wife, but the only child*
> *Of a widowed mother, and the only surviving*

*Parent of an orphan daughter*
*The duties of which interesting occupation*
*Were performed by her in a manner worthy*
*Of the emulation of an older Christian*
*She endured a long and painful illness*
*With an entire resignation to the divine will*
*And a cheerfulness of mind peculiarly her own.*
*(Oh! She was gentle, virtuous, and sincere)*
*Too pure a spirit to continue here.*[334]

Lydia was the wife of Dr. James Stringham, who taught chemistry at Columbia and may have written the blank verse epitaph.

## Sumner and Lucas

A little behind the markers of Purdy and Springler are two matching dark gray ledger stones, pushed askew by the roots of a tree beneath them. They are for two Revolutionary soldiers: John Lucas (1785–1789, I5) and Job Sumner (1754–1789, I6). The inscriptions read:

*This tomb is erected to the memory of Major John Lucas of the Georgia line of the Army of the Revolution; and Treasurer of the Society of the Cincinnati of that state. He bore a severe and lingering decay with that Fortitude which ever marked his character as a Soldier and Died in this city on Tuesday the 18th of August 1789. Aged 33 Years.*

*And this tomb contains the remains of Major Job Sumner of the Massachusetts line of the same Army. Who having supported an unblemished Character through life as The Soldier Citizen and Friend. Died in this city after a short illness universally regretted by his Acquaintance on the 16th day of Sept 1789. Aged 33 years.*

A shared couplet runs along the bottom of the two stones, though the shifting ground has knocked them out of sync:

*Alike in arms they ranged the Glorious Field*
*Alike in turn to Death the Victors Yield*

The Sumner and Lucas graves.

Lucas helped organize the Georgia branch of the Society of the Cincinnati; he had served as aide-de-camp to General McIntosh during the war.

Sumner had just started at Harvard when the Revolution broke out. He was in command of Major Andre while the treasonous major awaited execution, then ended up second-in-command of American forces when the British were evacuated from New York in 1783. When General Washington rode out from Fraunces Tavern after his farewell speech to his troops, Sumner's troops gave him his final salute.

Sumner was recalled as a good-tempered man, a lover of music who preferring hunting songs to psalms and a voracious reader of Shakespeare and Cervantes.[335] A son described him as "rather stout in person, [he] walked rapidly, bending forward and seemingly intent on some errand." But Sumner's open and trusting nature hurt him while he worked as a commissioner in Georgia after the war; he noted, "I have been robbed by almost every man I have put any confidence in."

It has often been said that both Sumner and Lucas died of yellow fever, but contemporary accounts of their deaths don't indicate as much. Of Lucas, it was said, "He bore a tedious and lingering decay with all that fortitude which his character as a soldier was strongly marked with."[336] Sumner's death the next month "was occasioned by poison received by eating a Dolphin which was taken off Cape Hatteras."[337] Vice President Adams and Secretary of War Henry Knox came to Sumner's funeral;

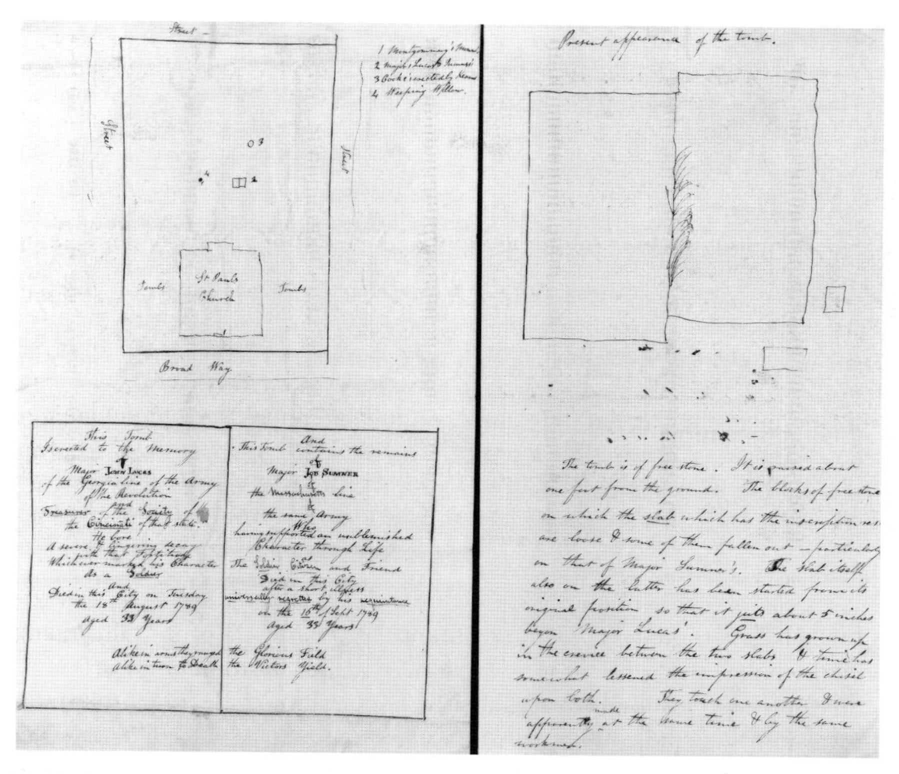


Sumner's grandson, the noted abolitionist Senator Charles Sumner, was beaten nearly to death by a proslavery senator in 1856. He visited the grave in 1829 and made this drawing of it for his father. *Harvard.*

Alexander Hamilton and Marinus Willet were pallbearers. The Society of the Cincinnati likely paid for the twin monuments.

It's hard to say whether the two men, bound together in death, ever met in life.

Walking along the southern path, at H1 and I2, are markers, one faded and one broken, for the Lambert-Browne vault. The white marble marker used to feature an epitaph added by Margaret Browne in 1861: "My Grandfather, My Grandmother, My Mother, My Father, My Little Sister, My Uncle."

Farther along the path, on the slanted top of one otherwise blank stone, one can faintly read the name "Oswald."

## THE SHAMELESS OSWALD

ELEAZOR OSWALD (1750–1795, N1) helped capture Fort Ticonderoga in the early days of the Revolution. He was captured in the Battle of Quebec and then freed in a prisoner exchange a year later to serve under John Lamb (page 52). After resigning from the army in a dispute over promotions, he launched the *Independent Gazetteer* in Philadelphia. He was a son-in-law of printer John Holt (page 194).

After attacking Alexander Hamilton in the press over the ratification of the Constitution, which Oswald opposed, the two nearly fought a duel in 1789, though mutual friends helped put a stop to it before it began.[338]

Oswald had already fought in a few duels by then. In 1786, rival publisher Matthew Carey suggested a school to teach immigrants to speak English. Oswald, who didn't approve of immigrants holding office, attacked the idea and made a point of insulting Carey's deformed leg, which he likened to a satanic cloven hove.

An Irish immigrant himself, Carey replied with a pamphlet-length poem, *The Plagi-Scurriliad*, which featured some particularly colorful and obscene insults, telling Oswald he had a "brainless head and shameless face / Devoid of smallest spark of grace." It concluded with a call for a duel (in a line that rhymed "dare say" with "Jersey").

Oswald accepted. The inexperienced Carey missed with his first shot and was shot in his deformed leg when the seasoned Oswald fired. Carey recovered, and both men issued apologies in print, as was the protocol for duels.

In 1792, Oswald commanded artillery units in the French Revolution and then worked as a spy for the French in Ireland for a time. He returned to Philadelphia to resume his journalistic career but took ill and died in New York in 1795.[339] An obituary noted, "True he was not exempt from some failings; and show me the person without them? The sun has never yet shown on such a person!"[340]

This late nineteenth-century stone replaces an older brownstone marker. Before the inscription faded, it read:

*E. Oswald, Colonel of Artillery in the American Army*
*An officer of noted intrepidity and usefulness*
*A sincere friend and an honest man. Died Sept 30, 1795.*
*Erected by his Grandson Dr Eleazor O. Balfour, Norfolk, VA*

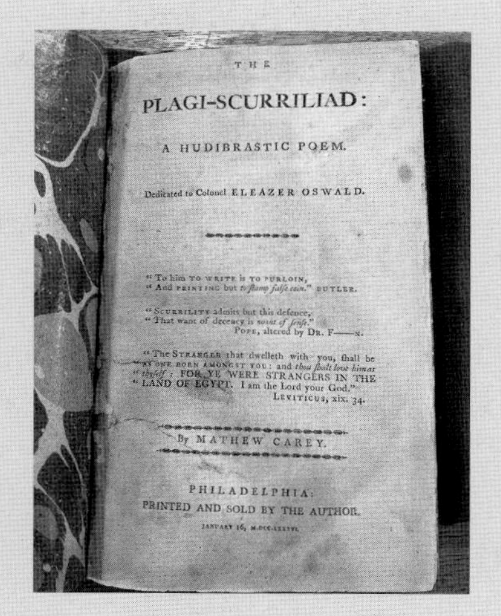

THE

PLAGI-SCURRILIAD:

A HUDIBRASTIC POEM.

Dedicated to Colonel ELEAZER OSWALD.

"To him TO WRITE is TO PURLOIN,
"And PRINTING but *to stamp false coin.*" BUTLER.

"SCURRILITY admits but this defence,
"That want of decency is *want of sense.*"
POPE, altered by DR. F——N.

"The STRANGER that dwelleth with you, shall be
"AS ONE BORN AMONGST YOU: and *thou shalt love him as*
"*thyself*: FOR YE WERE STRANGERS IN THE
"LAND OF EGYPT. I am the Lord your God."
LEVITICUS, xix. 34.

By MATHEW CAREY.

PHILADELPHIA:
PRINTED AND SOLD BY THE AUTHOR.
JANUARY 16, M.DCC.LXXXVI.

Carey's *Plagi-scurilliad* was a book-length poem challenging Oswald to a duel. Oswald accepted—and won.

There is a story that when Aaron Burr was in his final infirmity, a friend read him the section of Laurence Sterne's *Tristram Shandy* in which Uncle Toby lets a bothersome fly out the window, remarking, "This world is surely wide enough to hold both thee and me." Burr said, "If I had read Sterne more and Voltaire less, I should have known that the world was wide enough for Hamilton and me."*

It hadn't worked on Carey. In his *Plagi-Scurriliad*, he recounted the tale of Toby and the fly and then said, "Mind not fools, who say in Sterne / We might with ease and profit learn."

* J. Parton, *The Life and Times of Aaron Burr* (Mason Bros., 1857).

Carey had suggested a two-page epitaph for Oswald that began: "Inhumed beneath this stone lies...a man distinguished by a malignance and rancor, Whereof (great as is human depravity) the instances are rare."

Around the bend at the west end of the section is the large restored marker for a French engineer who found better recognition in America than at home.

## Rochefontaine

*My noble adversary, enraged at not assassinating me on the spot, was furiously asking powder of his second, "To kill," said he, "that S of a B." This was his noble expression on that occasion.*

—*Rochefontaine*

Unable to get a good position in France, Étienne Béchet, Sieur de Rochefontaine (later known as Stephen Rochefontaine) (1755–1814, U2) volunteered for Washington's army, bearing a recommendation from Benjamin Franklin. He was quickly made a captain in the corps of engineers and was sent to meet Commander Rochambeau when he arrived with thousands of French troops to aid the American cause. Rochefontaine's actions at the Siege of Yorktown earned him a promotion to the rank of major. After the war, he returned to France, but when King Louis XVI was beheaded, he fled back to America, where Washington made him chief engineer for the new government.

In 1795, Rochefontaine started the first military school at West Point, but discipline was lacking in the early days. The soldiers were little more than an unruly mob. They bristled at taking orders from a Frenchman and certainly didn't wish to attend classroom lectures as part of their training.[341]

When one young soldier, William Wilson, made a show of shouting from a window that Rochefontaine was a "damned rascal," Rochefontaine confronted him and drew his sword. Wilson (who had killed a fellow soldier in a duel a year before) called for his own sword and then admitted that he wasn't good with swords and requested pistols instead. They met with their firearms fifteen minutes later.

When neither managed to hit the other on a first shot, even from standing just a few steps away, Rochefontaine believed the affair was settled. But Wilson insisted he was still due satisfaction and that another duel must be fought, so Rochefontaine wrote to Alexander Hamilton for advice. Hamilton's response does not survive, though perhaps his intervention prevented another encounter. The matter apparently blew over.[342]

Anti-French sentiment in the John Adams administration forced Rochefontaine into retirement in 1798. Perhaps tired of fleeing from one army that unjustly distrusted him to another, he settled in New York, where he seems to have lived quietly until his death in 1814. His daughter built his original monument of marble with a brick core; the marble was replaced with granite in the 1950s.

Facing the section from the northeast corner, one can see one of the more legible markers, that of John Boardman (1752–1795) and Mercy Boardman (circa 1757–1811, B7), featuring a couplet that does not express an unusual sentiment but appears to be original:

*O death how bitter is thy sting*
*That age and youth to dust doth bring*

Along the north path, several rows back, are three brownstone graves, the most legible of which is for James Targay Jr. (circa 1773–1795, K13), containing two verses of a Wesley hymn. Beside his marker and to the right is that of his father, James Targay Sr. (circa 1737–1805, K14). His inscription, now worn away, read:

*From death no age nor no conditions save*
*As goes the freeman so departs the slave*
*The chieftain's palace and the peasant's bower*
*Alike are ravaged by this haughty power.*[343]

The verse had been published in an 1803 newspaper commemorating the death of a boy named Freeman, which made the second line a pun.[344] Little is known of Targay, but city records show that at a common council meeting in 1787, "James Targay, laborer," was respectfully admitted and sworn "a freeman of this city," a rank granting him special rights replacing the old Dutch "burgher" and accounting for why the poem was picked for Targay's epitaph. It wasn't the same pun, but it was still a pun.

Nearby is the marker of Captain Cornelius Swartwout (circa 1733–1787, J8). The stone has been broken for decades, but it once read:

*He took an early and active part in the service of his country and justly merited the character of a brave and good officer, particularly at Fort Montgomery and at the siege of Yorktown, in Virginia. His remains were interred with military honors, much regretted by every officer and his fellow citizens.*[345]

# MICHAEL MCLACHLAN

In the northwest corner of the section are two ledger stones, one of which is broken into two pieces. The other (V13) features a worn carving of a castellated tower once circled by the words "Fortis et Fidus" ("Strong and Faithful"), the Clan MacLachlan crest. It used to bear the following inscription for MICHAEL MCLACHLAN (CIRCA 1745–1802):

> *Here lies Michael McLachlan, a native of Scotland, who in infancy was made an orphan by the rebellion of 1745. He resided many years in the Island of Jamaica, and during the latter part of his life in this city. Died 1802.*[346]

The Jacobite uprising of 1745 was an abortive attempt by Charles Edward Stuart to attack Scotland (while most of the English army was busy on the European continent) and place his father, the Catholic James Francis Edward Stuart (page 18), on the throne. The attempt was soon aborted, but not before many of the Stuart-supporting MacLachlan Clan were killed at the Battle of Culloden. In one account, Michael's mother escaped to Jamaica while pregnant with him.

Records show that he served with the British in the French and Indian War and then sided with the Revolutionaries. In New York, he amassed a fortune as a brewer.[347] He is likely the M. McLachlan who, in 1793, placed advertisements for the capture of an enslaved man named Guy, who worked as a cook and washer "as he understands each equal to any woman." It is not known whether Guy was ever found.[348]

After Michael's death, his wife, Jane, married one of his employees, Phillip Garniss, who was soon taking out advertisements accusing her of having *several* husbands and warning people not to sell her any gin or snuff on credit.[349] Late in life, Jane reverted to the name McLachlan and exchanged letters with Aaron Burr, who denied owing her any money, and reminded her that "you once lost an estate by the unguarded use of your tongue."[350] (Or, as his character in the musical might say, "Talk less, smile more.")

Jane and Michael's son, ALEXANDER MCLACHLAN (CIRCA 1797–1819, V14), whose resting place is marked by the broken stone next to Michael's, was only about five years old when his father died, but he inherited his property. This kept the family in reasonable wealth, whatever estate Jane may have lost.

Their daughter, Julianna, married David Gardiner of Gardiner's Island. Her own daughter, Julia, was twenty-four when she married fifty-four-year-old President John Tyler in 1844, after which she became a vocal advocate for slavery. First Lady Tyler occasionally came up in the news in the early twenty-first century when people were amazed to learn that two of her and President Tyler's grandchildren—great-great-grandchildren of Michael McLachlan—were still living.

## Lost Markers in C2

There was once a marker for tinsmith Dewsbury Crawley (circa 1764–1815), which read:

*Soft was the hand and gentle was the blow*
*That summoned Crawley from this Vale below*
*Death like an angel came and beckoning stood—*
*His willing soul took wing and soared to God*

An 1868 article described the stone as a "marble slab, half buried in the sod, moistened by so many storms."[351] Kelby's 1875 transcription suggests no particular shape, and it was apparently gone or illegible by 1897.

The epitaph was taken from a long poem, "An Elegy Occasioned by the Death of the Rev. Dr. Gifford, Who Fell Asleep in Christ, the 19th of June, 1784, in the Eighty-Fourh Year of His Age," by Maria De Fleury, a London Baptist poet. De Fleury dove headfirst into the religious controversies of her day and argued that women's right to free speech was God-given. Of course, in the poem, she used the name Gifford, not Crawley.

There was also a marker for Catherine Owens (circa 1784–1808), which included a religious verse in Welsh below an English epitaph; an 1875 sketch shows a "tree of life" image in the stone's tympanum. The epitaph was still legible enough to transcribe in 1897:

*This monumentary testimony of true affection is erected by Henry George, in memory of Catharine Owens (his intended bosom companion), who suffered long affliction with patience and resignation.*

Someone also painted "My Mother" onto an otherwise blank grave, apparently copying the then-famous grave at Trinity (page 42). In 1861, it was said to be a small marker close to Cooke's.[352]

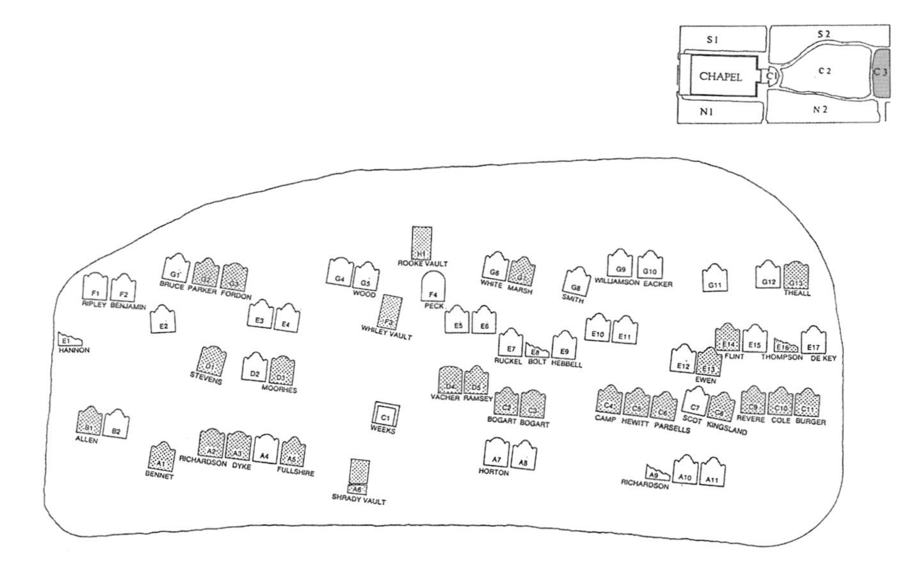
S1
S2
CHAPEL
C1
C2
C3
N1
N2
H1
ROOKE VAULT
G1
G2
G3
BRUCE
PARKER
FORDON
F1
F2
RIPLEY
BENJAMIN
E2
E1
HANNON
G4
G5
WOOD
F3
WHILEY VAULT
F4
PECK
E3
E4
E5
E6
G6
G7
WHITE
MARSH
G8
SMITH
G9
G10
WILLIAMSON
EACKER
G11
G12
G13
THEALL
E7
E8
E9
RUCKEL
BOLT
HEBBELL
E10
E11
E12
E13
EWEN
E14
FLINT
E15
E16
THOMPSON
E17
DE KEY
D1
STEVENS
D2
D3
MOORHES
D4
D5
VACHER
RAMSEY
C2
C3
BOGART
BOGART
C4
C5
C6
CAMP
HEWITT
PARSELLS
C7
C8
SCOT
KINGSLAND
C9
C10
C11
REVERE
COLE
BURGER
B1
B2
ALLEN
A1
BENNET
A2
A3
A4
A5
RICHARDSON
DYKE
FULLSHIRE
C1
WEEKS
A6
SHRADY VAULT
A7
A8
HORTON
A9
A10
A11
RICHARDSON

# SECTION C3

Section C3 runs along the western central edge of the churchyard; it is bisected by four underground vaults. Today, it runs alongside Church Street; there were once buildings backing up to it, including Trinity offices and apartments. They were torn down when the street was widened during subway construction in the 1920s. During work building the tunnel the previous decade, the ground in the graveyard sank fifteen inches, and many stones were moved out of position. They were presumably fixed.

Among the monuments facing the path in C3, near the section's southeast corner, is that of MERREN BENNET (DIED 1805, A1). The prose epitaph is vaguely legible:

*Consider this mourning parents and*
*Dry up your tears. Why should you lament*
*Your little ones are crowned with victory before*
*the storm of adversity was begun. O, remember,*
*They are not lost but taken away from the evil to come*

This passage is adapted from a paragraph of *Meditations Among the Tombs*, a popular 1746 book by English "graveyard school" poet James Hervey. It was influential for the gothic movement and for poet William Blake, who based paintings on it.

## "Our Client Levi Weeks Is Innocent"

Three of the four vaults bisecting the section, the Shrady, Wiley, and Rooke vaults, are marked with common vault stones. Perpendicular to most of the upright gravestones in the section is an upright stone marking the vault of architect Ezra Weeks (circa 1771–1849); his wife, Elizabeth Weeks (circa 1774–1826); and their children (C1). The Weeks were at the center of the Manhattan Well Mystery of 1800, the best-documented murder trial of the era.

In late December 1799, a woman named Elma Sands left her house and vanished. On January 2, as the 1800s dawned, she was found dead at the bottom of a well in what is now SoHo. Ezra's brother Levi was accused of impregnating and promising to marry her, then murdering her and throwing the body into the Manhattan Well.

Levi claimed that he'd been at Ezra and Elizabeth's house the night Elma disappeared, and Ezra hired the unlikely duo of Alexander Hamilton and Aaron Burr to team up to defend his brother in court at Federal Hall. Transcripts show that court language had not totally evolved from the days when New York was a part of the Church of England: the state charged that Levi had murdered Elma "[without] the fear of God before his eyes, but being moved and seduced by the instigation of the devil."

At one point, either Burr or Hamilton supposedly came to believe that one of the witnesses was the real killer, held two candles to his face and shouted, "Behold the murderer, gentlemen!" It became a famous anecdote; Burr later claimed he'd pulled the dramatic maneuver, and Eliza Hamilton said it was Alexander, but records don't establish that the candle incident happened at all. Elizabeth Weeks's testimony that Levi had been at her home that night and seemed relaxed was more crucial to his acquittal.

One legend, in print since at least 1872, says that Elma's cousin pointed at Hamilton and cursed him as Levi was freed, shouting, "If thee dies a natural death I shall think there is no justice in heaven."[353]

Ezra was a successful builder who worked on Grace Mansion the year before the trial and on Hamilton Grange shortly after. The brick Manhattan Well can still be seen in the basement of 129 Spring Street, which is currently a clothing store, where it has inspired numerous ghost stories.

## Dr. Vacher

North of the Weeks's marker is a restored monument to John Francis Vacher (1751–1807, D4). The French-born Vacher accepted the Marquis de Lafayette's request to come to America as a surgeon for Washington's army, where he served for several years, even though he was once tried (and acquitted) by court-martial for "using menacing language to his colonel."

In 1791, Baron Von Steuben responded to a letter in which Vacher had sent him lyrics to a French song and, apparently, an apology for all sorts of personal foibles. Steuben assured Vacher that he held him in high esteem: "I know my [foibles] and require that my friends look upon them with indulgence. Justice demands reciprocity. Such men as have more virtues than weakness are estimable beings in my eyes."[354] Vacher's original letter does not survive, so we can only imagine what foibles he was apologizing for.

Vacher was a charter member of the Society of the Cincinnati and wrote letters to Thomas Jefferson that could be described as fan mail. Following the war, he practiced medicine on Fulton Street.

The French inscription translates to "Good father, unique object of their loves, his desolate children will always mourn him."

## George Eacker: "I Expect to Hear from You"

> *Ecclesiastical influence, in the hands of* [political] *faction, is an instrument more dreadful than the dart wielded by death!*
>
> —*George Eacker, July 4, 1801*

In 1801, it may have seemed odd to see a Fourth of July oration from a man too young to remember 1776. Yet the speech George Eacker (circa 1774–1804, G10) made was enough of a hit to be published. It also may have gotten him into a duel.

Eacker was a promising young lawyer who'd supported Thomas Jefferson in the recent election; one person who knew Eacker wrote that he was "violent and bitter" in his politics.[355] In his fateful speech, he made some dire warnings about the influence of religion on government, presumably a response to the Hamilton-led Federalists accusing Jefferson of not being religious enough. "All the modern nations of Europe testify the havoc produced by hierarchical tyranny!" he roared. "Its abuses ultimately destroy the veneration due to true religion, and its holy advocates are the fruitful sources of immorality and crime."

Alexander Hamilton was never mentioned by name, though a few lines probably alluded to his financial policies. One letter to a newspaper written in response said that it wasn't uncommon for public speakers to engage in hyperbole, but in saying that Federalists had nearly ruined the country "with intention to injure the best characters," Eacker had gone too far.[356] The letter was signed only "A"; it's possible that it was Hamilton himself gently scolding the young lawyer.

Altogether, though, it's difficult to imagine that four months later, Hamilton's son would still be full of righteous rage over the speech.

On November 20, the Park Theatre presented a 1771 comedy called *The West-Indian* and a musical panto called *Obi; or, Three-Finger Jack*.[357] Phillip Hamilton and future Park Theatre owner Stephen Price (pages 72, 86, 214 and 232) found themselves seated behind Eacker and began making fun of him.

When Eacker called the two "damned rascals," he could have simply been annoyed that they were being obnoxious during the play. *The Evening Post* said that Phillip and his friend "began in levity a conversation respecting an oration delivered by [Eacker] in July," but the *Post* was, after all, a Federalist paper, launched by Phillip's father and friends barely a week before.[358] Editor James Cheetham (page 177) of the *American Citizen* said the *Post*'s account was a "premeditated misstatement of facts," and the *Post* responded that Cheetham was a "base wretch."[359] It's possible that both were correct: the *Post* really *was* trying to cast Phillip as valiantly defending his father's honor more than he really was, and Cheetham really *was* a base wretch.

In any case, Eacker calling the two "damned rascals" led to a formal challenge with each. The next Sunday, Eacker and Price met in New Jersey, where each fired four shots without causing harm. In a duel with Phillip the following day, Eacker fired first and landed a fatal hit.[360]

A later account said that Eacker suffered intense remorse, and "life became a misery to him" to such an extent that he began working recklessly as a volunteer firefighter, trying so hard to lose himself in the dangerous work that he made himself sick.[361]

Eacker died of tuberculosis barely two years after the duel. Cheetham wrote, "Few men have quitted this sublunary scene of bustle and anxiety with a fairer reputation."[362] His fiancée later married Robert Fulton, who may share a vault with Phillip Hamilton's aunt Angelica (page 165). One can still very faintly make out Eacker's name on the headstone; the full monument read, "In memory of George Eacker, who departed this life on the twenty-fourth day of January, in the year of our lord 1804, aged 29 years."

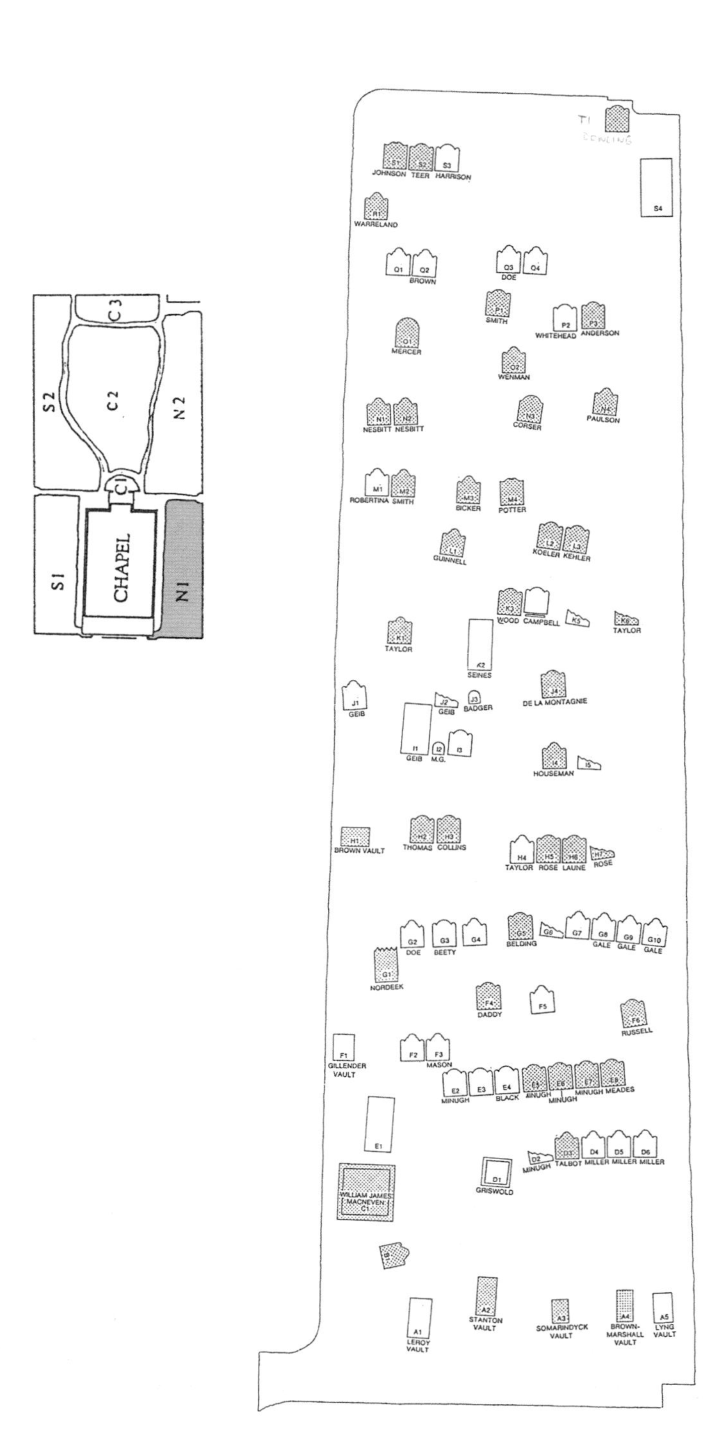
C3
S2
C2
N2
C1
CHAPEL
S1
N1
T1
S1 S2 S3
JOHNSON TEER HARRISON
S4
R1
WARRELAND
Q1 Q2
BROWN
Q3
DOE
Q4
P1
SMITH
P2
WHITEHEAD
P3
ANDERSON
O1
MERCER
O2
WENMAN
N1 N2
NESBITT NESBITT
N3
CORSER
N4
PAULSON
M1 M2
ROBERTINA SMITH
M3
BICKER
M4
POTTER
L1
GUINNELL
L2 L3
KOELER KEHLER
K3
WOOD
CAMPBELL
K5
K6
TAYLOR
K1
TAYLOR
K2
SEINES
J1
GEIB
J2
GEIB
J3
BADGER
J4
DE LA MONTAGNIE
I1
GEIB
I2
M.G.
I3
I4
HOUSEMAN
I5
H1
BROWN VAULT
H2 H3
THOMAS COLLINS
H4 H5 H6 H7
TAYLOR ROSE LAUNE ROSE
G2
DOE
G3
BEETY
G4
G5
BELDING
G6
G7
G8 G9 G10
GALE GALE GALE
G1
NORDEEK
F4
DADDY
F5
F6
RUSSELL
F1
GILLENDER
VAULT
F2 F3
MASON
E2
MINUGH
E3
E4
BLACK
E5
MINUGH
E6
MINUGH
E7
MINUGH
E8
MEADES
E1
D2
MINUGH
D3
TALBOT
D4 D5 D6
MILLER MILLER MILLER
D1
GRISWOLD
WILLIAM JAMES
MACNEVEN
C1
B1
A1
LEROY
VAULT
A2
STANTON
VAULT
A3
SOMARINDYCK
VAULT
A4
BROWN-
MARSHALL
VAULT
A5
LYNG
VAULT

# SECTION N1

Section N1 is the northeast section of the churchyard, fronting Broadway and Vesey Street. The most visible vault marker lies in the corner near Broadway and is the vault of a gambler and fight promoter.

## John R. Lyng

John R. Lyng (1820–1888, A5) probably wasn't the first to call people "suckers," but he was certainly a pioneer in the field. During an 1855 trial, he used the term for people who were easy to beat at cards, and the press referred to it as his "signature" word for years.[363] P.T. Barnum, who operated the museum across the park, is often credited with coining the phrase "There's a sucker born every minute," but the actual origin of the phrase is hotly disputed; Lyng probably could have claimed it and surely would have if it could have made him any money.

Lyng was a distinguished member of The Fancy, the subculture of bare-knuckle boxing enthusiasts who haunted both low-down gambling halls and upscale resorts. The Fancy weren't known to behave well in any surroundings; in 1859 at Delmonico's, Lyng pulled out a revolver and threatened to shoot a man named Figzy over some old dispute. He might have done it, according to a reporter, but for the intervention of "several persons who were averse to blood, brains, and the smell of villainous saltpeter."[364]

The Lyng vault marker.

It was just another night in the life of "Old Johnnie Lyng." He'd been a pugilist, a card player, the keeper of a disorderly house, and a firefighter in the days when firefighting companies were extensions of street gangs. He was associated with the famous 1842 bare-knuckle fight between Lilly and McCoy that went 120 rounds and ended with someone—reportedly Lyng himself—carrying McCoy's dead body away.

On the night when Bill "The Butcher" Poole, the gang leader, was fatally shot, his assassins ran to Lyng's tavern at Broadway and Canal Street. Lyng was briefly jailed for helping Lewis Baker, one of the suspects, escape and was a witness at Baker's eventual trial.

Lyng was baptised at St. Paul's in 1820 and was known to brag that he'd one day rest under Broadway. Though it's tempting to imagine that he won the vault in a card game or something, it appears that his paternal grandfather, silversmith John Burt Lyng, had built it over a century before; he presumably would have been interred there when he died in 1785, but there's no record of it. Likewise, John's father, Jandine Lyng (1764–1724), who sold a concoction called Jandine's Family Salve, may have been interred there in 1828. But as of 1888, when John R. Lyng died, the vault was said to contain only the remains of a child (two Lyng children were interred somewhere at St. Paul's in 1809 and 1815). Of course, it's possible that no trace of the senior Lyngs' remains were left by 1888.

By the time of his death, Lyng and his fellow members of The Fancy were seen as relics of a long-lost past, but his interment in a vault at St. Paul's made national news. The opening of a tomb so close to Broadway was fairly rare by then, and one story at the time held that Lyng's grown son only learned of his father's death when he came upon the funeral party in the churchyard by chance.[365]

The large marker near the church (C1) is a monument to William Macneven, an Irish patriot and chemist. It serves as a counterpart to the obelisk on the other side of the church for his friend, the Irish hero Thomas Emett. Like Emett, Macneven was not buried here; his remains are in Queens.

In between the Lyng vault and the Macneven monument, the large white urn-topped marker is for Elizabeth Huntington Griswold (1793–1822, D1), and it once identified her as "wife of Mr. John Griswold, merchant, of this City, and daughter of General Zachariah Huntington of Norwich, Connecticut."[366] A woman who knew Elizabeth in school recalled she was "earnest in her studies, and in the recesses for play, our leader....The sensation of fatigue was unknown to her. Together we scaled the ledges of gray rock...and knitted at the same time, with primitive simplicity, our own stockings."[367] She moved to New York after marrying Griswold.

To the right of Elizabeth's marker is a broken white stone for John W. Minugh (1802–1819, D2), one of several Minugh children who were buried nearby. The faded stone once said that John "Unfortunately perished on board the ship America stranded on Sandy Hook, Dec 13, 1819."[368] When the *America* began to sink, Second Mate Minugh, Captain Vibberts and half of the crew jumped into a lifeboat, but the mainmast fell. One report said it "struck the boat and dashed it to atoms, and, shocking to relate, every person in it perished."[369]

Next to John's marker is a brown stone (D3) on which the inscription once read:

*In memory of* CAPTAIN WILLIAM HENRY TALBOT, *late of the 17th Regiment Light Dragoons, who departed this life March 6, 1782, aged 37 years.*[370]

Though this marker is often listed and even decorated as an American soldier's grave, Talbot was part of a British regiment that fought alongside the notorious "Bloody" Banastre Tarleton.[371] There is a rumor that he married Sarah Wilson, an indentured servant who stole jewels and a dress from Queen Charlotte and used them to pass herself off in the colonies as "Princess Susanna," the queen's sister. Historians are doubtful of the supposed marriage, but good con artists seldom leave a simple trail behind.[372]

Walking along the southern edge of the section, west of the Macneven monument, is a flat stone for CHARLES NORDECK (CIRCA 1755–1782, G1). Featuring a carved crest, it reads "In memory of CHARLES NORDECK, Baron zur Rabenau, Captain in the Hessian Regiment De Ditfort who departed this life Novr. 30th 1782 age 27 years."

Despite Nordeck's title of nobility and military rank, little is known of him. An obituary merely says, "Last Saturday night died of a consumptive [tuberculosis] disorder, Captain De Rabenau, of the Regiment Dittfort—His Friends sincerely lament his Death; and the Military regret the Loss of a fine Officer."[373] The stone was refurbished at the request of a mysterious anonymous donor in 1929.[374]

Along the path between the fence and the church, there are matching monuments for MEHITABLE NESBIT (CIRCA 1748–1807, N1) and DR. SAMUEL NESBIT (CIRCA 1746–1811, N2), a prominent physician and druggist. Mehitable's epitaph is in prose:

*She was an affectionate wife, a kind parent*
*And an humble follower of the blessed Jesus*
*Under a full persuasion of whose prevailing*
*Merits she calmly resigned her spirit*
*to GOD*

A solitary marker by the south fence marks the resting place of James Warreland (circa 1775–1808, R1), with the same verse from Pope's "Elegy to an Unfortunate Lady" ("How loved, how valued") seen on John Smith and Elatha Dale's markers (page 191).

Along the fence on the Vesey Street side, only a tiny stub remains of the grave of Matilda Rose (1772–1801, H7). It read:

*As those we love decay we die in part*
*String after string is sever'd from the heart,*
*Til loosen'd life at last, but breathing clay*
*Without one pang is glad to fall away.*[375]

It came from the poem "On the Death of Mr. Aikman," by James Thompson, who is best known for writing "Rule, Brittania."

## John Geib: The Organ Maker

*I found out sence in London, that it takes op a long while before a man is Knowing in a Strange Country, withouth Recommentation, and happens often, that the best Artist are lost for vand of it, therefore I ame most a frait to unter take Soch a jurney with out it.*

*—John Geib, requesting letters of recommendation from Benjamin Franklin, 1783 (spelling preserved)*

In the middle of the section are two white box-style graves. The one closest to the fence is John Geib Jr. (circa 1779–1821, I1). The faded white marker beside it, near the path, is that of his father, John Geib (1744–1819, J1). Geib Sr. was an organ and piano builder best remembered for inventing the "grasshopper" mechanism that made keyboards more dynamic.

The best data about his early life comes from a letter Geib wrote to Benjamin Franklin in 1783, in which he describes being raised as an instrument maker and tells how he'd left Germany for America but stopped in London and stayed until the war was over. Now, he wanted someone prominent to write him a letter of recommendation, and Franklin was the most famous American he would have known of. It's not known whether Franklin offered his assistance.[376]

When Geib exhibited an eight-hundred-pipe organ for the Lutheran church on William Street, an advertisement read that "the builder flatters himself that the fullness and melodiousness of its tone, together with the neatness and durability of the work, and particular new movement, which renders the touch so easy as to be playable by a child, cannot be excelled."[377]

Several of the organs he built are still extant.

The box grave near Geib Jr.'s is for MOISE MENDES SEIXAS (OR SEINAS) (CIRCA 1751–1817, K2). The inscription, no longer legible, gave his birth and death dates in French.

Moise (or Moses) is said to have been a relative of Gershom Mendes Seixas, the city's first American-born Jewish religious officiant. Some early writers who wrote about the churchyard were puzzled about how a Jewish

A worker on a lunch break reclines against the now-faded grave of John Geib, circa 1910. *Library of Congress.*

person came to be buried at St. Paul's, though one account says Seixas became an Episcopalian when he arrived in New York from France in 1794.[378] An obituary merely states that he died of "a long and painful illness."[379] He is easily confused with the Moses Mendes Seixas, a brother of Gershom, who wrote a letter to George Washington held by the St. Paul's Church in Rhode Island.

C3
S2
C2
N2
C1
S1
CHAPEL
N1

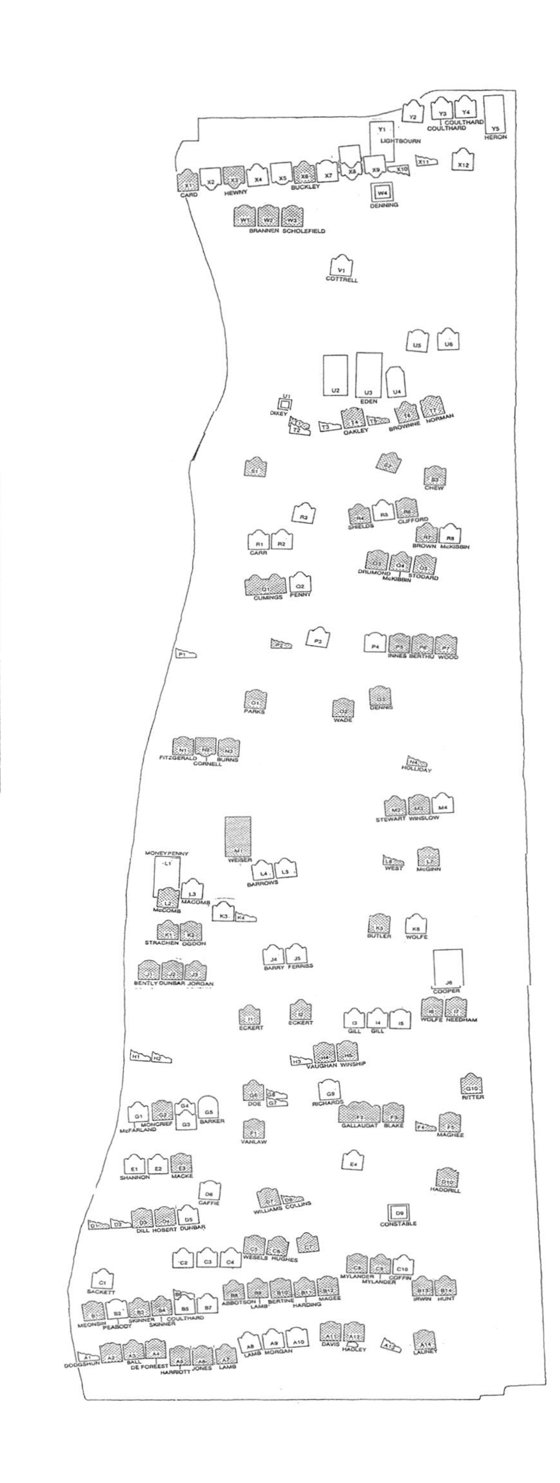

# SECTION N2

Section N2 is in the northwest corner, fronting Vesey Street. In the first row, visible when standing between N1 and N2, is a well-preserved marker with a soul effigy for James Davis (circa 1730–1769, A11), a blacksmith for the Royal Artillery.

A few markers to the left is John Jones (1764–1768, A6), who has a relatively common epitaph:

*O most cruel suden* [sic] *death that*
*Did take his harmless breath but*
*The lord hath thought it best*
*To take his soul with him to Rest*

In some older mentions of this grave, the words "his harmless" were transcribed as "her husband's," leading writers to guess that the epitaph was written by John's wife, though John was certainly not married. He was, after all, only a toddler.

Behind Jones is a broken marker (B6) for Maria Coulthard (1787–1810) that was found under the center aisle of the chapel in 1962, where it had been placed "for reasons unknown."[380] It was likely initially placed near the stone of brewer Isaac Coulthard (circa 1726–1812, Y4) on the opposite corner of the section.

On the left-hand side of the second row of graves is a stone for Eziral Mwnin (circa 1761–1796, B1) (spelled "Meonsin" in parish records). The inscription is legible, but the last line is often covered by grass. It reads:

*Go home my friends and cease*
*Your tear, I must lie here till*
*Christ appears*
*Repent in time while time you haiv* [sic]
*There's no repentance in the grave*

The epitaph is seen on a few gravestones elsewhere, though none are so oddly spaced, and none probably use the odd spelling of "have" to make it rhyme with "grave."

The middle of the second row includes the grave of ALEXANDER LAMB JR. (1805–1810, B9), whose now-buried epitaph appeared on a number of graves from the era and is notable for the use of a pun:

*As such a flower is from the garden gone*
*Who could have pluckt it but the Lord alone*
*Be silent grief; though lovely here he grew*
*He's now transplanted to a garden new*[381]

Still extant behind Alexander's stone is a marker for BETHUEL WILLIAMS (CIRCA 1782–1807, D7). The name is still visible, but the epitaph is gone. It once read, "No mortal care or grief shall ever tempt his mind."[382]

A few rows in is a pointed white monument (D9) on which the name "Constable" can be faintly made out.

## WILLIAM CONSTABLE

*We are mad for India trade.*
*—William Constable*

When lawyer Ogden Edwards first saw WILLIAM CONSTABLE (1751–1803) at a dinner party that included Hamilton and Burr, he wrote that "even in such good company, all eyes and ears were turned to [Constable], and he appeared to be the master spirt [*sic*]."[383] Constable wasn't a politician, but he was incredibly well connected, a close friend or business partner of seemingly every famous name of the era. His children married into the Livingston and Pierrepont families.

Born in Dublin, Constable took on the American cause and served as an aid to Lafayette in the war. Afterward, when the Crown could no longer expect colonists to respect the East India Company's monopolies on many goods from the far east, he became one of the first Americans to trade with China and India. He lost money on the Asian trade in the end, but through land deals and supplying the British army in the West Indies, he built up a massive fortune. He's perhaps best remembered for commissioning one of Gilbert Stuart's famous Washington portraits.

Though most histories of him focus on his business dealings and how much land he owned, by all accounts, Constable was the life of every party. Ogden Edwards recalled him as "a man of sound comprehension and fruitful mind, of high-toned feelings and vivid imagination. He saw clearly, felt keenly, and expressed himself pungently." One man even noted that even though he'd never met Constable, "Such was his appearance that [I] felt as though [I] should be pleased to pass a day in his company."[384] As Constable was an international trader of his era, though, it will come as no surprise that he enslaved people; he sent one enslaved man, named Adam, to live in the almshouse to get free care for his frosted feet.[385] Letters survive in which Constable muses about how much money could be made importing and selling people.[386]

His wife, Ann White Constable (1762–1826), was a childhood friend of the future Martha Washington.[387] William and Ann lived for a time in a townhouse on the site that would eventually hold the Astor House Hotel, right next to St. Paul's. It would have practically overlooked their eventual grave.

Along the south fence of N2, there is a particularly large concentration of intact headstones, many with legible inscriptions. Most of them have relatively common epitaphs for their era.

A white box grave, nearly worn away, is for John Moneypenny (circa 1779–1821, L1), who was in the scouring and dyeing business at Greenwich and Chambers Streets; his wife and sons carried on the business after his death.[388]

Nearby is the box grave (M1) of Jacob Weiser (circa 1745–1785), which read:

*Farewell vain world I know enough of thee*
*And now I'm careless what you say of me*
*Your smiles I court not nor your frowns I fear*
*My Cares are part my head lies quiet here*
*What faults you saw in me, take care and shun*
*And Look at Home Enough there's to be done.*

A *New York Leader* article in 1861 chuckled that Weiser must have been a man "for whom the world had no smile."[389] The bitter poem appears to be original and was later published in a number of epitaph collections. Little is known of Jacob, though probate records indicate that he was a shoemaker.

Beyond Weiser's marker lies the grave of Giles Parks (circa 1756–1792, O1) of London; it features the common epitaph from Alexander Pope's "Elegy" ("How lov'd, how valu'd") (page 128) below the legend "This stone is erected by one who knew his worth and still laments his loss."

People who "knew his worth" may have been in short supply; such records of Giles that exist are mostly of him getting in trouble—he was once tried for larceny and indicted for running a "disorderly house."[390] In 1789, he was fined ten pounds for "harboring loose women."[391] One can read the epitaph in different ways: Does the one who erected the stone still lament his loss long because of his great worth, or think little of his worth but lament his loss in spite of it?

Nearby is a blank white stone (Q2), its inscription long obliterated. It is a marker for John Penny (circa 1793–1823), a native of England. His epitaph was frequently transcribed when it was legible:

*No kindred sigh, nor soft parental tear*
*Soothed thy pale form or graced thy mournful bier*
*With strangers was thy dying trust reposed*
*By strangers hands thy dying eyes were closed*
*By strangers is thy humble grave adorn'd*
*By strangers honor'd and by strangers mourn'd*

This is taken from another portion of Pope's "Elegy to the Memory of an Unfortunate Lady," which, so close to the more common lines on Giles Parks's grave, would have made this a veritable Alexander Pope section. The original uses "foreign" in some places where the epitaph uses "strangers." One can surmise from the epitaph that Penny was a visitor in the city, though an obituary, which blames his death on "a short but severe illness," indicates that he had friends and family in New York.[392]

## John Dixey, the Sculptor

The conical-shaped white marker toward the back is for John Dixey (1763–1820, U1). The faded inscription read, "To the memory of John Dixey, sculptor by profession. Native of Dublin and a member of the Royal Academy London, who arrived in this his adopted Country 1789."

John Dixey was best known as a sculptor but worked in other fine arts, such as painting and paper-staining as well. One obituary said he was "by occupation a carver…by profession a sculptor." At his looking glass shop on William Street, he offered mirrors, frames, figures, building ornamentations and artwork of all sorts.

From his newspaper advertisements, it's apparent that Dixey did a good trade in portraits and busts of Hamilton following Hamilton's death and then had another small boom selling portraits of Captain Lawrence (page 21) when Lawrence died.[393]

Other advertisments Dixey took out in papers show a lot about the culture of apprenticeship in his era. Teenagers would start apprenticeships at around fourteen, and until about twenty-one, they'd be bound to a "master" who taught them a trade and paid in room and board. Apprentices who'd learned enough to get work for pay would sometimes run away before their contract was up. Dixey took out several advertisements looking for runaways, offering rewards and stating, "All persons are cautioned against employing him, as they shall answer it at their peril."[394] His rewards usually ranged from five to twenty dollars, though in 1816, he offered just one cent ("and no charges") for the return of one William Wood.[395]

Upon his death, Dixey was noted for having "a mind well stored with knowledge that has proved useful to his adopted country, a cheerful disposition…and affability that endeared him to an extensive audience." It was hoped that his example would "induce those desirous of such regard to go and do likewise."[396]

# MEDCEF EDEN

Nearby are two white box graves that appear half-sunken into the ground.

One (U3) is that of MEDCEF EDEN (DIED 1798), a Golden Hill brewer who made hopped ale and spruce beer during and after the Revolution.[397] He was helped by people he enslaved, who, judging from advertisements, escaped frequently, including a teenager named Bill, and a Guinea-born man named Limas who was "scarred on his face with the country mark" and who "when in liquor talk[ed] silly."[398] Eden died of yellow fever; his will said an enslaved man named Hagar would go to his wife and be freed upon her death, with many others to be freed at various times. One, Hannah Palmer, was to be freed immediately and given a $100 per year annuity; court records show she later married a man named Griffin.[399]

Besides his brewery, Eden owned a farm that stretched several blocks in what is now Midtown and Hell's Kitchen. There was a dispute over his estate based on changes and nuances between the old English and new American property laws (just the sort of issue John Coghill Knapp, page 205, warned about). Hamilton and Burr sparred in court over the estate, with Burr representing the family's side and losing. In 1803, the Astors bought the land for about $25,000.

Years later, after much travel and mischief, the cash-strapped Burr convinced Eden's heirs they still had a case and got them to hire him again. The Medcef Eden case was full of strange turns; Burr brought in future president Martin Van Buren as an assistant (later fueling rumors that Burr was secretly Van Buren's father), and Medcef Jr.'s 1819 will stated that if any of his stepdaughters "should marry without the consent of my friend Aaron Burr, she shall forfeit her share" of the estate.[400] The case wasn't decided until more than thirty years after Eden's death. The family won, but it's possible that only Burr made much money out of it.

The large rectangular block monument near the western edge (W4) still faintly features the name of WILLIAM DENNING (1740–1819), a merchant. It once read:

> *To mark the spot most sacred and interesting to his children where the remains of William Denning are deposited A tender affectionate parent, a*

*benevolent indulgent friend, An enlightened liberal disinterested Patriot In full possession and active employ of his mind this valuable and virtuous life terminated without pain.*

It also noted,

*Elizabeth Denning Rosetta M. Denning Sisters, taken from their afflicted family in the bloom of youth....Buried near their grandfather.*

William came from the island of Antigua, where family stories say that he was treated so brutally by a stepfather that he stowed away aboard a ship to Canada, where he became an apprentice to a New York merchant.[401]

After making his own fortune, Denning served on several state and local bodies, including the Committee of One Hundred, which met in 1775 to form armed resistance to Britain's continuing Intolerable Acts. He was elected to the U.S. House of Representatives in 1808 but resigned without ever taking his seat. No one seems to know why he never claimed the office, but it may be related to the fact that his wife died right after the election—or the fact that he seemed to walk into accusations of scandal all the time. In April 1808, he wrote, "It is to be regretted that every sentiment of social intercourse and sometimes actual friendship are to be sacrificed to gratify political rancour."[402]

Library records show that he was a voracious reader, checking out over four hundred volumes in a five-year period.[403] Manumission records show that he freed three enslaved people, Primus, John and Sylvia, in 1800.

His granddaughter Rosetta Denning (1812–1819) died about a week after William did; her sister Elizabeth Denning (died 1820) died less than six months later.

## Lost Markers in N2

A stone for John Queen Jr. (1786–1817) simply read, "Here lies the remains of an honest man."[404]

The box grave beside Eden's (U2) is not identified but is a good candidate for a lost monument that was transcribed in 1830 but illegible or missing by 1897. According to the old article, newspaper editor John Crookes (circa 1768–1818) had a marble slab in the northwest corner, and it must have been a large one. It read:

> *Sacred to the memory of John Crookes, many years editor of the* New-York Mercantile Advertiser, *who died June 27, 1818, aged 50 years. Actuated by the tender charities which adorned his life, his heart was ever accesible* [sic] *to the tale of suffering humanity; and, in sympathizing with its distress, like the good Samaritan, he passed it not by, till his hand had administered that practical benevolence which best proves the law of kindness*
>
> *"Some weep in perfect justice o'er the dead."*[405]

The last line is adapted from "graveyard school" poet Edward Young's "Night Thoughts," which was published in 1745 with illustrations by William Blake.

Though so many publishers were known to be combative, a memorial poem about Crookes said, "Mild were your manners, and your chief delight / to cherish friendship, and act whate'er was right."[406]

There was also a marker that gave the date of death as "1084." It was a favorite of Rector Morgan Dix, who joked that those who assumed it was a typo for 1804 were of "that school which delights in finding solutions for every thing mysterious." He said it was very near the rail on the north side of the yard, about three-fourths of the distance west from the porch.[407] An 1868 article said the name on the marker was EDWARD HARRISON (CIRCA 1744–1804), though records don't confirm such a burial that year.[408]

# MONUMENTS INSIDE THE CHAPEL

Several memorials are built in and around the chapel. The most prominent is the one by the front doors.

## Richard Montgomery

The handsome and magnetic Richard Montgomery (1738–1775) rose through the ranks of the British army in the French and Indian Wars and then took up life as a civilian. He married into the anti-British Livingston family, which pretty well required him to cement his long-held feelings that the colonies should be independent of the Crown. He set up a farm in Rhinebeck and reportedly said he was "never so happy in all my life" before adding "it cannot last."

When the Continental army was formed in June 1775, Montgomery was made a general. One of the new army's first actions was launching an invasion of Quebec in an effort to persuade the French to join in the fight on the American side.

Montgomery's forces took control of Montreal in November, which made him one of the war's first heroes. John Hancock wrote him a letter, congratulating him on "exploits so glorious" that they would be remembered forever.

The Montgomery monument. He is likely buried under the porch.

In December, his forces joined with Benedict Arnold's to attack Quebec City. Montgomery led the charge, shouting, "Men of New York, follow your general!" He was killed in the battle and given a burial with honors by the British; early stories that Aaron Burr attempted to recover his body from where it lay helped build Burr's reputation, even though they probably weren't true (page 38).

Weeks later, Congress voted to have a monument to Montgomery made and advanced £300 to Benjamin Franklin to have one created in Paris. Most likely sculpted by Jean Jacques Caffieri (who sculpted a bust of Franklin as well), the monument was shipped first to North Carolina to avoid capture during the war. It was the first monument ordered by the United States government.

Lewis Livingston, a nephew of Montgomery, went to Quebec to retrieve the body in 1818. A soldier who'd seen the burial pointed out the spot. A report at the time said, "The coffin which contained the remains had not fallen to pieces. It appears to have been of a rough structure, with a silver plate on its lid—there is no inscription visible on the plate. The anatomy is a perfect state of preservation. The skeleton of the head, with the exception of the jaw, which was shot away, is perfect."[409]

Satisfied that the bones were the right ones, Livingston had them transferred to a mahogany coffin with a new silver plate. Montgomery's widow watched the steamship carrying the remains down and wrote, "When the steamboat passed…the splendid coffin canopied with crepe and crowned with plumes, you may conceive my anguish. I cannot describe it."[410] Like Eliza Hamilton and Julia Lawrence, she survived her husband by half a century; she was buried in Rhinebeck.

The new coffin was buried, with great ceremony, in the ground below the monument. Matthew Clarkson (page 70) was a pallbearer.[411]

Near the altar inside, beneath which her remains were buried, is a marker for Elizabeth Franklin (1728–1778). Born in Barbados to a wealthy sugar planter, Elizabeth married William Franklin, the son of Benjamin Franklin and an unknown mother. William became the royal governor of New Jersey in 1763. After clinging to power longer than most colonial royal governors, William was forced into exile in Connecticut in 1775 (a move his father voted for), leaving Elizabeth alone at home. Accustomed to luxury, in her reduced circumstances, she moved to Loyalist-friendly New York and wrote to her father-in-law asking him if he could arrange for William to join her. Dr. Franklin did not respond, though he did send her money.[412]

When Elizabeth died in 1778, the still-exiled William was not permitted to attend her funeral but drew up a sketch for the memorial tablet. His bitterness can be clearly read in the inscription:

> *Compelled, by the adverse circumstances of her times, to depart from the husband she loved, and at length deprived of the soothing hope of his speedy return, she sunk under accumulated distress.*

William was freed in a prisoner exchange later that year and moved to occupied New York, where he remained a Loyalist leader and actively tried to interfere with his father's efforts to negotiate a treaty after the war (page 176). The monument was installed in 1787, by which time William had moved to England.[413] He and his father had one brief meeting there to tie up business matters but never truly reconciled.

## SIR JOHN TEMPLE

A tablet in the entryway commemorates the first consul for "His Brittanic majesty." Born in Noddles Island, near Boston, JOHN TEMPLE (1731–1798) served as lieutenant governor of New Hampshire and then spent most of the Revolution in Great Britain. He took the side of the rebels and lobbied hard to be allowed to return, but Congress didn't trust him and repeatedly rejected his requests. After the war, he was appointed the first British consul to the United States in 1785.

The next year, upon the death of his father, a baronet, he assumed the title of Sir John Temple. The title may have worked against him. According to nineteenth-century retellings of the anti-doctor riots of 1788 (page 98), he was nearly attacked when the half-literate mob read the name "Sir John Temple" on his door and believed it said "Surgeon Temple."

# UNKNOWN BURIALS

## Richard Coote, Lord Bellomont

*You will see in the middle of the inventory of a parcel of* [Captain's Kidd]*'s treasure and jewels delivered by Mr. Gardiner of Gardiner's Island...the recovering of which treasure is owing to my own care and quickness.*

—*Lord Bellomont, letter to the Board of Trade*[414]

Richard Coote, first Earl of Bellomont (1635–1701), may be the earliest-born person interred at St. Paul's, having died several decades before it was built.

Bellomont was said to have killed a man in a duel over the affections of a woman in his youth, but the woman in question *wasn't* Catherine Nanfan, his eventual wife, whom he married in his forties (her age at the altar is variously given as having been between eleven and fifteen). In Parliament, he helped clear Jacob Leisler's name (page 118) and then was made governor of New York (and several other colonies) in 1697, with special instructions to crack down on the pirates who operated freely in the area at the time.

Having decided that the best way to combat pirates was to hire a someone to capture their ships, he engaged Captain William Kidd, a former privateer. Kidd had married a wealthy widow, making him one of New York's largest property owners, and even contributed to the construction of Trinity

Church. Now, he felt the call of the sea again (or perhaps his new governor persuaded him that he didn't have much of a choice) and was sent off to battle pirates. The British government was leery of funding the voyage, so Bellomont invested in it privately and directed Kidd to prowl known pirate hangouts far from New York, which wouldn't really help the stated goal of combating local piracy as much but would yield more profit.

The voyage was a failure, and rumors swirled that Kidd was resorting to actual piracy to keep his crew, who were to be paid in plunder, from a mutiny. Bellomont decided to turn against Kidd before being accused of piracy himself. The captain was arrested in Boston, and Bellomont wrote to the Board of Trade that Kidd had offered to retrieve some hidden treasure in exchange for a pardon. Some treasure was retrieved from Gardiner's Island, and Bellomont's letters suggesting that Kidd had alluded to *more* stashes of riches have been pored over by treasure hunters ever since.

Though modern historians tend to believe Kidd was largely innocent—and certainly not deserving of his later reputation as a bloodthirsty buccaneer—he was hanged in London.

In between writing himself into pirate history, Bellomont worked on colonial relations with the Abenaki and Iroquois tribes, largely unsuccessfully. He died of gout in 1701 and was buried under the old chapel at Fort George, near Bowling Green.

In 1790, the ruins of that chapel were demolished to make way for a mansion for George Washington. Several skeletons were discovered, as were three stone vaults, one of which contained Lord Bellomont's lead coffin, apparently marked as such by a silver plate. Next to his was another lead coffin, initially presumed to be that of his wife, though it was soon learned that she died far later in England, having married three more times.

The skeletons were brought to the "Charnel House" at Trinity; Bellomont's coffin and the mysterious second lead coffin were reburied in an unrecorded spot within St. Paul's Churchyard.[415] As the nation's capital was moved to the District of Columbia before the mansion was finished, Washington never moved in, and the structure became known as the Government House.

Tales spread over the next century that Bellomont's coffin plate was eventually made into teaspoons. Indeed, there were later stories that the Government House was haunted and that the coffin plate spoons were later stolen by a "night thief" and sold off one by one to buyers who had no idea that they carried a terrible curse.

It was a legend written only long after the reburial, but if you're feeling unlucky, you might wish to check your silverware drawer.

# Midshipman Price

John Price was a midshipman on the British HMS *Poictiers*, a seventy-four-gun ship used as part of a blockade against the United States in the War of 1812. Sometimes, the ship would send out smaller ships attached to it, such as the tender *Eagle*, to rob local fishermen and burn the coaster ships that sailed between ports.

In 1813, U.S. commodore Lewis arranged to borrow a fishing boat, the *Yankee*, and put men dressed as fishermen on the deck, along with a cow, a sheep and a goose. The *Eagle*, staffed by about a dozen, chased it down and called out an order for it prepare to be plundered. Once it sailed close enough, someone on the *Yankee* shouted the code word "Lawrence!" at which point around thirty armed soldiers jumped from the cabin and attacked, capturing the *Eagle* and its crew.

The captured ship and its crew were brought to Whitehall in time to be seen by cheering crowds at a Fourth of July celebration.[416] "Thus was the lamb preserved," wrote one historian, "and the proud and cunning men of Britain outwitted with a fatted calf and a Yankee goose."[417]

Price was mortally wounded in the attack, a fact that Lewis noted he was sorry to report in his letter to the secretary of the navy.[418] He died in a hospital in New York and was buried at St. Paul's with military honors that were "due to the memory of a brave enemy."[419]

# Elizabeth Hazard (and Other People of Color Known to Be Buried at St. Paul's)

Rules about the burials of Black individuals at St. Paul's are even more nebulous than those at Trinity (page 178). A number of burials of people of color have been identified, but ethnicity was not recorded in burial records, making it particularly difficult to know how many there might have been.

Among the most intriguing of these individuals is a man listed only as King, a "free Negro" (circa 1722–1803). New York manumission records show only one man named King, with no last name, who was given his freedom by Declaration of Independence signer Francis Lewis, who was buried at Trinity several months before King died (page 100). The paperwork in that case specified that King would be freed upon Lewis's death, so if this is the same man, his freedom lasted only from January to July.

Another is Elizabeth (or Betsy) Hazard (1719–1818), whom the burial registry noted was "99 years, 9 months, and twelve days" old. A death record shows that she was born in Rhode Island and lived on Fulton Street.[420]

There is an obituary for Hazard, which says she was a member of the Episcopal Church for sixty-seven years and that "her conduct through the whole course of her life was eminently pious, and she died in full assurance of a happy state in the world to come."[421] This doesn't tell us much, really, and another woman of the same name who died in New York in 1811 complicates the search for more information about her.

Isabella Williams (1740–1818) was buried on September 15, 1818. Her name is also common enough to make reliably connecting stories of people of that name to her a challenge. A death record shows that she was born in New Jersey and lived on Barclay Street.

The other known burials of people of color at St. Paul's include:

Joseph, age five, died of scarlet fever on February 3, 1801.
An unidentified child, eight months old, died of "fits" on February 25, 1801.
An unidentified woman, eighty-three, died of "decay" on May 29, 1801.
An unidentified child, six months, died of "fits," on August 19, 1801.
An unidentified child, three, died on January 18, 1803.

# OTHER LOWER MANHATTAN GRAVEYARDS

Though Trinity and St. Paul's are the best-known of the extant graveyards in lower Manhattan, there are a few others, which will be featured in a future volume. These include:

**New York Mable Cemetery and New York City Marble Cemetery**
This pair of small lower East Side cemeteries, both consisting entirely of marble vaults, opened after in-ground burials were stopped. President James Monroe was initially interred in the New York City Marble Cemetery on Second Street; like so many in this book, he nearly fought in a duel with Hamilton. A grandson of Hamilton died in an accident while serving aboard the ship that transported Monroe's body to Virginia.

**St. Patrick's Old Cathedral**
Construction on this Mulberry Street church began in 1811, and burials began there two years later. Between the graveyard and the catacombs, some thirty-two thousand burials were noted over the next twenty years.

**St. Mark's in the Bowery**
A graveyard consisting almost entirely of vaults, burials at St. Mark's include the Stuyevant tomb, the now-empty vault of merchant A.T. Stewart (whose bones were famously stolen and held for ransom) and recent memorials to writers such as Sam Shepard and Allen Ginsberg.

**Shearith Israel**
An extant burial ground used by the city's first Jewish congregation, near what is now Chinatown.

# SOME LOST BURIAL GROUNDS

Several other graveyards in the area were built over or turned into parks during the nineteenth century. In most cases, an attempt was at least made to move remains to new cemeteries, though bodies continue to be found at some sites. In cases such as Bryant Park and Washington Square, little or no attempt to move bodies seems to have been made at all.

**The African American Burial Ground**
Just north of city hall, this was the primary burial place for Black New Yorkers in the eighteenth century. It was nearly forgotten until construction uncovered remnants in the late twentieth century.

**St. John's Burying Ground**
Managed by Trinity until the late nineteenth century near Greenwich Village, the site is now Walker Park. The headstones were buried when the graveyard became a park. The parish offered to move bodies on the request of family members; the small handful of handwritten requests they received are preserved in the Trinity Archives, many from people who only believed that they might have family there. Often, they were incorrect. Few removals took place.

**"Old Graveyard"**
West side of Broadway near Morris Street and Bowling Green, replaced by what is now the north churchyard at Trinity.

**Dutch Church**
North side of Exchange Place, between Broad and William Streets. Destroyed in a fire.

**French Church**
Northeast corner of Nassau and Pine Streets (1704–1830).

**Presbyterian Church**
North side of Wall Street on the opposite end of New Street (1717–1844).

**Middle Dutch Church**
East side of Nassau Street from Cedar to Liberty Streets (1729–1844).

**Brick Church**
Beekman Street between Chatham and Nassau Streets (1768–1856).

**North Dutch Church**
William Street between Fulton and Ann Streets (1769–1875).

**Spring Street Presbyterian**
Northwest corner of Spring and Varick Streets. The vaults were active from 1820 to 1846.

**St. Luke-in-the-Field**
Hudson Street between Christopher and Barrow Streets. The vaults were used from 1821 to 1852, and the bodies were moved in 1891.

**Carmine Street Cemetery**
Adjacent to St. John's, Carmine and Clarkson Streets. The burial ground was active from 1808 to 1846, and the bodies were moved in 1869.

**Lutheran Burial Ground**
Southwest corner of Broadway and Rector Street, across from Trinity. Once this land was purchased by Trinity to build the first Grace Church, the bodies were moved circa 1805. By some accounts, it went as far south as Bowling Green. In 1897, during the construction of a new skyscraper on the site, bones were found deep underground.

**Potter's Field**
The eastern portion of what is now Washington Square Park. The burial ground was active from 1797 to 1820.

# NOTES

## *Preface*

1. Mines.
2. "A Brooklynite in NY Churchyards," *BDE*, July 7, 1846.
3. *Documents of the Assembly of the State of New York*, vol. 69 (Albany, NY: Carroll and Cook, 1846), 31.
4. "Sacrelige," *NYP*, February 15, 1838.
5. "Old New York," *NYTr*, February 10, 1890.

## Part I

### *Introduction: Trinity Church*

6. "279 Peppercorns Used to Pay Debt to England," *The Reporter Dispatch*, July 8, 1976.
7. "Queen Liz Is Dubbed a New Yorker," *New York Daily News*, July 10, 1976.
8. John Flavel Mines (as Felix Oldboy), "Who Was Charlotte Temple?" *Frank Leslie's Popular Monthly* (November 1890).
9. Strong.

## *Sections S1-A and S1-B*

10. *NYA*, September 9, 1807.
11. *NYA*, September 10, 1807.
12. Broke to Lawrence *Weekly Register*, September 11, 1813.
13. Afidavit of Benjamin Trefethen, 1869.
14. Robert Ludlow Fowler, "The *Chesapeake* and Lt. Ludlow," *Magazine of American History*, April 1891.
15. Ludlow to Ludlow, June 24, 1813.
16. "The Illustrious Dead," *The Pennsylvania Gazette*, September 22, 1813.
17. "Monument to Captain Lawrence," *NYS*, March 19, 1830.
18. *Sunday Dispatch*, December 7, 1845.
19. "A Beautiful Monument," *NYE*, March 24, 1847.
20. "Brooklynite," *BDE*; "Lawrence's Monument," *New York True Sun*, November 5, 1845.
21. *Weekly Museum*, September 18, 1813.
22. List of people made freemen of the city, 1744.
23. "New York," *NYJ*, April 28, 1768.
24. "Fashion," *The Crayon*, November 1765.
25. Burnet Landreth to Trinity Church, January 5, 1926.
26. Notes of Miriam Silverman, Trinity Archives.
27. *NYM*, January 6, 1755.
28. Mines.
29. *New York Columbian*, May 19, 1819.
30. *NYAm*, June 17, 1825.
31. "Snobs," *NYAt*, March 28, 1847.
32. 1839.
33. Ibid.
34. *NYT*, August 14, 1855.
35. Thomas Egleston, *The Cause and Prevention of the Decay of Building Stone* (American Society of Civil Engineers, 1886).

## *Section S1-C*

36. 1980s Trinity database.
37. "Died," *NYA*, October 15, 1801; Advertisement, *NYA*, October 22, 1801.
38. John Kippax, *Churchyard Literature* (Chicago, IL: SS Griggs and Co., 1877).

39. Claire Bellerjeau and Tiffany Yecke, *Espionage and Enslavement in the Revolution* (Lyons Press, 2021).
40. *NYG*, July 28, 1783.
41. Strong.
42. "Obsequies of Mrs. Hamilton," *NYH*, November 12, 1854.
43. *NYAm*, July 31, 1829.
44. Walt Whitman, *Life and Adventures of Jack Engle: An Autobiography* (University of Iowa Press, 1852).
45. Pollock.

## *Section S1-D*

46. "Liveliest Cemetery in Town," *NYSu*, June 5, 1904.
47. *Suffolk Gazette*, October 12, 1807.
48. Francis.
49. Cynthia Own Philip, "Robert Fulton, Genius Ahead of His Time," *Hudson River Valley Review* (Autumn 2007).
50. Francis.
51. "The Robert Fulton Memorial," *Scientific American*, December 21, 1901.
52. J.A. Scoville, *Old Merchants of New York* (Carleton, 1865).
53. J.E. Quinlan, *History of Sullivan County* (G.M. Beebe and W.T. Morgans, 1873).
54. "Last of the Old Beaux Gone," *NYH*, November 15, 1859.
55. J.A. Scoville, *Old Merchants of New York* (Carleton, 1865).
56. "Washington," *NYH*, March 3, 1843.
57. "Last of the Old Beaux," *NYH*.
58. *NYMa*, June 11, 1891.
59. "Buried in Trinity Churchyard," *BDE*, June 14, 891.
60. Benjamin Moore, letter to Mr. Coleman in "Monitorial Department," *The Balance*, July 24, 1804.
61. "Died," *Commercial Advertiser*, September 27, 1798; Advertisement, *Commercial Advertiser*, May 22, 1797.
62. "Died," *Commercial Advertiser*, September 24, 1798.
63. Will of David Ogden.
64. Isaac Leake, *Memoire of the Life and Times of General John Lamb* (1850).
65. Obituary, *New York American Citizen*, June 3, 1800.
66. "Petition," *Columbian Gazette* (Washington, D.C.), February 10, 1807.
67. *NYG*, September 3, 1818.

68. *NYT,* October 25, 1875.
69. Scoville, *Old Merchants.*
70. *NYH*, March 26, 1854.
71. 1897.
72. 1868.

## *Section S2*

73. William Digby, *The British Invasion of the North.*
74. Advertisement, *NYA*, August 8, 1771.
75. NYSL.
76. Maitland Armstrong, *Day Before Yesterday* (Scribners, 1920).
77. *Acts of the General Assembly of the State of South Carolina From Dec 1795 to Dec 1804*, vol. 2 (J.J. Faust, 1808).
78. *Letters of Robert Mackay to His Wife* (UA Press, 2010).
79. Slidell file, Trinity Archives.
80. *NYG*, October 1, 1770.
81. Burial registry, Trinity Archives.
82. Abraham Helffenstein, *Pierre Fauconnier and His Descendants* (privately published, 1911).

## *Section S3*

83. *Boston Transcript*, June 18, 1850.
84. Obituary, *NYH*, June 23, 1850.
85. Ibid.
86. *NYAt*, August 11, 1850.
87. Jerome Mushkat, "Matthew Livingston Davis and the Political Legacy of Aaron Burr," *New York Historical Quarterly* (April 1975).
88. *NYA*, February 26, 1838.
89. Quoted in *Jacksonville Republican*, March 29, 1838.
90. "Meeting to Oppose Slavery," *NYP*, November 17, 1819.
91. "Commemoration by the Africans," *NYS*, July 10, 1827.
92. Strong.
93. *Burlington Weekly Sentinel*, November 29, 1861; *Kansas Tribune*, January 1, 1865.
94. Marian Gouverneur, *As I Remember* (Appeton and Co., 1911).

95. *NYT*, May 10, 1915.
96. *NYT*, January 18, 1884.
97. *NYT*, January 18, 1884.
98. Will of William Brownejohn; Obituary, *New York Packet*, October 6, 1785.
99. A.V. Phillips, *The Lott Family in America* (1942).
100. Daniel Aaron, "The Greatest Diarist," *American Heritage*, March 1988.
101. Strong.
102. Dates from Gautier file, Trinity Archives.
103. *NYP*, February 26, 1750.
104. 1897.
105. Luther Martin, *Modern Gratitude* (privately published, 1902).
106. "Men and Things of the Past," *Sunbury Gazette*, January 24, 1857.
107. "Communication," *Baltimore Federal Gazettte*, November 21, 1807.
108. Ibid.
109. *NYP*, October 29, 1807.
110. *New York News*, reprinted in *New Albany Daily Ledger*, November 28, 1856.
111. Strong.

## *Section S4*

112. Nathan Schachner, "Alexander Hamilton Viewed by His Friends," *The William and Mary Quarterly* (April 1947).
113. John Church Hamilton, *History of the Republic of the United States* (Appleton, 1857); Michael O'Brien, *Hercules Mulligan* (P.J. Kennedy, 1937).
114. *NYJ*, November 2, 1774.
115. "To the Honorable of the Senate…," *NYA*, March 14, 1786.
116. *Freeman's Journal*, May 16, 1787.
117. O'Brien, *Hercules Mulligan.*
118. *NYG*, May 8, 1775.
119. "Legislative," *NYJ*, March 14, 1776.
120. "The Late Stephen Price," *Morning Herald*, January 22, 1840.
121. "The Late Stephen Price and His Father," *Morning Herald*, February 4, 1840.
122. Barnard Hewitt, "King Stephen of the Park and Drury Lane," in *The Theatrical Manager* (Princeton, 1971).
123. 1839.
124. *New York Express*, October 9, 1874.
125. Charles Winfield, *History of the County of Hudson* (Kennard & Hay, 1874).

126. "The Late Stephen Price," *NYH*, January 22, 1840.
127. *NYH*, August 12, 1846.
128. 1839.
129. "Shipping News," *Commercial Advertiser*, October 9, 1820.
130. 1897.
131. *NYA*, October 2, 1805.

## *Section S5*

132. *Mercantile Advertiser*, September 11, 1810.
133. Jill Lepore, *New York Burning* (Knopf, 2007).
134. Note in Stirling file, dated 1903, Trinity Archives.
135. Aaron Burr, to Joseph Alston, November 20, 1815.
136. Washington, to Lady Stirling, January 20, 1773.
137. William Duer, *The Life of William Alexander Earl of Stirling by His Grandson* (New York: Wiley and Putnam, 1847).

## *Section N1A*

138. "Restoring Trinity's Stones," *NYP*, May 22, 1907.
139. Scott to Gates May 16, 1778.
140. Adams to Morse December 2, 1815.
141. William Marinus Willet, *Narrative of the Miliary Actions of Colonel Marinus Willet* (G. & C. & H. Carvill, 1831).
142. Dorothy Rita Ditton, *The New York Triumvirate* (Columbia University Press, 1948).
143. *New York Packet*, September 16, 1784.
144. *New York Gazetteer*, July 21, 1775.
145. S.D. Nevets, "Historic Characters," *Potter's American Monthly* (July 1877).
146. *NYG*, September 22, 1796.
147. James Thatcher, *American Medical Biography* (Richardson & Lord, 1828).
148. Richard Harris, "Laporotomy...," *American Journal of the Medical Sciences* (October 1878).
149. *National Advocate*, November 9, 1822.
150. *Mercantile Advertiser*, November 1, 1810.
151. Washington, to Frederick Jay, August 16, 1775.
152. 1871.

153. *NYG*, June 15, 1747.
154. Julia Delafield, *Biography of Francis Lewis and Morgan Lewis* (Randolph, 1877).
155. Jefferson to Meriwether Lewis, January 22, 1804.
156. NYSL.
157. *Register of the Empire State Society of the Sons of the American Revolution* (1899).
158. *NYG*, March 30, 1805.
159. 1830.
160. "Charlotte Temple," *Albany Journal*, November 13, 1869.
161. Mines, "Who Was Charlotte Temple?"
162. C.J. Hughes, "Buried in the Churchyard: A Good Story, at Least," *NYT*, December 12, 2008.
163. *New York Weekly Post Boy*, September 2, 1745.
164. 1897.
165. *NYA*, October 27, 1787.

## *Section N1B*

166. *NYP*, May 15, 1749.
167. *NYP*, November 20, 1749.
168. 1871.
169. "New York," *NYP*, August 27, 1745.
170. *Weekly Journal*, September 23, 1734.
171. *NYA*, June 3, 1794.
172. *Loudon's Register*, October 3, 1794.
173. "Letter from New York," *Mining Record* (Pottsville, PA), September 3, 1859.
174. *Argument of Edward Sanford, Esq.* (New York: Baker and Goodwin, 1854).
175. "Trinity Church," *NYT*, December 2, 1854.
176. "To the Editor," *The Churchman*, June 10, 1854.
177. "War Dungeons of the Revolution," *NYT*, February 14, 1855.
178. Will of Anthony Ackley, 1775.
179. 1871.

## *Section N2*

180. *NYG*, May 23, 1798.
181. Mines.

182. *Advertiser*, July 2, 1799.
183. Sarah Breese Walker, *Personal Reminisces* (privately printed, 1884).
184. Ibid.
185. Advertisement, *New York Weekly Postboy*, January 27, 1752.
186. *An Act for the Payment of the Debts*, April 1, 1756.
187. Walker, *Personal Reminisces*.
188. Advertisement, *New York Gazette*, May 16, 1763.
189. Genealogical records.
190. 1897.
191. "Trinity Church," *NYP*, March 13, 1875.
192. *NYT*, August 14, 1855.

## *Section N3*

193. "Things Wise and Otherwise," *Harper's Weekly*, September 5, 1857.
194. "Charles Venables," *NYA*, November 20, 1792.
195. "From the Indian Country," *NYA*, October 18, 1793.
196. Jacob Lindley, "Expedition to Detroit, 1793," in *Friends' Miscellany* (1836).
197. Pickering to Washington, October 15, 1793.
198. Autumn Whitefield-Madrano, "Treaty of Canandaigua Remains a Powerful Symbol of Native Sovereignty," ICT News, September 13, 2018.
199. William Dunlap, *History of the American Theatre* (London: Bently, 1833).
200. James Grant Wilson, *Memorial History of the City of New York*, vol. 4 (New York History Company, 1893).
201. Advertisement, *Pennsylvania Gazette*, September 13, 1759.
202. William Sangster, *Umbrellas and Their History* (Cassell, Petter and Galpin, 1871).
203. *Valentine's Manuel of New York* points to this spot, and "Buried Centuries Ago," *Buffalo News*, May 29, 1899, notes that it's near Nelson.
204. "Arrived," *Commercial Advertiser*, October 16, 1805.
205. "Highway Robbery," *NYP*, September 1, 1806.

## *Section N4*

206. "Shipping News," *NYM*, November 14, 1757.
207. "New York," *NYG*, September 20, 1762.

208. Nan Rothschild, "Digging for Food in Early New York City," in *Gastropolis*, edited by Jonathan Deutsch and Annie Hauck-Lawson (Columbia Universtiy Press, 2009).
209. Charles W. Bair, *History of the Huguenot Emigration to America*, vol. 2 (Dodd, Mead, 1885).

## *Section N5*

210. Neau to Hodges June 22, 1704.
211. Elias Neau, *An Account of the Sufferings* (privately printed, 1699).
212. Translated from Neau to Chamberlain, August 24, 1708.
213. Ibid., July 24, 1707; Ibid., July 22, 1707.
214. Ibid., October 3, 1705.
215. Neau to Hodges June 22, 1704.
216. Neau to Chamberlayne, July 11, 1711.
217. Davis Humphreys, *An Account of the Endeavors Used in the Society for the Propagation of the Gospel in Foreign Parts to Instruct the Negro Slaves in New York* (1768).
218. Anne Fontaine Downs Richter, "I Sing Night and Day: The Spiritual Songs of Elias Neau" (master's thesis, University of the South, 2023).
219. Pollock.
220. Will of William Taylor, 1721.
221. Janine Skerry, *International Silver and Jewelry Fair Handbook* (1992).
222. John E. Tourette, "Pastor Pierre Peiret and Family," http://www.latourrette.net/pastor_peiret.html.
223. Abram English Brown, *Faneuil Hall* (Lee and Shepard, 1900).
224. Michael O'Brien, *In Old New York: The Irish Dead in Trinity and St. Paul's Churchyards* (American Irish Historical Society, 1928).
225. *American Aurora*, November 3, 1798.
226. William Sullivan, "The Rising of 1798 and the Political Foundation of Irish Identity" (master's thesis, College of William and Mary, 2005).

## *Section N6*

227. *Mercantile Advertiser*, June 29, 1803.
228. *NYG*, December 22, 1777.
229. Edward Winslow Martin, *Secrets of the Great City* (Philadelphia, PA: Jones Bros and Co., 1868).

230. *An Account of the Free-School Society of New-York* (Collins and Co., 1814).
231. *Biographical Register of the Saint Andrew Society of the State of New York*.
232. David L. Johns, *Convincement and Disillusionment: Printer William Bradford* (Kent State University, 1992).
233. Elizabeth Bradford, in preface to *War With the Devil* (1705).
234. "The Bradford Commemoration," *New York World*, May 21, 1863.
235. Isaiah Thomas, *History of Printing in America*, vol. 2 (1810).
236. Jefferson, to John Henry, December 31, 1797.
237. Robert G. Parkinson, "From Indian Killer to Worthy Citizen: The Revolutionary Transformation of Michael Cresap," *William and Mary Quarterly* (January 2006).
238. Letter, *Virginia Gazette*, November 17, 1775.
239. Parkinson, "From Indian Killer to Worthy Citizen."
240. Mines.
241. Advertisement, *NYG*, October 7, 1771.
242. "City Graves 200 Years Old," *NYSu*, July 5, 1885.

## *Section N7*

243. "Historic Trinity Building Chapel," *NYT*, June 7, 1964.
244. Hannah Gallatin, to Dolley Madison, August 12, 1816.
245. "Alexander Hamilton's Unfought Duel of 1795," *Pennsylvania Magazine of History* (July 1954).
246. Strong.
247. Henry Adams, *Life of Albert Gallatin* (1849).
248. "George Drummond," *Chicago Tribune*, September 19, 1885.
249. Charles Bird, "In Memory of Lord Drummond," *BDE*, August 14, 1887.
250. "Buried Far from Home," *BDE*, August 7, 1887.
251. *New York Diary*, September 2, 1794.
252. J. Brooke, *History of Parliament 1754–1790* (1964).
253. "Died," *The American Minerva*, September 3, 1794.
254. Mrs. William Jones, "Catherine Schuyler," *American Monthly Magazine* (February 1898).
255. Advertisement, *NYG*, February 18, 1771.
256. "Dead Man's Lane," *NYTr*, February 8, 1854.
257. Obituary, *NYG*, July 22, 1745.

## *Burials in the Church*

258. William McVickar, *Life of the Rev. John McVickar* (Riverside Press, 1872).
259. 1868.
260. Adams's diary, August 25, 1774.
261. "New York," *NYM*, August 4, 1760.
262. Advertisement, *Weekly Journal*, January 12, 1735; David Horsman, *New York Conspiracy Trials* (transcript).
263. Kathleen Staples and Madelyn Shaw, *Clothing Through American History* (Greenwood, 2013).
264. "Hermit's Letter," *Fall River Globe*, October 10, 1904.
265. William L. Stone, "The Administration of Lord Cornbury," in *The Memorial History of the City of New York*, vol. 2 (New York History Company, 1892).
266. John Sharp, *A Sermon Preached at Trinity Church in New York in America, August 13, 1706, at the Funeral of the Right Honourable Katherine Lady Cornbury* (printed by William Bradford, 1706).
267. Stone, "Administration of Lord Cornbury."
268. Diary of Philip Hone.
269. Diary of William Byrd.
270. *NYG*, May 26, 1740. (Though numerous sources give Anne's death year as 1760.)

## *Known Burials, Unknown Graves*

271. Pennington court-martial.
272. "New York," *NYG*, September 29, 1777.
273. Richard Fitzpartrick, to Lady Ossory, October 26, 1777, in *The Letters of Horace Walpole*, vol. 7 (London: Richard Bentley, 1858).
274. James Gordon, to George Washington, May 27, 1782.
275. Alexander Hamilton, to Harry Knox, June 7, 1782.
276. *NYP*, September 20, 1802.
277. *American Citizen*, April 23, 1804.
278. "A Warning to Libelers!" *American Citizen*, April 25, 1804.
279. *NYP*, September 20, 1810.
280. Mines.

# Part II

## *Introduction: St. Paul's*

281. Morgan Dix, *Historical Recollections of Trinity Church* (1867).

## *Section S1*

282. Sarah's birth year is sometimes given as 1764.
283. George Warner Nichols, *Miscellanies* (Bridgeport, CT: Marigold Printing Co., 1893).
284. *Report on American Manuscripts in the Royal Institute of Great Britain: Aug 1779–June 1782* (London: John Falconer Printer, 1906).
285. Polly Hoppin, "The Thomas Swords Family," Saratoga NYGenWeb, http://www.saratoganygenweb.com/swords.htm.
286. Washington, to Nathanael Green, October 7, 1779.
287. Bailey to George Washington, April 17, 1790.
288. 1861.
289. "Some Famous Heiresses," *St. Paul Globe*, February 3, 1889.
290. "The Social Sin of William Rhinelander," *NYSu*, July 19, 1914.
291. Holt to Wm Goddard, February 26, 1778.
292. Thad W. Tate, "The Negro in Eighteenth Century Williamsburg," *Colonial Williamsburg Foundation Library Research Report Series* (April 1957).
293. Alen Dyer, *A Biography of James Parker, Colonial Printer* (Troy, NY: Whitston Publishing, 1982).
294. Ibid.
295. James Parker to Jared Ingersoll, July 2, 1769, Ingersoll Papers, NHCHS; Adams's diary, August 25, 1774.
296. Thomas, *History of Printing.*
297. William Campbell, "To the New York American," reprinted in *Alexandria Gazette*, March 8, 1844.
298. Daniel Roberts, "The Wayward Path of an American Hero," *International Journal of Maritime History* (March 2021).
299. The 1875 Kelby transcriptions are held by the New York Historical Society, but due to construction, they were only partially available during the research for this project. His brother, William Kelby, is said to have transcribed inscriptions at Trinity Churchyard at the same time, but if they are extant, they could not be located.

300. "Masonry in Marble," *New York Dispatch*, October 7, 1866.
301. *NYG*, May 4, 1815.
302. 1830.

## *Section S2*

303. Will of James Lacey Mariner.
304. "Theatric," *NYA*, June 2, 1787.
305. Jason Shaffer, "The Female Martinet: Mrs Harper, Gender and Civic Virtue on the Early Republican Stage," *Comparative Drama* (Winter 2006).
306. Advertisement, *NYM*, December 1, 1766.
307. *Leicester and Nottingham Journal*, July 9, 1763.
308. Advertisement, *NYG*, July 1, 1771.
309. Advertisement, *NYM*, June 9, 1766.
310. *NYG*, August 25, 1766.
311. *NYG*, October 22, 1781.
312. *NYG*, August 26, 1782.
313. *The British Critic* (1798).
314. Ann Gorman Condon, "The Family in Exile: Loyalist Social Values After the Revolution," in *Intimate Relations*, edited by Margaret Conrad (Fredericton Acadieness Press, 1995).
315. Ted Jones, *Historic Fredericton North* (Nimbus, Halifax, 2007).
316. F.B. Kelly, *Historical Guide to the City of New York* (Stokes, 1909).
317. *NYG*, May 18, 1802.
318. "Fatal Accident," *NYS*, September 11, 1811.

## *Section C1*

319. "Double Funeral," *NYTr*, January 16, 1901.
320. *NYG*, September 6, 1773.

## *Section C2*

321. Wm Dunlap, *Memoirs of George Frederick Cooke* (Colburn 1813).
322. Diary of William Dunlap.
323. Dunlap, *History of the American Theatre*.

324. 1830.
325. Hawkins, *Life of Edmund Kean* (Tinsley Bros., 1869).
326. Wm Dunlap, *Memoirs of a Water Drinker* (Saunders and Otley, 1837).
327. Francis.
328. *NYP*, October 17, 1833.
329. Dunlap, *Memoirs of a Water Drinker*.
330. John Eisenberg, *The Great Match Race* (Boston, MA: Houghton Mifflin, 2006).
331. "Alderman Purdy," *NYE*, December 17, 1836.
332. "Alderman Purdy," *NYE*, December 5, 1836.
333. "A Tribute to a Great Sportsman," *The Thoroughbred Record*, May 26, 1933.
334. Wingate.
335. Grimke, *The Life of Charles Sumner* (Funk and Wagnall's, 1892).
336. "Deaths," *NYG*, August 19, 1789.
337. *NYA*, September 17, 1789.
338. Leake, *General John Lamb*.
339. "Mortuary Notice," *Albany Gazette*, October 9, 1795.
340. "Col. Oswald," *NYJ*, October 17, 1795.
341. Raleigh Buzzair, "Washington's Last Chief Engineer," *The Military Engineer*, March 1953.
342. Rochefontaine to Hamilton, April 28, 1796, in *The Intimate Life of Alexander Hamilton* (Scribners, 1910).
343. 1897.
344. *Vermont Gazette*, July 19, 1803.
345. 1897.
346. 1861.
347. William M. MacBean, *Biographical Register of St Andrew's Society* (privately published, 1922).
348. "Absconded," *NYG*, July 26, 1793.
349. Advertisement, *NYA*, December 6, 1804.
350. Burr, to McLachlan, June 2, 1831.
351. "New-York Churchyards," *NYTr*, July 13, 1868.
352. 1861.

## *Section C3*

353. *Intimate Life of Alexander Hamilton*; "The Manhattan Well Murder," *Harper's Weekly*, May 1872.

354. Steuben to Vacher, March 1791.
355. Robert Troup to Rufus King, December 5, 1801.
356. "Communication," *NYG*, August 14, 1801.
357. *Mercantile Advertiser*, November 20, 1801.
358. "Died," *NYP*, November 24, 1901.
359. *American Citizen*, November 25, 1801; *NYP*, November 25, 1801.
360. *NYA*, November 25, 1801.
361. "The Week in New York," *Cincinnati Gazette*, October 2, 1880.
362. *American Citizen*, January 25, 1804.

## *Section N1*

363. "The Baker Case," *New York Dispatch*, December 9, 1855.
364. "Row Among the Fancy," *NYH*, December 5, 1859.
365. "An Old Sport Gone," *San Francisco Examiner*, June 21, 1888.
366. Wingate.
367. Mrs. J.H. Sigourney, letter, in *A Genealogical Memoir of the Huntington Family in This Country* (1863).
368. 1897.
369. *NYP*, December 21, 1819.
370. 1897 transcription; it's worth noting that a note beside it says "NS 2," so this may be misidentified.
371. *NYG*, March 11, 1782.
372. R.J. Clarke, *The Impostress* (The History Press, 2019).
373. *NYG*, December 2, 1782.
374. Nordeck File, Trinity Archives.
375. 1897.
376. Thomas Strante and Jenny Nex, *John Geib: Beyond the Footnote* (Cambridge University, 2010).
377. Advertisement, *Greenleaf's New Daily Advertiser*, December 27, 1798.
378. Allan Amanik, *Dust to Dust* (NYU Press, 2019).
379. *Commercial Advertiser*, July 12, 1817.

## *Section N2*

380. Addendum to 1897 transcription.
381. 1897.

382. 1897.
383. Franklin Hough, *History of Lewis County* (1860).
384. Ibid.
385. David Gellman, *Emancipating New York* (LSU Press, 2008).
386. Constable to John White, August 3, 1779.
387. Hough, *History of Lewis County*.
388. *NYA*, May 13, 1823.
389. 1861.
390. New York City Court Records, 1760–1797.
391. Marvin Lowenthal, *This Was New York* (Doubleday, 1943).
392. *National Advocate*, January 27, 1823.
393. *NYP*, August 23, 1813.
394. *NYG*, September 2, 1795.
395. *NYP*, May 30, 1816.
396. Obituary, *National Advocate*, August 3, 1820.
397. The parish calls him "Medger," which is probably a mistranscription.
398. *NYG*, September 25, 1780; *NYJ*, June 2, 1784.
399. "Romance of the History of the Eden Farm," *NYT*, February 29, 1920.
400. Will of Medcef Eden Jr., 1819.
401. *The MacDonugh Hackstaff Ancestry* (1901).
402. *Albany Register*, April 12, 1808.
403. NYSL.
404. 1897.
405. 1830.
406. Obituary, *NYS*, June 30, 1818.
407. Morgan Dix, *Historical Recollections of Trinity Church* (1867).
408. *Sunday Dispatch*, July 2, 1868.

## *Monuments Inside the Chapel*

409. "General Montgomery," *NYP*, July 8, 1818.
410. Wingate.
411. *NYA*, July 9, 1818.
412. Elizabeth Franklin to Benjamin Franklin, August 6, 1776.
413. *NYA*, October 24, 1787.

## *Unknown Burials*

414. Lord Bellomont, to Board of Trade, July 26, 1699.
415. *NYA*, June 28, 1790.
416. "A Coup de Main," *NYP*, July 5, 1813.
417. Gilbert Hunt, *The Late Ware Between the United States and Great Britain* (New York: Daniel Smith, 1819).
418. J. Lewis, to Secretary W. Jones, July 6, 1813.
419. *NYG*, July 9, 1813.
420. New York City Municipal Deaths.
421. "Died," *New York Columbian*, October 12, 1818.

# FREQUENTLY CITED SOURCES

The following abbreviations are used for frequently cited sources.

*Newspapers*

*BDE*: *Brooklyn Daily Eagle*
*NYA*: *New York Daily Advertiser*
*NYAm*: *New York American*
*NYAt*: *New York Atlas*
*NYE*: *New York Express*
*NYG*: *New York Gazette*
*NYH*: *New York Herald*
*NYJ*: *New York Journal*
*NYM*: *New York Mercury*
*NYMa*: *New York Mail*
*NYP*: *New York Post*
*NYS*: *New York Spectator*
*NYSu*: *New York Sun*
*NYT*: *New York Times*
*NYTr*: *New York Tribune*

*Frequently Cited Articles and Records*

1830: *Cabinet of Religion, Education, &c.* "Monumental Inscriptions." 1830.
1839: *New York Truth Teller*. "An Hour in Trinity Church." November 2, 1839.
1861: *New York Leader*. Reprinted in *Sacramento Bee*. "Dead of St. Paul's." February 16, 1861.
1868: *New York Tribune*. "New York Churchyards." July 13, 1868.
1871: *Rochester Democrat*. "New York Letter." August 19, 1871.

1897: Transcriptions of inscriptions recorded in 1897; Trinity Church Archives.
NYSL: New York Society Library Records, https://cityreaders.nysoclib.org.

## *Books*

Francis: Francis, John W. *Old New York*. Charles Rosk, 1857.
Mines: Mines, John Flavel (as Felix Oldboy). *Walks in Our Churchyards*. Peck, NY: Jazzybee Verlag, 1896.
Pollock: Pollock, Allan. *History of Trinity Church and Its Graveyard*. Self-published, 1880.
Strong: Strong, George Templeton. *Diary of George Templeton Strong*. 4 vols. New York: Macmillan, 1952.
Wingate: Wingate, Charles F. *St. Paul's Chapel*. Albert King & Co., 1901.

# ABOUT THE AUTHOR

Adam Selzer is a tour guide, historian and podcaster primarily in Chicago and New York, and he is the author of more than twenty books, including *Graceland Cemetery*, *H.H. Holmes: The True History of the White City Devil* and several novels.

Find him online and sign up for a tour, either virtual or in-person, at AdamChicago.com.